For Pramit,

Delhi 1990 Sunanda.

M12/7

COLONIES AND THE EMPIRE

Colonies and the Empire

India 1890–1914

Sunanda Sen

Orient Longman

ORIENT LONGMAN LIMITED

Registered Office
3-6-272 Himayatnagar, Hyderabad 500 029

Other Offices
Kamani Marg, Ballard Estate, Bombay 400 038
17 Chittaranjan Avenue, Calcutta 700 072
160 Anna Salai, Madras 600 002
1/24 Asaf Ali Road, New Delhi 110 002
80/1 Mahatma Gandhi Road, Bangalore 560 001
3-6-272 Himayatnagar, Hyderabad 500 029
Birla Mandir Road, Patna 800 004
S. C. Goswami Road, Panbazar, Guwahati 781 001
'Patiala House', 16-A Ashok Marg, Lucknow 226 001

First Published 1992
ISBN 0 86131 970 2

Published by Orient Longman Limited
17 Chittaranjan Avenue, Calcutta 700 072
and printed in India at
Swapna Printing Works Pvt. Ltd.
52 Raja Rammohan Roy Sarani, Calcutta 700 009.

Preface

The present work embodies the research undertaken over a fairly long period. It reflects my attempts to understand economic backwardness in a historical perspective, for nations which are subject to economic and/or political subjugation in relation to the external world. The central theme of the book has been developed in the context of India as a part of the British empire during the late nineteenth and early twentieth centuries. The method of analysis used to study the economic retardation and surplus appropriation in colonial India generates a set of broader perspectives which relate both to the formal empires and to the neo-colonies of the contemporary world. Thus, while the present study emerged out of the curiosity of an economist towards historical data on underdevelopment in colonial India, the end-product addresses a wider spectrum of questions most of which have an appeal to social scientists interested in the historical roots of underdevelopment. While the present study is concerned with the surplus appropriation in the colonies and the internal-external dimensions of the disbursement and transfer of such surpluses, the method of analysis adopted may be of relevance in understanding the contemporary processes of underdevelopment under neo-colonialism. Indeed, the imperial domination of colonial finance, which got entrenched during the age of high finance between 1890–1914, offers a parallel to the present-day pattern of subordination for the Third World as a whole on matters concerning national monetary policy. The links between the past and the present broadens the potential readership of the book since it can have an appeal to a wider group of social scientists.

The long period of incubation of the present work makes it difficult to locate and identify the help I received from various colleagues and institutions. Comments received on earlier drafts of the present manuscript from colleagues in India and abroad are gratefully acknowledged. I am especially thankful to Amiya Kumar Bagchi, Sabyasachi Bhattacharya, Dietmar Rothermundt, Tapan Roychaudhury, and Immanuel Wallerstein for their suggestions and for the active role to encourage me to eventually complete the project. Institutions which offered invitations and generous research facilities include the Clare Hall (Cambridge), Maison des Sciences de L'Hommes (Paris), and Sudasien Institute (Heidelberg). I am grateful to them for the arrangements at the formative stages of my work. Workshops were attended and seminars were given on the present work at the institutions mentioned above, and in addition, at the faculty of Economics and Politics at Cambridge University, St. Anthony's College, Oxford, University of Sussex, the Centre for Studies in Social Sciences, Calcutta, and at the Jamia Milia Islamia and Jawaharlal Nehru Universities in New Delhi. I appreciate the constructive comments I received from various colleagues and students. The Indian Council of Social Science Research, the Clare Hall, and the Masion de Sciences de L'Hommes provided financial assistance which helped me to collect primary material while JNU, my university, allowed me to undertake the work by granting a sabbatical year. I would like to thank these institutions for the facilities provided. Colleagues at the Centre for Economic Studies and Planning and at the Centre for Historical Studies of Jawaharlal Nehru University were generous in terms of their time, patiently hearing my arguments and offering comments. The students who were destined to share my enthusiasm for this rather unconventional route to economic history did provide fresh air by equipping me with an audience which proved always ready and alert to test out the truth. I am grateful to all of them for what they offered towards the study. T.K. Arun volunteered help in reading the proof which proved valuable. I would like to thank Om Prakash who helped in typing out the final version of a difficult manuscript within a very short period.

New Delhi 1991 Sunanda Sen

Contents

List of Tables

To
Professor Bhabatosh Datta

CHAPTER 1

Introduction

1.1 Theories of imperialism and colonialism

The early doctrines of imperialism, advanced in the classical writing on the subject by Hobson, Lenin, Hilferding and Luxemburg,[1] had a great deal to offer on the historic specification of world capitalism in the industrially advanced nations during the late nineteenth and early twentieth centuries. The dynamics and the conjuncture of events which culminated in the World War of 1914 were both predicted and analysed in the above writings, which viewed the war as a measure to secure control over external markets through open aggression. Tendencies towards underconsumption, the falling rates of profits, and the related problems of realization in the industrially advanced nations made it imperative for them to reach out to the external markets, a large part of which was in the colonies.

Colonies can be viewed as a support to the imperial network in a multiple capacity. First, the colonies have been a source of profit in trade, by providing raw materials at depressed prices as well as a captive market for manufactured wares from the ruling nations. Second, they also provided a source of profit on investments which found an easier and lucrative outlet in the empire. Third, the colonies provided, in addition, steady sources of surplus which were remitted as political tributes on a contractual basis and legitimized as 'home charges' on the colonies. More often, these proved to be a sustainable source of surplus which was transferred to the ruling nation through a network of specially instituted channels of remittance. Finally, the colonies, by administrative diktats, maintained their official monetary reserves with the banking system and the security market of the ruling nation, which was thus enabled to make free use of the additional source of finance towards domestic or overseas spendings (including new overseas investments). As part of the surplus appropriation and transfer, the colonial economies underwent structural changes incorporating monetization and commercialization of the production and exchange processes. The impact of these changes, however, failed to initiate growth in these economies. We will return to the theme advanced here when we dwell, later in this volume, on colonial India and its imperial connections.

Classical writings on imperialism, with their emphasis on the problems central to the industrially advanced nations, have often left the process of expropriation within the formal empire unspelt. The relative neglect of the processes operating at the level of the colonies reflect, to a certain extent, the Euro-centric bias in the early writings on imperialism, which was defined as the highest stage of capitalism. We propose to redress the balance, by concentrating the focus of our analysis on India which was one of the major colonies in the British empire at the turn of the last century.

The lapses in the early writings on imperialism on the question of the colonies and their significance within the formal empires have been sought to be remedied in the more recent literature. Labelled as neo-Marxian, some of these constructions have dwelt on the links between advanced industrial nations and the rest of the world. Colonies within the formal empires of the earlier years have been matched by their analogues of neo-colonies which have been utilized by the capitalists in the industrialized nations as the external markets for surplus commodities as well as for investment of savings. The capitalist state which supported the earlier arrangements appropriated, in addition, the flow of political tributes from the colonies, often raised without any quid pro quo. A hierarchy of power structure, encompassing the colonies and the ruling nations, emerged in the process, introducing an element of dominance and power relations within the empire.

The emphasis given to trade as a major channel of resource transfer from the colonies (or the periphery in general) has been contested by some writers in the neo-Marxian tradition who have viewed the flow of capital as the major source of such surplus and its transfer.[2] Contrasted with the orthodox view, capital exports to the colonies were no longer seen as investment of surplus savings from the capital-rich industrialized nations who were in fact receiving, on a net basis, an excess of investment income over the new investments (goes investment less amortization). Attention has often been drawn to what is known as a 'reverse flow' of capital in the direction of the industrially advanced nations.[3] Such processes, in our judgement, confirm the loigical historical sequence when the initial flows of capital had been in the opposite direction. Instances are not difficult to provide of similar tendencies, especially for countries which started early as capital exporters on a large scale. It was logical for these nations (e.g. Britain) to experience deficits in their balance of merchandise earnings when investment income from abroad tended to exceed the capital exports.[4] Thus it was natural for England, by mid-nineteenth century, to enter upon a phase of external economic transactions with inflows of investment income large enough to finance both merchandise deficits and gross export of capital. The scenario fits in with the experience of the colonies, e.g. India under British rule—a point we would develop later in the next few chapters as we discuss the specific case of India. As for the implication of the reverse flows, the syndrome has been cited in the New-Left writings as a rebuttal of the direction of capital exports observed in the orthodox writings on imperialism. The reverse flow of capital from the colonies in the direction of the metropolitan countries enabled them to launch and continue large investments in new areas (e.g. Argentina in the case of Britain), thus indicating an ongoing process of ploughing back of investment in the colonies within the formal empire and ensuring a continuity of income from fresh investments in other areas not always falling within the formal empire.

The discourse on the role of commerce in the expropriation of surplus from colonies (or neo-colonies) has led, in new-left writings on imperialism, to a debate concerning the primacy of exchange relations under capitalism. Initiated during the sixties by Dobb and Sweezy,[5] the controversy has harped on the relative significance of circulation or production relations as a means of surplus appropriation under capitalism. According to one school of thought, commerce amongst nations has held the key to a 'peripheralization' of new territories and a transfer of resources to 'core' areas. The 'core–periphery' distinction has been a central part of the arguments advanced in the literature on 'world systems'.[6] In the New-Left writings, emphasis has also been laid on the 'trade-cum-investment' flows as the basis for a global process, characterized as the 'development of underdevelopment'.[7] Elsewhere we have dismissed, as misleading and conceptually inaccurate, some other approaches to the significance of trade advanced as 'free-trade imperialism'.[8]

Literature on colonialism includes recent debates on the use of the 'nation' as a unit of analysis. In terms of one argument, the prevailing pattern of exchanges in the international economy has already transcended the identity of nation-states. Banks, industries, and even the capitalist states[9] are observed to be subject to supra-national alliances transcending the interest of individual nation-states. At another level of analysis, counter-arguments to the above point of view are offered in writings which have looked at the 'nation' as a unit of analysis, providing a powerful tool for an understanding of the emerging tendencies on part of nation-states.[10] It has been emphasized that the doctrinal thesis on imperialism, especially by Lenin, needs to be 'read' along with his work on the question of nationalism.[11] For others, the nation-states has been crucial in setting up an environment where surplus extractions are feasible, not only under capitalist but also under precapitalist forms of production and exchange relations. In the colonial regimes this was achieved through the property relations, the trade laws, the transport, and even the irrigation network supplanted within the nation-state.[12] In some extreme versions of analysis of the colonial state, the process of colonial transformation has been linked to the forms of precapitalist production and exchange relations which identifies a 'colonial mode of production'.[13] The legitimacy of the notion, however, has often been questioned in Marxist writings on related themes. Compared to what is offered elsewhere in the literature, the last-mentioned discourse on the colonial economy pays more attention to the issues of production and distribution processes in areas which have historically continued to remain backward. The conceptual basis of analysis underlying the thesis on 'colonial mode of production' relates to aspects which are not necessarily based on happenings in advanced capitalist economies alone. However, the analysis offered in this thesis—especially on the precapitalist formations—fails to provide the requisite tools for an understanding of the historical processes of backwardness in the colonial economies.

1.2 Colonialism in India

In the present work we propose to undertake a study of India under the colonial rule. Our study relates to the period 1890–1914—years when the British-Indian economic relations achieved considerable significance in the context of the imperial network which was consolidated by the financial relations dominant during the period.

The scope of our analysis is confined to an identification of the transfers, both financial and real, from the colonial economy of India and an assessment of the macro-economic implications of such transfers for the domestic economy, both in regard to the financial and to the real spheres of economic performance.

To set the stage for the point of departure in our study and interpretation of the experience of colonial India during 1890–1914 in the context of the British empire, we, in the previous section, had surveyed in very broad outlines both the classical writings on imperialism and the more recent neo-Marxist writings on colonialism. The limitations of the analysis in both classical and modern writings on imperialism to provide an explanation of the backwardness of the colonies in terms of the actual processes at work therein have persuaded us to undertake the present work, which might be treated as complementary to literature as are available on the subject.

Anticipating the major observations and the method of analysis adopted in the book, we provide a preview in the next few pages. While the present chapter aims to provide, as a background to an analysis of backwardness in colonial India, themes from the literature on colonialism and imperialism, Chapters 2 and 3 identify the magnitude and the domestic impact of financial surpluses transferred from colonial India. Dominance of the financial houses in the London City on matters concerning Indian finance, as is evident from these chapters, indicate the pattern of imperial connections during the period of finance capital. Chapter 4 unfolds the pace of corresponding real transfers to Britain, procured through export surplus earned by India.

The pace of surplus expropriation and their utilization through commercialization of agriculture as well as a colonial transformation of the economy provide an explanation of its growth-retarding process which continued despite expansion in exports, rise in prices, and increase in the production of commercial crops. The historical experience of the colonial economy in terms of underdevelopment provides a parallel to the ongoing processes in the developing countries in the contemporary world. A broader perspective has been offered in Chapter 5 which draws conclusions dwelling on a) the economic significance of the empire to Britain, b) the relative significance of surpluses extracted from India, and c) their broader significance for studies of underdevelopment. We now sum up, under (a)–(j) below, the more important arguments offered in the book.

(a) In the following analysis attention has been drawn to the role of capital flows and the institutional aspects of finance in effecting transfers from colonial India. The approach contrasts with the emphasis on trade alone as an integral part of colonial expropriations—a fact which has been mentioned earlier.

(b) In our attempt to identify the flow of unilateral transfers from India, we have noticed the flow of gold to England, often achieved by manipulating the official gold reserves maintained in India. The financial transfers were more than a sacrifice of short-run command over external resources, since these were matched by actual contractions in the parallel sources of money creation in the domestic economy, initiating contraction of credit therein. This point has been developed in the Chapters 2 and 3.

(c) We have identified, both in the London City and in colonial India, elements of monopoly and discretionary use of power relations in matters connected with finance (including credit in India), the procedure and the channels of silver import (for coinage of silver rupees in India), the 'use and location' of official reserves by the Government of India, the question of taxes (direct taxes were rather insignificant during the period), policies concerning borrowings abroad and the procedures relating to the accounting norms, and finally, the use made of the remittance network to maximize the transfer of financial surplus from India. Most of the above arrangements were influenced by the evolving power structure in the management of the empire, with the inevitably growing contradictions between the centers of power, which included, in an ascending order of significance, the commercial community in India, the India government, the India Office in London, and the Bank of England (or the British government). Use of absolute state power in determining the rules of the game within the empire resulted in a hierarchy of finance relations as was consistent in terms of the prevailing monopoly phase of imperialism. Details of these power relations, spelt out in the context of colonial India in Chapters 2 and 3, include some dimensions in the study of empire–colony relation which have, as yet, remained undefined in the available literature.

(d) Questions relating to contraction of demand in colonial India—which is viewed as a direct consequence of the colonial transfers from the domestic economy—have been spelt out in Chapter 2. Alignments of institutional arrangements were made to set aside a part of the tax revenue raised in India for settling, in rupees, the counterpart sterling liabilities of India in London on account of colonial rule. Details of the process, discussed in Section 2.1, reveal a picture where India was, in fact, continually transferring its net export revenue over the period. The above argument, made explicit in Section 2.2, is different from the nationalist charge that exports from India remained unpaid. While exporters were duly paid, the nation's net revenue from exports was cancelled through budgetary provisions which arranged for a settling of net exports through tax revenue. The macro-economic reasoning on the offsetting of net export earnings by tax revenue raised in India amounts to a cancelling of net exports or a surplus in the domestic budget. This point has received little attention in the literature. What, then, were the short-term effects of export expansion in colonial India in terms of a standard Keynesian multiplier? Assuming no change in consumption propensities in the economy before and after taxes, one can formulate the results in the following terms: In colonial India the expansionary effects of an export surplus were dampened with equivalent taxes which were imposed on the domestic economy. The contraction in demand which thus resulted was due both to the above fiscal restraint and to the contraction in money supply and the credit squeeze which resulted from the process of transfers. Details of the process of transfers and related income and/or credit contractions in colonial India have been worked out in Chapters 2 and 3. As a stylized observation, it is possible to construct the modified foreign trade multiplier[14] for a similarly situated economy, which responds to changes in the propensities to save and import differently from what is ordinarily expected in terms of a standard Keynesian multiplier. Thus an economy, constrained to set aside as, say, budgetary surplus the sum which it earns as net exports would experience a foreign trade multiplier effect which is larger/smaller depending on the relative values of the marginal propensities to consume and to import. Clearly, the income-generating capacity of the export sector operates in reverse gear in such an economy since it has to transfer abroad, by political necessity, the entire value of the net export earnings. The argument, while logically valid as an explanation of demand deficiency in a colonial economy, should not be taken at its face value. Thus it would be unrealistic and theoretically unsound to expect changes in demand to cause proportionate changes in output in the case of colonial India—as might have happened in terms of a strict Keynesian model of output adjustment. Instead, the stagnation of output, as observed in colonial India, was the outcome of a complex structural process, which not only included the demand-depressants but also the sectoral trends in production and prices included in the changes in the forms of surplus that were generated and the pattern of their utilization. The commercialization of agriculture, which resulted from the rising levels of exports from the economy, was in fact concommitant with a process of deceleration or stagnation of output—a sequence which cannot be explained by simple demand-based models of the Keynesian variant. In Chapter 4 we have looked into the processes which determined the utilization of surplus in the colonial economy which was dominantly agrarian, and in a manner which definitely retarded the yield-augmenting processes in agriculture. The syndrome of high prices, high exports, and low output or yield responses which prevailed during the period was clearly different from what should have resulted in terms of a typical Keynesian understanding of the basic issues.

(e) Alliance between big business (industry) and finance (banks) in the industrialized countries which prevailed during the period fits in with the hierarchy of power relations prominent in the domain of British–Indian economic relations during the colonial period. The structure and the interplay of power relations defined the realities of the behaviour of the concerned agents which, as mentioned above, included in India, in an ascending order of importance, the Indian government, the India Office, the Bank of England, and the British government.

(f) The new-left writings on imperialism point to the following limitations in the orthodox Marxist position on imperialism. First, the literature underplays the parallel process of surplus appropriation and transfer from the colonies. Secondly, there is a consequent underplaying of the precapitalist forms of production and exchange relations relating to the colonies. Both critiques provide a starting point for our analysis of the colonial economy in India.

(g) The expropriation and transfer of surplus from the colonies, including those from India, were achieved during the period through a network of multilateral finance relations, where surpluses originating from one direction could be disbursed as new investment in another. The system was perfected with the London City being able to work as a clearing house since the late nineteenth century, offering the financial infrastructure to settle the transactions on trade as well as investment. Finance, in the context of the closely knit financial combines which controlled the London City (banks and other financial houses), was thus significant in providing a transfer of resources from the old colonies within the empire to the new,[15] and Britain was in a position to expropriate surplus from the old colonies like India in order to reinvest them in new areas within the empire. The multilateral network of flows and the role of trade as well as finance relations are crucial to an understanding of the empire–colony relations which have been explored in the present study. International commerce as well as capital flows, in our opinion, had been crucial for transfer of resources from the colonies.

(h) The point raised in (d) above, on the relevance of the surplus approach as an explanation of the economic backwardness in colonial India, leads us to address questions which concern the precapitalist forms of surplus appropriation and utilization. In our analysis we have used the methods available to analyse the colonial transformation, the beginnings of which are traceable to the previous century. Emphasis laid on the above aspects enables us to identify the institutional processes in the economy which explain the tardiness of growth or absence of dynamism in the face of the export boom from the colonial economy.

(i) In analysing the question of financial and real transfers, use has been made of 'nation' as a unit of analysis. In colonial India, with the British authority over the disposal of resources, transfers which took place from the national economy were legitimized and the process of surplus extraction consolidated in terms of the legal jurisdiction and authority of the ruling state. A part of the surplus, in addition to the 'loot' overseas, did, of course, stay within the national economy. The pattern of expenditure by the resident Europeans and other nationals, however, often generated demand for imported articles (e.g. sugar, textiles etc.) to meet U-sector consumption, or increased demand for gold to be held as private assets. In general, expenditure within the economy stimulated activities (e.g. money-lending, land transfers, grain trade) none of which could generate investment demand either in the agrarian or in the industrial sector (most of these activities being confined to the sphere of circulation rather than production). Thus our emphasis on 'nation' as a unit in analysing transfers from colonial India to Britain does not undermine the significance of the parallel process of surplus expropriations which were internal to the economy and simultaneous with the external transfers. We have thus adopted the approach to analysing surplus appropriation in the economy which dwells on the internal-external dimensions of the national surplus. This is distinct from both the nationalist point of view or the world system approach on the question of transfer of surpluses (in both of which the nation has similarly been used as unit of analysis).

(j) The quantitative estimates, arrived at in Chapters 2 and 3 (on the magnitude of external transfers, or the value of sterling investments by India, etc.) do not undermine the historical-institutional approach of historiography which has been the basis of our analysis. We have tried to maintain a balance between the qualitative and the quantitative dimensions, in order not to lose sight of the historical dialectics implicit in the latter.

It is necessary, at this point, to draw attention to the gaps which have remained in our study. For reasons of feasibility and expediency, we have avoided attempts to interpret the industrial performance and the related fiscal policies in the economy (e.g. tariffs, excises, etc.). This is not to deny the relevance of the reinforcing mechanism between industry and agriculture, of which we are conscious. Policies of free trade adopted in the colonial markets by the British had destroyed, through indiscriminate encouragement of imports from abroad, the remnants of manufacturing skill and activities by the 1860s (the phenomenon is also described as de-industrialization in India). Between 1860–1914 the spurts in imports of cotton textiles and sugar were phenomenal, the level reaching 41.3

per cent of import value in 1910.[16] Both items met the demand of the upcoming bourgeoisie in India, which included the merchants, bankers, government officials, and landlords. For the group as a whole, the ostentatious living of the European residents in India often served as the model for consumption standards. It was not surprising that a lack of demand was experienced in India for home-made textiles and other manufactures, and even for inferior grains (the supply of which, as pointed out in Chapter 4, actually shrank during the period).

Another theme which could have been discussed in this work relates to the possible losses through terms of trade changes experienced by the country in international commerce during the period. By the 1860s India's trade reflected a pattern which was common to other underdeveloped, primary-producing countries. We suggest as an agenda for future research, an analysis of the possible real income shortfalls which might have resulted in the economy from the fluctuations and secular declines in its terms of trade—an aspect not analysed in this book. Another area of potential research that has similarly been inadequately dealt with here relates to the network of multilateral adjustments within the empire.[17] This could supplement the analysis offered in this book on the surveillance by the London City of financial policies in British India, and on the strict control exercised by the Bank of England on the disbursing of India government's sterling revenue and/or tributes to other white-settled colonies via the intermediation of London City. Lastly, the present study has refrained from offering a full-fledged analysis of the issues of bimetallism during the period (which, incidentally, proved rather crucial in fulfilling the goals of imperial financial policy with the help of the large, silver-using colonies like India or China). The issues listed above deserve mention as possible areas for future research. The present study remains an experiment in the application of an analytical-historical method, one which combines the tools of economic analysis with historical evidence. The events covered amply illustrate a process of precapitalist expropriation in colonial India, linked to the interests of the advanced industrial economy, viz. Britain, which was also the ruling nation. Rather deliberately, we have offered a set of general observations in this chapter to which the reader may like to come back. The purpose of the study will be served if the general observations offered here are borne out by the details analysed in the subsequent chapters.

Notes

1. Authors writing in this tradition include Hobson (underconsumption), Lenin (fusion of big business and major banks under monopolistic control, exports of capital and merchandise, repartitioning of world's territories), Hilferding (dominance of banking capital, monopoly, capital, exports), and Rosa Luxemburg (external trade to overcome limits to accumulation arising from underconsumptionist tendencies in the domestic economy). Themes mentioned against individual authors in brackets indicate the broad range of their concerns which, very clearly, centred around the happenings in the mainstream areas. V.I. Lenin, *Imperialism, the Highest Stage of Capitalism*, Peking, 1960.

   V.I. Lenin, 'Notebooks on Imperialism (1915–16)' in *Collected Works*, Vol. 39, Moscow, 1968. C.K. Hobson, *The Export of Capital*, London, 1904. Rosa Luxemburg, *Accumulation of Capital*, Translated in English by Tom Bottomore, London, 1963.
2. Immanuel Wallerstein, *The Capitalist World Economy*, Cambridge, 1979, pp. 119–65.
3. Michael Barratt-Brown, *Economics of Imperialism*, Penguin. Also Al Szymanski, 'Marxist Theory and International Capital Flows', *RRPE Review*, 6(3), 1974.
4. W.A.P. Manser, *Britain in Balance*, Penguin, 1971. p. 220–3.
5. See, in this context, the mode of production controversy under 'The Transitions from Feudalism to Capitalism', and in particular, contributions by Maurice Dobb, Paul Sweezy and others in *Science and Society*, 1950–53.
6. Immanuel Wallerstein, *The Modern World System: Capitalist Agriculture and the Origins of the European World Economy in the Sixteenth Century*, New York, 1976, Chapter 1. Also Immanuel Wallerstein, *World Economy*, 1979.

   A. Gunder Frank, *Capitalism and Underdevelopment in Latin America*, 1971.

   Ravi Palat et al., *Review*, I, Summer, 1986.
7. Gunder Frank, *Capitalism, 1979. See also*, Gunder Frank, 'On some Questionable Questions about Marxist Theory and International Capital Flows', *RRPE Review*, 1976.
8. J. Gallaghar and R. Robinson, 'The Imperialism of Free Trade', *Economic History Review*, 1953. See, for a critique, Sunanda Sen, 'Free Trade Imperialism in Southeast Asia', *Studies in History*, January–June, 1980.
9. Bill Warren, 'How International is Capital?', and Robin Murray, 'The Internationalisation of Capital and the Nation-State' in Hugo Radice ed., *International Firms and Modern Imperialism*, Penguin, 1975, pp. 107–140.

10. In terms of the arguments advanced, nationalist movements in colonies have been rated as precursors for an eventual bourgeois democratic revolution. See, for the arguments, V.I. Lenin, *The National Liberation Movement in the East*, Moscow, 1969.
V.I. Lenin, *Collected Works*, Vol. 22, Moscow, 1964.
Bipan Chandra, 'Lenin and the National Liberation Movements' in *Nationalism and Colonialism in Modern India*, Orient Longman, Delhi, 1979, pp. 297–322.
11. A.K. Bagchi, 'Towards a Correct Reading of Lenin's Theory of Internationalism' in P. Patnaik ed., *Lenin and Imperialism*, Orient Longman, Delhi, 1986, pp. 27-55.
12. Krishna Bharadwaj, 'A Note on Commercialization in Indian Agriculture', in K.N. Raj et al. ed., *Commercialization in Indian Agriculture*, Delhi, 1985.
13. Hamza Alavi et al., *Capitalism and Colonial Production*, London, 1982.
14. Using a simple Keynesian income-expenditure equation

$$Y = C + I + X - M - T \qquad \ldots(1)$$

where taxes reduce the disposable income left for consumption alone (i.e. taxes are all on consumption), we get

$$C = c\,(Y - T) \text{ and } M = m\,(Y - T)$$
$$\text{or } Y = c\,(Y - T) - m\,(Y - T) + X - T + I$$
$$= cY - T\,(1 + c - m) - mY + I + X$$

Differentiating, we get the loss in income for unit increase in taxes as

$$\frac{dY}{dT} = -\frac{(1 + c - m)}{s + m}$$

The above can be set off against unit expansion in exports which would change income as follows:

$$\frac{dY}{dX} = \frac{1}{s + m}$$

Assuming net rise in taxes (dT) as equivalent to net rise in exports dx, thus implying that all increases in export surpluses are inevitably balanced by net taxes in the domestic economy (a situation resembling fiscal arrangements in colonial India) we get the net change in income as

$$\frac{dY}{dT} + \frac{dY}{dX} = \frac{m - c}{s + m} = \frac{1}{\frac{1}{m - c} + 1}$$

The above explains the rather paradoxical result, highlighted in the text, that for a situation where export revenues are withheld from the circular flow of income within the country through net taxes, losses in income are minimized at smaller values of marginal propensity to consume relative to the marginal propensity to import. The symbols: Y = national income, C = consumption, I = investment, X = exports, M = imports, T = Net taxes equivalent to budgetary surplus, c, s, m are the marginal propensities to consume, save, and import respectively.

15. R. Nurkse, *Patterns of Trade and Development*, Stockholm, 1979.
16. *Statistical Abstracts of British India.*

CHAPTER 2

Tributes and Transfers from Colonial India

Introductory remarks offered in the previous chapter on the method and scope of the present study justify an attempt—made in the present chapter—to identify and measure the tributes which flowed from colonial India. Evidence of transfer of the tributes will be offered in this chapter, reinforcing our central thesis that expropriation and transfer of surplus in an empire–colony set up was an ongoing process.

We have chosen 1890–1914—years of high finance in the world economy—as the period of our analysis. During this period banks and industries in the advanced countries were geared, for the first time in history, to maximize the rates of return on investment which was also invested overseas. This period marked the heyday of finance capital in Europe and witnessed the coming of age of the financial institutions, especially in the London City, which provided for a multilateral clearing of trade and capital flows across the empire and other overseas nations.

As pointed out in the introductory chapter, our method of analysing the process of expropriation of surplus and its transfer overseas is relevant in understanding both the empire–colony configurations and the neo-colonial experiences. Parallels drawn between the colonial mode of surplus extraction and neo-colonialism in the periphery lends topicality to our reasearch on late nineteenth and early twentieth century experiences.

For India the beginning of the 1890s marked a period when British rule appeared to be fairly well-entrenched in terms of its claims on the domestic economy. This was reflected in the growing volume of 'home charges' (or the contractual overseas expenses) of the Indian government, the annual value of which was around £18 million by the turn of the century. This sum was substantial relative to the level of national income of India which was estimated at £120 million in 1900.[1]

Institutional support to transfers of financial resources was provided by the exchange banks, operating in the City of London and in the financial centres of India (Calcutta or Bombay). These banks were financing the growing financial transactions—both public and private—between the two countries. In London, all the sterling funds due for remittance to India (mainly on account of export surpluses) were mopped up through the intermediation of the exchange banks and the India Office. The latter, representing the foreign office of the India government, was under the direct surveillance of the British government. No less significant, however, was the influence of the financial centre, the London City, which, as will be pointed out in the next chapter, circumscribed the sphere of operation of the India Office. Home charges of the Indian government were disbursed in London in sterling procured from the exchange earnings, while the unspent part was maintained as a steady and growing sterling balance with the Bank of England. Funds deployed by the India Office, especially as cash reserves and other sterling assets in the City, had a significant role—as will be argued in the next chapter—in easing the liquidity situation in London City. (India government's involvement in the London money market was considered crucial for maintaining, in accord with the imperial interests, the market trends in silver. The Indian government was actually forbidden, even during situations of silver shortages at home, to procure silver from the market which would have produced sharp increases in silver prices.)

In Section 2.1 we provide an account of the mode of effecting the transfers, through the specially instituted devices under the Council Bills (henceforth CB) which settled the remittances. Attention is drawn to the legal–contractual aspects supporting the network of financial settlements across the two nations, especially in the context of the colonial regime in India. The crucial role of the exchange banks and trading houses is unveiled in the process, all of which were significantly controlled by Europeans. Financial transfers to England, legalized under the pretext of the manifold claims on the India government, were entirely met through export earnings in London. A closer analysis reveals the underlying process of political domination in which the government as well as the private individuals in Britain wielded the power to set the norms for transactions with the colonies. As would be indicated in this chapter, it is possible to identify an element of unilateral transfer in what otherwise can be viewed as a regular flow of remittances between the two countries. The official and private agencies in both countries took active interest in ensuring, through the CB network, a channel for a steady flow of financial transfers between India and Britain. Additional support was lent through private financial institutions (like exchange banks) which were mostly controlled by the Anglo-Indian or European commercial and financial interests in India. It is thus convincing to take, at its face value, the generalization arrived at the end of Section 2.1 that the major instruments of financial transfers between the two governments were, by and large, initiated at the behest of the British government or the European commercial agencies (which included the banks). Attempts to lay bare the specific political context of the various financial transactions bring to focus the subservient colonial status of the country in relation to Britain, in terms of both administrative and commercial arrangements. Our approach to an understanding of the external economic transactions rejects typical mechanistic interpretations of these arrangements which are often evident in similar other studies.[2] The specific slant in our emphasis on the political factors behind the international economic transactions in colonial India, while germane to the nationalist writings on Indian economic history, was hardly spelt out in these studies. Section 2.2 draws attention to the implications of the silver currency in India, especially during the period of depreciating silver.

Section 2.3 identifies and measures the flow of financial transfers between the two countries. For the sake of convenience it has been subdivided into two sub-heads, addressing two specific questions. In Section 2.3.1 we look into the details of the 'Expenditure Abroad', the compelling factor behind financial transfers. While a major part of these transfers consisted of interest payments on productive loans, incurred to meet productive expenditure (railways and irrigation) in the past, closer analysis reveals that even such interest payments could be classified as unproductive expenditure. Unearthing some accounting devices, which were used in the official budget, we find it possible to conclude that almost the entire amount of the home charges could be regarded as unilateral transfer from India. Section 2.3.2 addresses the question posed by the Indian nationalists around the turn of last century concerning the so-called drain of wealth from India. We have sought to bring out the basic strength as well as weaknesses of the nationalist position on this question. We have contested the claim of the nationalists that: (*a*) the whole of India's export surplus remained unpaid, and (*b*) the entire amount of home charges, including servicing of irrigation and railway loans, was part of a political tribute. Both issues can be examined by looking into the budgetary transfers. The first claim is found to be formally invalid since the exporters were, in fact, duly paid through the mediation of exchange banks. But the practice of using the local tax revenue to settle the net export earnings within the country imparted a deflationary bias in terms of aggregate demand in the economy. In fact, the unilateral transfer of the tribute (comprising home charges) created, in addition to an equivalent transfer or drain of wealth, a potential for income contraction. The second claim is examined as we look into the details of the controversy on the drain. Attention, in particular, is paid to the sharp attacks on the nationalist arguments by both Alfred Marshall and John Maynard Keynes in their official papers and other writings (which include private correspondence). That Keynes was an official at the India Office during 1906–18 did not detract the analytical rigour of his writings and correspondence on Indian currency. Incidentally, both Keynes and Marshall lent full support to the prevailing system of monetary arrangement in British India. A general ethos thus prevailed amongst officials and intellectuals in England which provided uncritical support to the British empire. The view clearly dismissed the ongoing questioning of British rule in India. For Keynes, inflow of long-term capital into India was solid evidence of what could be characterized as a 'reverse' drain of wealth from England.[3] We have contrasted this view to that held by the nationalists[4] in their theory relating to the drain.

Section 2.4 dwells on quantification of the resource transfers from India. We have tried to arrive at an indirect measure by relying on the estimates that are available for external trade and other economic transactions over the period 1899–1900 to 1908–09. Data compiled by Theodore Morison, and revised later by Keynes, on a 'Conjectural Balance Sheet for India'[5] have been used to test out our arguments on external transfers. Statistics on the current account transactions in the above estimates do not, somehow, tally with the figures available from India Office sources on remittances. This has led us to cross-check and reconstruct the official series on India's trade data. Our doubts on the issue seem to have a point as Keynes himself appears to have been baffled over the same issue. In his private correspondence with an India Office official, he pointed out an inconsistency between India's official trade returns and the India Office's records on Council Bill remittances—a controversy of which we became aware at a late stage of our research.[6] It was indeed reassuring to discover that Keynes pointed at the same type of limitations in India's official trade data as have been identified by us in our attempt at constructing a new series of such data. Problems in reconciling the CB series and the trade data even after the possible corrections to the latter led us to treat the remittance figures at the India Office[7] as a better approximation of the net transfers from India. (Our practice of treating the data on remittances as a surrogate for data on trade balance between the two countries can be justified by the prevailing legal–institutional system in colonial India which entailed the use of her entire trade surplus to meet the home charges in England.) Our analysis in the rest of this chapter confirms the hypothesis advanced in Chapter 1 that there is an evidence of a continuing flow of transfers from colonial India.

2.1 Formal control over remittances: the Council Bill device

India's trade and exchange links with the rest of the world appear to have achieved a fair degree of sophistication by the 1890s. The decade witnessed the emergence of a whole network of banks and business houses in India, largely controlled by Europeans, which supported official attempts to achieve a smooth flow of remittances between the two countries. By the turn of the century, official remittances to England on account of the overseas liabilities were nearly as large as the sum spent to meet official liabilities in India. Increases in the contractual overseas payments—the typical pattern of which around 1900 can be judged from data given in Table 2.1—indicate that regularity in overseas remittances was essential for managing the external relations of the ruling government. Payments abroad covered the administrative charges at the India Office and other external liabilities, some of which were contractual in nature. Administrative arrangement to ensure a steady homeward flow of the earnings of the commercial community and other European residents in India were highly convenient. A brief account of the changing arrangements for remittances is given below.

A formal device was employed by the British rulers to siphon off the sterling proceeds of India's export surpluses to England. This marked the beginning of the CBs drawn on the treasury in India and sold by the India Office in London to exchange banks desirous of remitting (on behalf of their agents) the proceeds of India's net export earnings. In India the bills were honoured by the treasury where the exchange banks were reimbursed in Indian rupees out of the fiscal revenue earmarked in the domestic budget. The new system of remittances reduced the significance of flows of treasure which, along with the trade bills, were ordinarily the means of settling the balance of payment. The CBs were sold in London every Wednesday by the Secretary of State (SOS) at the India Office against offers in sterling from exchange banks. The prevailing exchange rate and currency system in India permitted, until the mints were closed to unlimited coinage of rupees by an official decree of June 1893, a parallel flow of remittances via flow of treasure (which included both gold and silver). Thus, till June 1893, silver rupees were available on demand from the mint against bullion offered by the remitting public. The exchange value of the rupee fluctuated in sterling according to the movements in the relative prices of the two metals in the world market. The prices of the CBs in rupees were closely monitored by the India Office, in order that the network of remittances under CBs was never unprofitable as compared to the direct remittances through flow of treasure (gold and silver bullions as well as gold coins).

Problems encountered by the ruling government and the European residents in India in the face of sharp declines in the rupee rate (which drifted downwards with the drop in the gold price and in the price of silver since the 1870s) led to the appointment of a Royal Committee on Indian Currency in 1893. This committee, known as Herschell Committee, recommended closure of the Indian mint to public so that no coins could be minted on public demand. While the exchange value of the rupee was officially announced at 1s 4*d*, minting of coins was left entirely to official discretion after 1893. As mints were closed in 1893, the unit price of the CBs sold was appropriately adjusted, allowing for the costs of remittance. (Rates fixed for the alternate route of remittance, the telegraphic transfers, were similarly adjusted.) The volume of CBs sold by the SOS went up over the years, providing the India Office direct access to the sterling proceeds of India's net export earnings. (The earlier practice—during the East India Company rule—of selling bills of exchange on India effectively achieved for the Company a similar goal of collecting the sterling proceeds of India's net exports in London.) The maximum value of CBs sold during a year, however, was limited to the respective annual home charges during the earlier years. The CBs were later allowed by the Act of 1905, to exceed the home charges and thus CBs sold were upto a value which was acceptable in the market (see Table 2.1 for CBs sold during 1861–1914). The CBs, therefore, provided a route for retaining in England the entire amount of India's export surplus which now could even build up externally held assets for the India Office. Actual use of these assets, however, was severely constrained by the directives of the Bank of England; which soon gained an authority over the financial policies of the India government. Purchase of sterling securities by the India Office improved, in general, the investment climate in the City. We will return to these aspects of India's financial links with Britain during the period of 'mature colonialism'[8] in the late nineteenth century after we have discussed the essence of the mechanism and the magnitude of the financial transfers.

Remittances through Council Bills were based on an undertaking by the Indian treasury that all bills drawn on it were to be reimbursed by it in Indian rupees. Funds earmarked in the annual budget as 'Expenditure Abroad' were used to honour the CBs in India, thus releasing the sterling proceeds (of the sales of CBs) for disbursement in England. Fiscal problems of providing for the home charges in rupees were sorted out in 1893 when uncertainties regarding the rupee rate were removed. Home charges, however, continued to grow in absolute terms in sterling, resulting in proportionate increases in domestic expenditure which was earmarked for overseas disbursements. The process, in terms of a simple Keynesian framework, implied a leakage in the income stream, as could be caused by an equivalent surplus budget.[9] Compounded with the monetary squeeze and credit stringencies which resulted from the policies

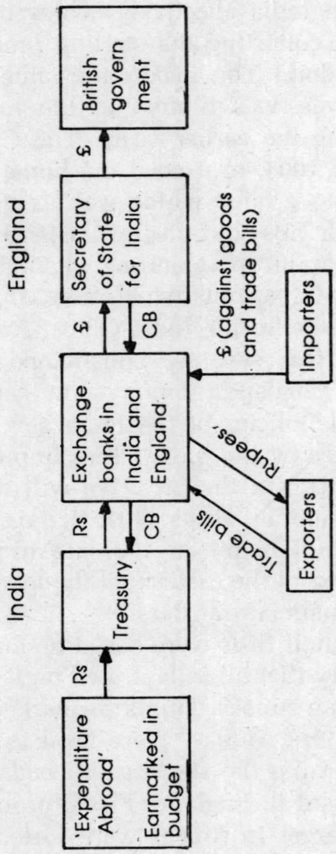

Fig. 1 Mode of remittances between England and India during British rule

followed by the ruling government, the colonial economy had reasons to experience a sluggishness in demand and a related depression in output growth.

The intricacies of the remittance scheme under the Council Bills or of their counterparts, the Reverse Councils (which were sold in years of adverse trade), persuade us to pay a little more attention to the mechanism. Figure 1 shows the network of payments and compensations which can be described in the following seven steps:

(*a*) CBs sold by the India Office to exchange banks served as a device to retain in London India's sterling revenue from net export earnings abroad.

(*b*) In India, the treasury paid to the exchange banks an equivalent sum in rupees as the CBs were produced for encashment. Implicit in the device was a transfer or compensation; while the budgetary sources of revenue in India provided for the entire payments to exporters on account of their net export earnings abroad, equivalent revenue was kept back in sterling at the India Office in England. The rupee payments were the counterpart funds to sterling disbursed (in England) under the budgetary head of Expenditure Abroad (or home charges).

(*c*) Bills sold by the SOS were denominated in sterling, the rupee value of which was consistent with the exchange value of the currency. Before 1893, when mints in India were open to unlimited coinage of silver currency, CBs (or telegraphic transfers) provided an alternate channel of remittance, supplementing the other option of a direct settlement by shipments of gold and silver bullion or gold coins. It had thus been always customary as well as compulsory on the part of the SOS to maintain the price of the CBs at a level which was consistent with the prevailing rupee–sterling rate.

(*d*) In England the India Office's annual expenditure abroad, known as home charges, included the India government's official liabilities to Britain. The more important heads of such expenditure (given in Table 2.1) included interest payments and debt management on past loans. In addition, home charges included payment of salaries and pensions to British officials employed with the (India) government, the India Office's administrative expenses, and finally, the charges on account of Britain's defence activities in India and abroad.

(e) The India Office maintained its residual sterling balance (which was left after meeting the annual expenses) with the Bank of England, the actual disbursement of which was a matter of serious controversy between the India government, the Bank of England, and the SOS. In the next chapter we give an account of such conflicts between the dominant financial interests in the City and the colonial administration in India.

(f) The upper limit upto which Council Bills could be sold was, till 1905–06, determined by the annual value of home charges. Later no such limits were observed and bills could be sold upto what the market could bear without a drop in the exchange value of the rupee in terms of sterling. Sales of bills were also co-ordinated to transfer gold from the treasury and from the two official currency reserves in India to their counterparts in London where gold could be put to use for purchase of sterling securities, providing sources of liquidity to the financial system in the London City.

(g) Sales of CBs on India gave way to Reverse Council Bills (RCBs) on England during 1907–08. The period was an unusual one with trade deficits for India, largely as a result of the extensive droughts and crop shortfalls in of the country. The practice was one of stopping the sale of CBs in London and their substitution by the RCBs. These bills could be encashed in sterling at the India Office. The unusual step was taken to meet the country's trade deficit and also to maintain the rupee rate at its official peg. In the absence of RCBs the trade deficits would have put pressure on the rupee rate.

Singularities of the remittance scheme under the Council Bill network of the Indian currency system were commented upon by Keynes who, among other contemporaries, was also highly appreciative of the device: '...Remittances by means of Council Bills is a feature peculiar to the Indian system [arising] partly from the historical circumstances that the Government of India is the successor of a trading company, partly from the necessity...of making very large remittances to England.' Furthermore, '...rupees to this amount, being part of the revenue from taxation, etc. accumulate in the Indian treasuries. This value is remitted to England by selling for sterling in London bills which can be cashed in Calcutta. Thus the Government of India pays out rupees in Calcutta where the bills are presented, and the Secretary of State's balances in the Bank of England are swelled by a corresponding amount.'[10]

It is reasonable at this stage to distinguish between two possible approaches to the mode of external settlements by Council Bills. In terms of the first approach, the CBs, in combination with the ordinary trade bills (also known as bills of exchange), can be viewed as ordinary means of settling India's external trade and payments. The Council Bills and trade bills, along with the domestic budget, were the three chief instruments available to finance the country's external economic transactions, and were used by a set of three official agents which included the India Office (or the SOS) in London, the exchange banks and trading houses operating between the two countries, and finally, the treasury in India.

We have offered, above, an alternative view on Council Bills, based on considerations which completely change the interpretation of the CB network as a mode of remittance. This former view reflects an awareness that, implicit in the CBs—apparently settled on a simple basis of reciprocity—there remained an imperial design to plough back the entire proceeds of India's export surplus and to retain it in England. In Section 2.3.1 we have posed the question of whether the process was at all legitimate, an answer to which helps us to identify the element of unilateral transfer in the flow of remittances between the two countries. The issue, as pointed out earlier in this chapter, can only be sorted out by recognizing the political realities of the empire–colony relations between India and Britain.

2.2 Depreciating silver and the fiscal burden on the India government: 1870–92

The CB network provided a handy tool to the finance department of the India government as it closed the mint to free coinage in 1893 on the recommendations of the Royal Commission on Indian Currency. The committee, under the chairmanship of Lord Herschell, wanted to delink the rupee rate from fluctuations in world silver prices. The silver prices fell in world markets with the steady displacement of silver by gold and the breakdown of bimetallism in the major industrialized nations of the West during the 1870s. As already hinted, maintaining silver currency in India implied a considerable strain on the country's fiscal resources, with almost half (or more) of official expenditure determined by contractual liabilities in sterling. It was, therefore, necessary to raise additional revenue which could meet the escalation in the rupee cost of sterling caused by the depreciating rupee. Moreover, the European community in India were concerned at the depreciated sterling value of their rupee remittances, and this provided additional grounds for a change in the official currency policy. Implementing the recommendations of the Herschell committee in 1893 by delinking the rupee rate from the market fluctuations in silver prices, thus, proved to be a mutually convenient solution to the government and the European residents in India. The continued use of silver as the metallic base for coins in India (and in China) suited well with the interests of the silver producing countries in the West which, according to a study, constituted an integral part of the imperial designs in the East[11].

Measures implemented during 1893–98 to stabilize the rupee rate at 1*s* 4*d* included, among others, the following:

(*a*) A willingness on the part of the Indian treasury to convert all incoming CBs at the official exchange rate. It is worth pointing out the implicit anomaly in the functioning of gold exchange standard in India as conversion of rupees into sterling was ruled out by the government, presumably on grounds of the poor rating of the rupee in world currency market. The official attitude indicated the prevailing state of colonial economic policies in India which ruled out all connections between export surpluses and the market strength or weakness of the rupee.

(*b*) Measures were taken to demonetize the rupee, as was recommended by the Herschell committee, in order to stabilize the rupee rate at the officially announced peg of 1*s* 4*d*. Rupee coins worth Rs. 10 million were melted while fresh coinage of the rupee was altogether stopped—the second measure amounting, according to a private estimate, to a net withdrawal of Rs. 525 million from circulation during 1893–98.[12] The package of measures, however, did not succeed in stabilizing the rupee before the reversal in world gold prices which started during 1898. In the next chapter we will return to the monetary implications of these policies in the domestic economy.

Closure of the mints in 1893 to coinage on public demand strengthened the demand for CBs in England as a form of remittance. The other route via treasure flows, however, continued, as can be verified from Table 3.1. While the treasure inflows helped sustain hoarding (or other industrial uses) of the metals, coinage was resumed in 1898 sustaining the regular source of demand for imports of silver in India. Gold sovereigns, however, were accepted by the treasury as revenue—a policy which channelized most of the gold sovereign imports into official reserves. The changing composition of the reserves which resulted from the disproportionate increases in the share of gold sovereigns, called for further changes in the official currency policy in India which now aimed at transferring them to England by using the remittance network of the Council Bills. Motivations and implications of such manipulations will be analysed in the next chapter.

2.3 Pattern of financial settlements between India and England around 1900: the direction, sources, and magnitude of the net flows

In this section we draw attention to the pattern and the magnitude of what we have identified as the flow of unilateral transfers from colonial India around 1900. It clearly requires more than a conventional textbook approach to look for an element of transfer in what apparently were legitimate contractual payments to the British government and its officials for 'services' provided and paid for under 'home charges'. An analysis of the specific political context of the so-called 'services' reveals an element of expropriation legitimized under colonial rule. Interestingly, the relatively non-controversial component of the home charges, viz. that on servicing the official loans contracted in the past for productive purposes seems, on a closer analysis, to have been the result of accounting transfers. Such transfers were deliberately used to hide the extent of borrowing which met the unproductive expenditure of the India government. Use of the net export earnings to meet the unproductive expenditure amounts to an act of unrequited exports or unilateral transfers—one without any quid pro quo (as indicated in Section 2.3.1). Understandably, it is relatively difficult to arrive at a measure of the unilateral transfers. The difficulties are compounded by the limitations of trade data and the consequent problems in compilation of India's balance of payments by a 'residual approach'.[13] Problems of using the official trade statistics of colonial India led us to base our measure of the transfer on estimates of remittance flows through sales of Council Bills at the India Office—records which were obviously more accurate compared to trade data. We will return to this theme in Section 2.4 which deals with the magnitude of transfers.

2.3.1. THE TRANSFERS FROM INDIA AND 'EXPENDITURE ABROAD'

The flow of finance between India and England was to a large extent determined by the sum annually remitted abroad to meet the government's home charges in England. Since the latter absorbed nearly the entire amount of India's overseas trade surplus, it is worth enquiring into its political legitimacy by scrutinizing the individual heads of expenses under home charges. The criterion of political legitimacy is given by the justifiability of such expenses in terms of the separate identity of India as a self-governing territory, as was often claimed by the British. Payments made out to procure goods or services which were absorbed by the national economy (in its separate identity shorn of colonial rule) were all warranted in terms of this criterion. Logically, the remaining charges which were directly related to the maintenance and promotion of commercial and political interest of the British empire could be identified as unilateral transfers from the national economy since these were never reimbursed or repaid in any form.

Let us dwell a little on the actual pattern of financial flows between England and colonial India during the half century preceding the First World War. As already explained, all official expenses of the India government in England were earmarked, in the India budget, as Expenditure Abroad by the India Office, which procured the sterling equivalents through sale of Council Bills in London. In Table 2.1 we have provided the details of overseas expenses during 1861–62 to 1913–14. The items listed under the different subheads can be divided into the following three major categories: (*a*) civil administration (items 3 and 5); (*b*) defence (item 4); (*c*) productive expenditure and/or management of debt chargeable under productive heads (item 1 excluding (*b*) plus item 2).

Quantitatively, the weight of debt service charges in respect of railway and irrigation loans appears to be predominant in the aggregate overseas expenditure during the period. These loans were chargeable under productive heads. The relative significance of the three categories (*a*) to (*c*) can be assessed from their respective weights which stood at 1:1:3 during 1910–11, indicating the very crucial importance of the expenditure designated as 'productive' in determining the magnitude of home charges, most of which was thus incurred on servicing irrigation and railway loans. In the year 1910–11, out of a total expenditure of £18.6 million on home charges, more than 60 per cent was spent in servicing past loans. At £8.7 million, railways alone accounted for around 47 per cent of the total

Table 2.1: Pattern of overseas expenditure under home charges: 1861–62 to 1913–14 (£ Millions)

Items	Annual Averages 1861–62 to 1874–75	1875–76 to 1897–98	1898–99 to 1913–14	1910–11
(1)	(2)	(3)	(4)	(5)
1. Interest charges and debt management: chargeable under head of	5.7	7.9	9.4	11.1
(*a*) railways and irrigation	3.5	5.3	6.9	8.8 (0.1)
(*b*) other interest	2.2	2.6	2.5	2.3
2. Stores purchased in England against revenue and for railways	1.1	1.2	1.6	1.0
3. Civil administration in India Office (excluding pensions)	0.2	0.6	0.2	0.1
4. Army and marine charges:	2.6	3.5	4.2	4.1
(*a*) effective charges including home charges for British officials in India				1.1
(*b*) Non-effective charges				3.0
5. Pensions and furlough	0.9	1.7	2.3	2.3
6. Total expenditure under home charges (items 1 to 5)	10.5	14.9	17.7	18.6

Note and Sources: Figure in brackets in col. 5 refers to irrigation. Sources: cols. 2 to 4, Dharma Kumar, 'The Fiscal System' in *Cambridge Economic History of India (1757–1920)*, Vol. II, ed. Dharma Kumar, p.938. Col.5 is taken from the Explanatory Memorandum, annually submitted by the Under-Secretary of State for India, cited in Theodore Morison, *Economic Transition*, p. 234.

expenditure. Interest payments and debt management in respect of other types of loans accounted for another £2.3 million, thus bringing expenditure under this head to £11.1 million, a sum which was substantial compared to other current productive expenditure earmarked for purchase of stores for railways, which at £1.0 million, was only 5.6 per cent of the total. Expenditure on defence, designated as 'Army and Marine Charges', comprised the second major component, which, at £4.1 million, constituted about 21 per cent while the third important component, viz. pensions and furlough, along with current civil expenditure stood at £2.4 million or 12 per cent of total overseas expenditure for 1910–11. The distribution of the expenses reflects the overall pattern of home charges during the pre-World War period.

One can argue, presumably without being accused of a nationalist bias, that most of the civil and military expenditures of the India government in England (items 3, 4, and 5 in Table 2.1) listed as (*a*) and (*b*) above, which accounted for one-third of overseas expenditure, were in the interest of the British.[14] The argument excludes the local expenses in rupees connected with the maintenance of the civilian government in India, which would clearly have been warranted even under a national government. Later in this section, we have looked into some of the current controversies on the expediency and justifiability of the enormous share of British military expenses which had to be borne by India.

Looking at the table one can identify about one-third of overseas expenses (which included defense and civil administration) as directly caused by British rule in India. This certainly does not warrant condemning the entire amount of home charges as a 'drain of wealth' from India as the nationalists had argued.[15] It has to be remembered that nearly three-fifths of the overseas expenditure was accounted for by 'interest charges and debt management' against productive loans for investment in railways and irrigation. Unless these payments can also be attributed to the machinations of the ruling imperial power in India it would not be logical to attribute the entire amount (or even the major part) of the home charges as expropriations due to the foreign rule. It is interesting to note that a distinction was maintained in contemporary official reports between productive and unproductive categories[16] of official loans in India. When the money borrowed was spent on public works like railways and irrigation, loans were treated as productive. Borrowing for all other purposes including administration, was categorized as unproductive. We do not, at this point, want to enter into the debate as to whether in India, expenditure in railways was oriented to serve national interests. Rather, we prefer to reserve our judgement on the extreme position taken by the nationalists that the entire amount of home charges, including the substantial sum incurred to service productive loans, were all a drain of wealth from the national economy.

It is worth mentioning, at this point, a rather curious device of accounting transfers which was hidden in the budgetary practices of the India government during the period. The practice, initially recommended by a select committee of the British parliament in 1867, amounted, for practical purposes, to a camouflaging—one where borrowing under productive heads were used, in effect, to cancel old unproductive debt while public works expenditure was in reality financed by a revenue surplus. In terms of the recommendation of the 1867 select committee, '...all capital expenditure on productive works supplied from revenue should be treated in the accounts *as if it had been borrowed*, that a sum equal to that which was thus supplied should be *transferred* from the ordinary debt to the productive public works debt, and that interest on that sum be charged on the works' (italics added).[17] In the year 1880–81 the Government of India added Rs. 5.4 million as outstanding productive loans—a sum which was simultaneously recovered from current revenue and utilized to cancel unproductive loans, the proceeds of which were spent on unproductive heads before 1867.[18] Since then new loans shown against productive heads of expenditure floated in the market, and the proceeds were made available to finance the capital projects (despite the availability of revenue surplus for the purpose). The notional (or accounting) transfers implicit in the scheme included the following stages:

Stage 1: A hypothetical sum, say Rs. 100, is transferred from the revenue account to finance an equivalent expenditure on public works in the capital account of the domestic budget.

Stage 2: An expenditure of Rs. 100 on public works expenditure in India and England is shown in the capital account.

Stage 3: Additional borrowings, under productive heads, worth Rs. 100 covers the capital expenditure.

Stage 4: Revenue from above borrowings are used to repay

Table 2.2: Changes in the composition of public debt in India: 1867–1897 (£ millions)

	1867	1897
1. Ordinary or unproductive	90.6 (93.3)	72.7 (31.4)
2. Productive (public works)	5.4 (6.7)	159.3 (63.6)
Total	96.0	232.0

(Brackets relate to percentages)

Note: 1. According to Balfour returns, unproductive debt held in March 1867 and 1897 were at £92.5 million and £63.7 million respectively. The divergent movements in the shares under the two heads over the periods were thus sharper under the Balfour returns.

2. Rupee figures converted into sterling at Rs.10:£1 and Rs.15:£1 for 1867 and 1897 respectively. *Sources*: Welby Commission, pp. 44, 47–48.

and cancel old unproductive loans which now goes down, as a consequence, by Rs. 100.

Adoption of the procedure described above in managing government's finances led, as could be expected, to a relative increase in the size of productive debt which was held as a proportion of the aggregate debt in rupee and sterling. The absolute figures for productive debt went up from £5.4 million to £159.3 million over 1867–97, and its share in total debt went up from 6.4 per cent to 63.3 per cent over the same period (*see Table 2.2*).[19] *The underlying process was the outcome of a policy contrived by the colonial rulers to camouflage the extent of public borrowings to finance the politically sensitive and commercially unviable expenditures of government.* Most of these expenditures, connected with the subservient political status of India in relation to Britain, was but overtly political in origin. It is pertinent to argue, by the same logic, that the servicing of productive debt, which accounted for almost two-thirds of aggregate home charges by 1913, was in effect financing unproductive expenditure. Thus interest paid and debt managed were, truly speaking, not in respect of productive debt, since the latter was a surrogate for the amount spent and borrowed in the past for unproductive purposes. This fact, we think, can be used as a very important step in constructing an argument on the justifiability or otherwise of the home charges from a national angle.

With notional transfers incorporated in the budget, revenue earmarked to finance public works was, in effect, used to subsidize unproductive expenditure by cancelling old, unproductive debt. Hence, a natural tendency on the part of the government was to feel encouraged in continuing with its growing level of unproductive expenses in the two countries and covering them by taxes or loans (in rupee or sterling) raised from the market. (All productive expenses, it might be recalled, were statutorily covered by fresh loans raised in the market.) Moreover, raising of sterling loans to cover capital expenditure and the subsequent transfers under service heads led to the possibility of sterling borrowed in excess being retained by the SOS in London. Sterling loans contracted against public works expenditures in India, which was statutory under the select committee recommendations, increased India Office's liquidity in England because a part of the public works expenses was met in rupees. The implications of a rise in the sterling assets of the SOS will be examined in the next chapter.

Outstanding loans of the India government held in sterling rose sharply relative to rupee loans during 1890–1913.[20] This was evident in the meagre 10 per cent increase in rupee loans over the period, which contrasted with the 32 per cent increase in sterling loans. Table 2.2 reveals the marked increases in outstanding loans under productive heads, matched by simultaneous declines of unproductive loans. It was thus natural that interest charges and management of productive debt comprised nearly 60 per cent of the home charges around 1910–11 (*see* Table 2.1).

Current expenditure, classified as unproductive in government budget was spread under three heads. These included famine relief, military operations, and civil administration. Interestingly enough, while the outstanding debt shown under unproductive heads went down over 1867–97, the scale of unproductive expenses, especially on overseas military operations, went up over 1861–62 to 1913–14. Contrasted with £2.6 million spent on 'Army and Marine' as annual average expenditure over 1861–62 to 1874–75, the expenditure under the same head was substantially higher later, with annual averages of £3.5 million and £4.2 million respectively between 1875–76 to 1897–98 and 1898–99 to 1913–14 (Table 2.1). The increased expenditure on army and marine was clearly encouraged by the provision for the notional transfers incorporated in the budget. As pointed out above, the practice amounted to 'subsidizing' of the unproductive heads of expenditure because of the facility to fund the latter through new debt under productive heads. This created a tendency on part of the government to continue with its growing level of unproductive expenditure in India and England. Thus, sterling loans, contracted against public works expenditure in India (which was only statutory), increased liquidity at the India Office in England.

Welby Commission's analysis of the implications of the fiscal transfers between productive and unproductive heads of expenditure (as well as of borrowing) puts to test the basis of the rather politically charged thesis advanced by Sir John Strachey—a contemporary British official. According to him, most of the increases in India's public debt between 1862–1909 were related to public works expenditure. Basing his argument on a rather simplistic use of official data on India's outstanding public debt and its distribution under productive and unproductive heads, Strachey drew attention to the fact that all increases in aggregate public debt occurring over the period 1862–1909 were matched by a fall in the unproductive category by £60 million (*see also* Table 2.2). Clearly, the argument is disproved if attention is paid to the accounting transfers mentioned above. The rate of return on irrigation projects, calculated by what came to be known as the Strachey method, was put at 0.2 per cent for 1885–86, and was thus considered rather low, especially when compared to the opportunity cost of capital employed elsewhere during the period. Calculation of returns under the Strachey method, according to the Welby Commission, entailed an underestimation and could be revised upwards to 2.2 per cent per annum by redefining the surplus on public works (given the fact that money spent on public works was actually not borrowed and was chargeable under revenue). Thus interest charges on borrowed capital, ordinarily treated as an item of cost, were no longer relevant in determining the rate of return on public works. The rate of return calculated by Welby Commission on irrigation was, therefore, at a higher level—at 2.2 per cent over the same period. The calculation removed, to a large extent, the impressions created under the Strachey thesis that much of the public works expenditure in India was non-remunerative.[21]

The Select Committee recommendation of showing all capital expenditure on public works as new loans also encouraged a different kind of financial transfer within the official budget. Funds initially allocated to the Famine Relief Fund—initiated in 1874 at the suggestion of Lord Northbook—were often set aside for expenditure on irrigation and railways.[22] Thus, out of Rs. 500 million allocated to the Famine Relief Fund between 1881–82 and 1923–24, the amount spent on direct relief was as little as 47 per cent while 21 per cent and 4 per cent were spent respectively on irrigation and protective railways.[23] For John and Richard Strachey both ardent advocates of the empire, such expenses could be justified as being incurred for '... the construction of canals and railways required for the protection of districts, especially liable to drought and consequent scarcity.'[24]

Of the total outstanding public debt held by the Government of India, the proportion held as sterling loans rose from 27 per cent (1860) to 47 per cent (1890), and to 59 per cent (1913).[25] This implied a fall in rupee loans as a part of total outstanding public debt held. If was thus only natural to find a rising trend in the debt charges on sterling loans over the period. Incidentally, it is worth mentioning here that the records availabe on rupee loans subscribed by the European community indicate that around 1899, resident Europeans had subscribed to Rs. 480 million of such loans (which was 46.6 per cent of the total rupee loans floated by India government). Their overseas counterparts managed to pool another Rs. 270 million (26.2 per cent) of the total rupee loans.[26] The predominance of Europeans was but natural in the other category of public loans, viz. those which were denominated in sterling and sold in London. The national bourgeoisie thus posed no effective threat to the European rentier class or to the commercial public who enjoyed a clear superiority in the Indian subcontinent.

The above discussion on interest charges and debt management—the major component of home charges—brings us logically to the second most important component of home charges, viz. overseas expenditure on military operations. This alone accounts for more than a quarter of aggregate home charges over 1898–99 to 1913–14, as we can see from row 4 of Table 2.1. An interesting debate was going on during the period amongst the different departments of the British government regarding the justifiability of levying the costs of the military operations of the empire on the India government. It brings back to our mind a parallel debate amongst nationalists and contemporary British officials on the justifiability of home charges as a whole. Interestingly enough, Welby Commission's views on the more general issue of apportioning home charges was very different from the mainstream official stand of the British rulers. The Commission drew attention to several anomalies in the prevailing pattern of military expenses, and especially to the share borne by India.[27] Following are some of the observations which, on a closer look, touch upon the critical points on the question of the apportioning of the official military expenses:

(*a*) Aggregate official overseas expenditure on 'Defence and Foreign Affairs' exceeded the official expenditure on civil charges, administration, pensions, and public works chargeable to revenue (compare sum of rows 2, 3 and 5 with row 4 in Table 2.1).

(*b*) During the period under consideration, the India government was increasingly involved in British defence and foreign affairs. This implied a proportionate and absolute rise in expenditure on related items (row 4 in Table 2.1).[28]

(*c*) The Welby Commission was openly critical of the fact that most of the expenses of British administration in its overseas territories (like Aden, China, or Persia) was borne by India, pointing out that 'the practice had no parallel in our relations with other colonies or dependencies'. Often the share borne by India was much larger than that borne by Britain—a fact pointed out by the Commission.[29]

Senior officials of the India government were quite aware, by the turn of the century, of the financial responsibilities of the India government in the military and foreign administration of the empire. Differences were thus only inevitable, even between the India government and the British government officials on the political justice behind the 'apportioning' of expenses. The debate provided interesting revelations of the actual pattern of expenditure, as are indicated by the following:

(*a*) Payments for Indian troops stationed outside the country were questioned by the Secretary of State. Despatches to the India government from Lord Hamilton (30 June 1896) and Lord Cross (3 February 1887), and the speech delivered by Henry Fowler at the British Parliament on 6 July 1896 all expressed a similar attitude.[30]

(*b*) 'Effective charges', consisting of the capitation cost to repay to the British exchequer the actual cost incurred by the

War Office at home in raising and maintaining the British force in India, were a matter of dispute, and the original rate, fixed at 10*s* per person, was revised at the end of a series of India government despatches over 1870–90 and the deliberations of a committee set up under Lord Northbrook. The new rate was fixed at 7*s* 4*d* in 1890–91.[31]

(*c*) 'Non-effective charges', on which payments had to be made by the India government to the War Office in London to meet 'pensions of officers and soldiers of British forces in respect to their service to India', was another source of discord on financial matters between India Office and the British government.[32]

(*d*) Disagreements relating to the apportioning of 'Naval Charges' led Lord Salisbury, the prime minister of England, to arrange a conference in 1891 of officials from India Office, the British Foreign Office, the Treasury, and the British Admiralty. (Incidentally, a mutiny broke out in the Indian Navy in 1862 at end of which the naval defence of the nation was handed over to the Admiralty in Britain.) The meeting, however, was inconclusive and in 1894 the India Office had to accept, unconditionally, the views expressed by Lord Rosebury, who was the new prime minister of Britain.[33]

We have so far focused our attention on two major heads of expenditure under the home charges—the costs of interest payment and the debt management, as well as those of defence and foreign administration. It is only logical at this point to discuss the remaining heads of expenses relating to the management of the civil administration in England and incurred mostly to meet the costs of the India Office. The amount spent on the civil adminstration (excluding pensions paid out) averaged around £200,000 over 1898–99 to 1913–14 annually. This sum was a little more than 1 per cent of the average annual home charges at £17.7 million over the same period. Despite being a relatively small part of the home charges, India Office expenses drew disproportionate attention and turned out to be a politically sensitive issue. A rather progressive view was held by the Welby Commission on the matter, representing a radical departure from the contemporary British ethic on home rule in India. The position was evident in the following extract from the report: '...in order that there may be no ground for allegation that India is treated less favourably than other part of Her Majesty's Empire, we recommend that Parliament should be asked to make a contribution towards the charge of the India Office'.[34] Interestingly enough, the Welby Commission chose to remain silent on matters relating to direct expenditure on defence (which contrasted with its critical look at the costs of foreign missions and those on managing the India Office), probably in deference to the view dominant in England. The Commission could thus avoid the dilemma experienced by the India government in its attempts to denounce, because of financial hardship, the various liabilities emerging out of India's 'association' with the 'British Crown'. A minority in the Commission submitted a note of dissent to the main report, the foremost among them being Dadabhai Naoroji, the nationalist spokesman, who could successfully persuade Sir Wedderburn and Mr Caine, two British members of the Commission, to sign the note of dissent.[35]

Our discussions so far on the nature of the home charges, the resistance on the part of the India government officials to the financial commitments arising therefrom, the difficulties experienced by them in view of the official British position supporting such expenses, and finally, deviations from the official line of thinking on the part of the Royal Commission (Welby Commission) as expressed in their *Report on Indian Expenditure* make it evident that the authority and justifiability of imposing these charges on India were questioned even by the British.

Economic historians, writing in the imperialist tradition, were naturally on the defensive on this count and on the financial arrangements during the period. We may mention in this connection the work of Theodore Morison, who was a contemporary, and of Vera Anstey, who wrote in the 1940s. Both authors identified a 'political' content in the expenditure and borrowing patttern of the government. A distinction was drawn by Morison between debts under 'economic' and under 'political' heads. Of a total debt of £17.2 million outstanding in 1910–11, £10.3 million comprised 'economic debt', the proceeds of which were used to meet the expenditure in the past '... an independent country might make in the early stages of industrial development and railway building'. The remaining £6.9 million was deemed to have been spent on 'political heads... related to the lack of independent status for the nation.'[36]

Attention was drawn in Vera Anstey's work to such official expenses as were incurred on 'particular civil and military items... on account of military expenses of conquering India and interest payments on the debentures of the East India Company, taken out by the Crown after the Mutiny and un*justly* debited from India' (italics added). Again, '... it is reasonable to agrue that payments on account of the military expenses of conquering India and interest payments on the debentures of the East India Company, taken out by the Crown after the Mutiny ought never have been charged to the Indian revenues'.[37] Questions raised by Vera Anstey on the justifiability of certain expenses of the India government abroad stand in sharp contrast to the analysis of Theodore Morison whose distinctions between 'economic' and 'political' debts were never extended to a questioning of the latter. Thus, in Morison's view, the £7 million which India paid because of her 'political connections with England', was in the nature of a 'political drain' and in return for the 'freedom from external aggression, and peace and order within the borders'. On the 'economic debt' Morison pointed out that 'such [economic] borrowing was probably justifiable by the same logic as with the political heads under home charges'.[38] Morison's approach was consistent with the general ethos prevailing amongst the British on the rather sensitive issue of the period, viz. that of the justifiability of overseas expenditure related to the British empire and its apportioning between India and England. However, the functional distinction between 'economic' and 'political' debts was widely in use in the debate current amongst the nationalists and official spokesmen of the period. The shift from an unquestioned approval in Morison (1911) to a moderately critical look at the 'political' debt (and overseas expenses) in Vera Anstey (1942) can be traced to the controversies current over the interim period. Even Vera Anstey had to concede that 'political, administrative and commercial connections with England,...far outweighed the corresponding payments',[39] presumably the home charges. The cautious and conservative stance of Anstey continues the condescending note of the Welby Commission on the huge military involvement of India government in the upkeep of the British empire. (Incidentally, the Commission also maintained a distance from sensitive issues like the 'drain' of wealth.) Most of the contemporaries, British and Indians alike, who were writing outside the nationalist tradition apparently seem to have shared the conviction that the home charges were mostly payments for invisibles purchased by India. Morison was no exception and his writings reflected a total rejection of any plea whatsoever as could question the responsibilities laid on the India government to finance the home charges. Incidentally, the slant was shared by his contemporary John Maynard Keynes, who, as mentioned earlier, commented extensively on Morison's work in the *Economic Journal* of 1909.[40]

The British official position on the legitimacy of the empire and the home charges on colonies was, in principle, never in doubt in the mainstream literature of the period. It however, underplayed the discontent and contradictions, even at the level of intra-governmental despatches between the India government and the SOS in London which often openly expressed displeasure over the military expenses. A picture of apparently harmonious relations also leaves out the critical analysis at the level of a royal commission (the Welby Commission) which was appointed in 1900 to study the sensitive issue of Indian overseas expenditure. A survey of the official reports or correspondences relating to the period reflect the undercurrents of tension in administering the financial arrangements, which became a sensitive issue with the growing nationalist sentiments against these arrangements.

We conclude the present section with an account of our impressions on the issues pertaining to 'overseas expenditure' by India. These concern (*a*) the dilemma of the India government in conceding to and abiding by the demands of the imperial authorities; (*b*) the revelations by the Welby Commission of the various accounting transfers practised by the India government, and (*c*) the characterization by the imperialist historians of the financial administration in British India. Our observations strengthen the thesis that most of India's 'Expenditure Abroad' during the period was political in origin and was avoidable in absence of a colonial rule. The above lends support to the proposition advanced earlier in this section that such expenditure constituted an element of unilateral transfer from the point of view of the national economy.

2.3.2 THE NATIONALIST ARGUMENTS ON 'DRAIN OF WEALTH' REVISITED

Nationalist perceptions on what they had chosen to describe as a 'drain of wealth' from India can now be reassessed. We propose to reopen the arguments put forward[41] on the issue and relate them to our position on 'transfer of resources' from colonial India.

Attention was drawn in the seventeenth century and earlier by mercantilist writers on possibilities of acquiring 'Treasure by Forraign Trade'.[42] Writings, defending the East India Company's practices, were all centred around the mercantilist notion of drain as a net outflow of precious metals. Thus the early writings on the subject by Thomas Mun and by Josiah Child in England emphasized that Britain's exports of specie to India fetched, in effect, a net inflow of the same to the country— earned through re-exports of Indian wares to European markets. Notions of drain in terms of an outflow of precious metals was often considered as too narrow a definition, even in the eighteenth and nineteenth century writings on Indo-British economic relations. Thus, despite net inflows of silver as well as of gold to India, external payments were considered responsible for a conceivable drain of wealth from the national economy and were attacked by various writers. India government's expenditure abroad and other private remittances by Europeans were quantitatively not significant before the Indian mutiny and the takeover of the East India Company by the crown during 1857–58. However, the East India Company administration was evidently exploitative. This was indicated by the sharp public criticism from British officials like Sir George Wingate who pointed at the '...*tribute* paid to Great Britain...(as)...the most objectionable feature in our existing policy' (italics added). Thus the '... cruel, crushing effects of the tribute upon India' entailed a policy with 'taxes raised in one country and spent in another' which implied 'an absolute loss and extinction of the whole amount withdrawn from the taxed country'.[43] Tributes from India increased to significant proportions by early nineteenth century and a large number of British civilian officers were concerned about the large outflow of funds from India. We may recall, in this connection, the writings and representations of Lord Cornwallis (the governor-general of India in 1790), Frederick John Shore (a Bengal civilian, writing in 1837), Saville Marriot (a revenue commissioner of Deccan), and C.J. Hamilton (a British economist writing in 1919).[44] Thus tribute paid out by India was often recognized in the commentary offered by some Englishmen. For understandable reasons, writings by the British stopped short of a questioning of the tribute—an attitude which was in line with the prevailing ethos on British rule in India. Questions raised, in late nineteenth century, by Indian nationalists regarding the propriety of British claims were based on a conceptualization of drain which was very different from the specie form prevalent in the writings of the mercantilists. The awareness shown by the British administrators of the tribute paid by British India helped the nationalists to articulate their challenge, which questioned the very basis of the British empire in India. In Europe the pace of Industrial Revolution and the consolidation of industrial capitalism led to the rise of free trade doctrines which advanced the role of comparative advantage in transmitting growth. The nationalists used these paradigms to highlight the experience of India under colonialism. In the West, similar dissents were articulated in the context of the Irish economy of the eighteenth and nineteenth centuries.[45] Thus the mercantilist preoccupations of the earlier centuries with the drain of specie gave way, in later writings, to a theoretical perception in which the drain was identified as unilateral transfers effected through commodity trade. This shift in position was evident in the writings on Irish colonies during nineteenth century. A similar recognition of drain ran parallel in the Indian context as the nationalists started writing, during the second half of the nineteenth century, on the intensity of famines in India and their incidence on poverty, and on the lack of fairness in the steady flow of remittances from India, a large part of which was connected with the upkeep of the British empire. Incidentally, the complacency and the self-righteousness of British officials who relied on the Strachey thesis regarding benevolent British administration of the public works programmes (despite their low rates of return) underwent a jolt with India experiencing some of the severest famines of the century over the same period.[46]

Writings by the nationalist writers in India, as could be expected, were at various levels of sophistication and political expediency. From an analytical angle, Dadabhai Naoroji's writings provided one of the earliest but relatively complete version of the nationalist argument.[47] Emphasizing on the drain of wealth from India through its export surplus which he thought to remain unpaid or unrequited from the angle of the domestic economy, Naoroji also drew attention to the profits on export trade. These profits, mostly enjoyed by Europeans, were also viewed as a part of the drain. According to Dadabhai Naoroji, 'Profits on India's export trade' (which ranged between 15 to 20 per cent of export earnings during 1883–92) were entirely appropriated by the Europeans. Imports were also overpriced during these years by at least 10 per cent. The two components, along with the unpaid (unrequited) margin of export earnings (which was another 30 per cent of latter) comprised, according to Naoroji, the drain from India. It ranged, according to him, between £20–30 million. The estimate was clearly larger than the annual averages of export surpluses which stood, according to official statistics, at £17million in the 1870s. We are tempted, probably at the risk of reproducing what might be considered as a piece of rhetoric, to quote the following passage from Naoroji's work. 'This, then, is the way the treasure goes, and poor British India gets all the abuse—insult added to injury. The candle burns not only at both ends but at all parts'.[48]

Naoroji's notion of drain, which had a wider coverage than those of other nationalists, was relatively difficult to quantify. Since profits in export trade and the overcharging of imports were both subject to the varying degrees of monopoly enjoyed by respective traders, these were difficult to estimate. In a recent work on India's economic relations over the second half of the last century, Banerji has stressed the need to look at the drain of wealth from India from an 'alternative' angle in order that the researcher could examine the 'entire spectrum of payments abroad' and identify varying elements of drain in them.[49]

Political leverage enjoyed in colonial India was clearly an important factor behind the ability of the British to extract monopoly profits (in both internal and external trade) and to earn high salaries. Thus the India government was committed, despite financial stresses in the domestic economy (details of which are provided in Chapter 3), to meet a myriad of overseas liabilities, most of which, as noted earlier, had their origin in the political subordination of India. This alternative notion of drain, according to Banerji, was potentially capable of capturing the element of compulsion in the colonial economy, to procure net export earnings in order to make them available for settling the overseas liabilities.

That export surpluses did not have a positive impact on the national economy—since net earnings from exports were all retained abroad (to meet the home charges and other expenses of the India Office)—provided the core of the argument for nationalists ranging from Naoroji to Dutt. All of them were critical of the prevailing procedure which, for practical purposes, amounted to a remitting of India's tax revenue abroad (*see* Fig. 1 and the related arguments). The above may in fact be interpreted as the anticipation of a Keynesian effective demand argument which was voiced in the nationalist protests to the prevailing financial practices.[50] The argument also contests the very basis of the notion of gains from free trade—one which was evidently denied to India under colonial rule. The nationalists, however, did not spell out their critique of the free trade doctrines. Nor did they visualize the parallel surplus expropriation process within the economy—one which, argued in Chapter 4, left very little potential for domestic investment. The issue gains a special perspective in some recent writings where the nationalist views are identified with an anti-imperialist position.*51 (It requires a close study of the political predilections of nationalist movements in order to judge their worth as an anti-imperialist force. In absence of such efforts, we hesitate to offer a judgment on the legitimacy of such generalizations.)

While the drain of wealth from colonial India had far-reaching consequences for the domestic economy, it is nonetheless important to arrive at a measure of the flow of the drain-related remittances. The flow, in our judgement, provides a good indicator of the possible extent of expropriation and spoliation of the colonized economy, some evidence of which has been presented in Chapters 3 and 4 which respectively deal with monetary stringency and the commercialization process in the agrarian economy in India.[52]

The prevailing financial arrangements in British India were questioned by the nationalist writers on three major grounds. First, in British India most of the significant positions in civil administration, in defence services, and in the commercially profitable ventures were controlled by Europeans. The related income enjoyed by the latter, which was considered as a 'moral drain' by Naoroji, was seen by the nationalists as a cost to British India. In terms of Naoroji's estimates, the sum comprised about one-sixth of total expenses of India government disbursed between England and India.[53]

Second, the India government was forced, under British rule, to meet a long list of official overseas expenses, described as home charges.

Third, India's net export earnings in sterling were never brought back to the country. This aspect confirmed the existence of unrequitted (unpaid) exports from India, the proceeds of which were financing, according to the nationalists, the flow of unilateral transfers from the country. The magnitude of the drain of wealth from India was thus approximated by the annual value of its export surpluses.

The nationalist arguments were articulated in the charter of demands pitted by the Indian National Congress around the turn of the century. The demands included (*a*) a reduction of home charges (which was considered as excessive), and (*b*) the Indianization of civil services.'[54] Lord Curzon—the then governor-general of India—however, asserted that of the salaried sections receiving Rs.75 and above per annum in 1867, about 55 per cent were either Europeans or Eurasians. The proportion fell, according to Curzon, to 43 per cent in 1903. G Subramania Iyer, the Indian nationalist, was quick to point out that the real picture was exactly the opposite—with share of Europeans rising over 1867–1903, provided one only considered the jobs fetching Rs.1000 and above. The Indian National Congress's demands were wholly rejected by the ruling government.[55]

Notwithstanding the stand taken by the nationalists in their challenges to the old imperialist order and colonial rule in India, the drain theory, which identified India's export surpluses as unilateral transfers (or unrequited exports), from country, is, in our view, faulted on the following two grounds. First, it is not logical to argue that India's export surplus remained unpaid. Revenue against such surpluses were duly remitted under the Council Bill schema (*see* Fig. 1 and Section 2.1) and actually paid out via the intermediation of exchange banks to exporters in India. Revenue earmarked in the domestic budget as 'Expenditure Abroad' was, however, effectively transferred abroad with home charges met in sterling without the necessity of an actual sterling remittance to England. Hence India's export surpluses, which roughly indicated the magnitude and the direction of financial transfer from the country, should by no means be deemed to constitute the transfer itself.

Second, it is difficult to accept, at its face value, the nationalist contention that the entire amount of home charges (including the sum spent in the servicing of productive loans) represented a drain of wealth to the national economy. Indeed, the absolutist position of the nationalists on their outright condemnation of public works programmes in India appears untenable, especially when one considers the material implications of public works programme in the domestic economy. One can here address the broader question as to whether public works expenditure programmes on railways and irrigation brought any net benefits to India. The available analysis of railroad investment in India fails to provide a conclusive thesis on the matter. The India government's purchases of erstwhile guaranteed railway companies in 1907 had often been cited as an indirect example of profitability. Profits, however, fructified only after the step was taken. It has also been pointed out that during the period concessional finance was often provided by Britain to meet the cost of railroad construction in India.[56] Railways have, in general, been viewed as 'profitable' ventures, capable of reducing discrepancies between social and private returns. To Vera Anstey, interest paid on productive loans (which covered expenditure on railways) 'brought in more revenue than suffices to cover the interest charges ... (it) does not contain any net drain from India. In addition railways and irrigation works have been of immense benefit to the country ... the money could not have been raised as cheaply anywhere else as in London.'[57] The above view contrasts the position held by nationalists on Indian railways, pointing at the fact that the network of railway tracks laid down in India more often served British commercial interests and not national interest.[58] It was often a common official practice to buy the entire amount of railway stores (raw materials, machinery, etc.) in England—a device which entailed an equivalent expenditure abroad to procure imports. The above considerably minimized the possible expansionary (multiplier) effects of initial railway investment in the national economy.[59] The arguments are by no means unfounded and one comes across, even in a more balanced study on Indian railways, comments such as '... railroad building in India did not give rise to a flood of satellite inovations and it destroyed more occupational opportunities than it opened up'.[60] The developments probably led a British contemporary to admit that 'Next to Australia, India is the largest consumer of Britain for locomotives... We have supplied all the material and all the equipments and we reaped the profits very largely.[61] Earlier years of railway construction in India was often geared to the strategic or political exigencies of British rulers in India, an evidence of which comes out clearly in the following statement from Lord Hardinge, the governor-general, in 1846: 'In this country... the facility of rapid concentration of infantry and artillery and stores may be (treated as) the cheap prevention of insurrection, the speedy termination of war, or the safety of the empire.'[62] Similarly, the strategic value of railways led Lord Dalhousie, the governor-general of India, to state in 1853 that railroads would provide 'full intelligence of any event to be transmitted to government at five times the speed now possible; as well as the concentration of its military strength on every given point, in as many days as it would now require months to effect.'[63] Interestingly enough, despite expansions which covered ventures along non-rewarding tracks, railways turned out to be a financially profitable proposition as was evident from the literature.

The diametrically opposite views on the implications of railroad investment in India have been mentioned above to serve an illustrative purpose. We certainly did not want to provide the whole debate on railway investment in India. Our purpose was to highlight the difficulty, even from a nationalist angle, of ignoring the material indicators of changes in the Indian economy which were introduced by railways (say, in terms of the increased traffic provided by the growing transportation facilities connecting the hinterland and the port, in the movement of goods in internal trade within the economy, and finally, with the relative standardization of prices, often at higher levels, for commodities grown in the interior areas). Some of these aspects were stressed by Marx as indicative of progress (actual or potential) in his attempt to identify the 'regenerative' role of railroad construction in Asian colonies. (Incidentally, Marx's comments on Indian railways have been later viewed with scepticism in the controversy on Marx's position on the Asian type of colonialism).[64] Our discussion shows the logical difficulty in accepting what we view as the rather absolutist position of the nationalists that the entire sum of home charges (including the servicing of the loans needed to finance public works including railways[65] or irrigation) could be reckoned as a drain of wealth from India.

A possible way of avoiding the impasse faced by the nationalists in their attempts to identify the drain can be found if we refer to the accounting transfers which were practised by the India government in the context of the domestic budget. As mentioned above (*see* pp. 31–3), in British India accumulation of productive debt had been achieved with equivalent cancellation of unproductive debt. Evidence of the above was provided by the Welby Commission. Thus interest and debt management charges on loans which in the past were contracted to meet railway and irrigation works (none of which could, by any fervour of nationalism, be branded as wholly related to British interests), were, in fact, services on unproductive or 'ordinary' debt. The surreptitious underplaying of the compounding or the servicing of unproductive loans lends credence to an argument that the entire amount of home charges covering both productive and unproductive heads of expenditure was attributable to colonial expropriation. The position, interestingly, removes the major fallacy or dilemma of the nationalists in their outright condemnation of public works expenditure and the servicing of related loans in India.

Before concluding our analysis of the nationalist position relating to the drain we feel tempted to draw attention to the question of what has been described as a 'moral drain'. The dominance of Europeans in most of the remunerative occupations in British India[66] implied a regular expropriation as well as remittance of the privately appropriated surplus. This led to outflows of funds on private account, the overall magnitude of which was large enough to balance (according to unofficial estimates) the private inflows of capital over the decade preceding 1908–09.[67] This aspect of the drain of wealth received relatively less attention from the nationalists who, for political reasons, were more concerned with the official remittances. A related flow concerns the surplus appropriated by the British residents in India, and especially those who opted to spend their earnings within the country. To the extent the above are overlooked, the nationalist approach to drain leaves out, in our judgement, an important aspect of the imperial impact on the Indian economy, with European residents controlling a sizeable part of the surplus. Colonial policies in India also generated a layer of surplus which was enjoyed by Indians in various capacities—through their land rights or through the relatively superior positions they enjoyed in government or business. As the demands of the Indian National Congress made it evident, the nationalists wanted to curtail the extent of European domination in government and business. It was, however, less important to them as to whether such domination also provided a source of private remittance. Similarly, their concern was even less on how the imperial connections transplanted, in the Indian soil, the machinations of an exploitative system where the loot were appropriated by Indians as well. We would attempt to analyse some of these issues in Chapter 4 when we discuss the pace of real transfers from India and their implications.

2.4 On quantifying the resource transfers from India

In this section we will make an attempt to assess the quantitative magnitudes of the resource transfers from India. A rough measure of the transfers will be approximated from the available series on external trade, capital flows, and remittances from the country.

A parallel process in Britain—the recipient country—might be worth considering at this point. We have offered below a brief digression on the 'reverse flow of capital', experienced by Britain—the lender nation—which started receiving net inflows of funds from abroad since mid-nineteenth century. Incidentally, our findings relating to the Indian experience refute the position that during the period under consideration, India was receiving, on a net basis, foreign investment from abroad. We will later counter the extreme position held by Keynes that India's borrowings implied an equivalent 'drain from England'.[68]

It may not be out of place to digress, at this stage, on two specific dimensions which are important for the resource transfer issue. The first concerns the perceptions relating to the external economic transactions of Britain over the period. The second relates to a broader context and points at the need to avoid possible ambiguities in interpreting the international accounts of individual nations. The two aspects would help in our understanding of resource transfers between colonial India and Britain.

In the literature on theories of imperialism there is mention of a 'reverse flow'[69] of capital, experienced by mature capitalist economies like Britain (*see* Chapter 1). Britain's early start as a capital-exporting nation initiated steady inflows of income to the country, the magnitude of which outstripped the flow of her overseas investment by the middle of nineteenth century. Looking at British national accounts statistics for 1870, the country's overseas investment (I_f) was less than her investment income from abroad (i). (Thus I_f at £55 million was clearly much larger than i at £35 million during the year.[70] The picture conforms to its mirror-image, the pattern relating to net financial (and real) outflows from colonies like India.

It is interesting to relate the above thesis on reverse flow to the argument that investment income flows from abroad were supporting the British domestic investment or consumption. Thus, during 1870, the sum of British overseas and domestic investment was actually smaller than the sum of savings at domestic origin and investment income from abroad. In symbols, $(I_d + I_f) < (S_d + i)$ where I_d and S_d respectively indicate gross domestic fixed capital formation and savings at domestic origin. Looking at the data for 1870,[71] we get the following:

I_d : £64 million
I_f : £55 million
S_d : £111 million
i : £35 million

The excess of $(S_d + i)$ at £146 million over aggregate investment (I_d+I_f) at £119 million indicates the possibility that overseas investment income was used to supplement domestic consumption during the year in Britain. It is not difficult, in this context, to find indirect evidence of distinct improvements which were taking place, by the late nineteenth century, in consumption standards of the British working class. Aggregate consumption of items like tea, which had a low income elasticity of demand, went up—a fact which indicates that tea entered the consumption basket of a wider section of British people, a large section of whom were presumably from the upcoming working classes.[72]

We now refer to the second theme which dwells on the basic principles governing the external accounts of nations including the double-entry book keeping devices. Credits (claims) arising from an outflow of real resources (exports) from a nation ordinarily gives rise to a claim over an inflow of financial resources. These inflows could lead to the following possibilities:

(a) imports of goods and services,
(b) purchase of foreign assets (e.g. securities, gold or foreign currencies) deposited with domestic/foreign monetary system, and
(c) unilateral transfers abroad.

Of the three, only the first contributes to the current flow of consumption or investment in the domestic economy while the second or the third option releases resources to the rest of the world. In fact a use of export proceeds for (*b*) amounts to lending on a short-term basis by the domestic economy over the period during which the foreign assets are held. Option (*c*) transfers abroad, on a permanent basis, the country's claims over the corresponding export earnings. Exports which finance this category of transactions are thus without a quid pro quo. In other words, the real transfers (via exports) make possible the unilateral transfers in financial terms.

We now get back to our task of quantitative identification of such transfers, if any, from British India. As revealed earlier in this chapter, most of the expenses of the India Office (i.e. the home charges) can be attributed to the imperial interests. We have already analysed the details of India's expenditure abroad. As has been argued earlier, even the servicing of productive loans were, in reality, towards the upkeep of the empire. The interpretation follows as we keep in mind the expenditure under different heads. (We have argued at end of our discourse on nationalist conceptualization of drain that most of the home charges on India were towards the empire and related interests.)

Flow of remittances between India and England were regularly recorded in the value of Council Bills sold in England. Since the sterling proceeds of the CB sales remained in England with the India Office, the above effected a flow from India to England, with bills being reimbursed in rupees at the Indian treasury. In addition, sterling could also be procured by the India Office through its borrowings in London capital market. Remittances largely channelized through sale of CBs (and trade bills) could in principle be supplemented by net flows of gold and silver. The overall picture relating to the flow of remittances and their components for India can be stylized in terms of the following equation:

$$B_T + K_f = CB \qquad \ldots(1)$$

where B_T and K_f respectively indicate the balance of India's trade in commodity plus treasure, and the flow of net capital imports during each period. The left hand side of the equation records the demand for the flow of remittances during each period. Sale of CBs by the SOS, recorded in the right hand side, measures the actual flow of remittances between the two countries which settled the balance of trade and other payments. Since K_f provided a part of import finance over the same period, the flow of K_f released the same value of export earnings which could be remitted to India. Thus the sum (B_T + K_f) measured the net remittances sent through CBs sold in England. However, in terms of the institutional arrangements, CB sales in England were not followed by actual remittances of sterling to India. Instead, India's claim was settled within the country by drawing on the budgetary resources, earmarked as expenditure abroad. Clearly, the availability of foreign finance in the form of external borrowings (K_f) effectively increased the stock of sterling with the SOS. To provide an example, a hypothetical merchandise surplus at an annual value of £100 could be partly financed or settled by net imports of treasure worth £25 over the same period, thus leaving a balance of £75. Again, direct borrowing of sterling by the SOS might amount to £25 which could settle an equal value of imports. The final settling of remittances then would amount to £100 (derived as the sum of trade and treasure balance plus foreign borrowings) which had to be transacted by CBs. Since the whole of the sterling proceeds of CB sales were maintained in England, if spendings by the SOS fell short of the value of those sterling proceeds (from sale of CBs and official borrowings) the SOS's reserves were likely to go up in London.

We can put back, in equation (1), figures which relate to the annual averages for the respective flows of B_t , K_f and CB during 1898–1908. Alternatively, we can compare the time series relating to CB and B_T over a longer period and find out the discrepancy (which, in principle, should reflect the net flows of foreign capital). The latter method provides a basis for cross-checking the margin of accuracy in the statistics by looking into their internal consistency. Incidentally, among the sources of statistics, data provided on the CB series by the SOS's office, or even the data on K_f collected by private researchers from London stock market (and other sources) were usually more dependable compared to official trade statistics which is originally collected from the customs returns.

Data on India's capital flows (K_f) during the period, as are available from different sources, do not seem to tally (see Table 2.4).

2.4). Using the available estimates of gross and net capital flows, Theodore Morison constructed, for the first time, an international accounts for India. This was described by the him as a 'Conjectural Balance Sheet of India 1898-1908'. The data was cross-checked and corrected by Keynes in the *Economic Journal* (1909).[73] We have rearranged them, in the following pages, in order to assess the magnitudes of financial flows from India during the above period. Later, we have used the same data source to test the validity of equation (1) which also cross-checks the internal consistency of the statistics.

Separate estimates of capital flows, done by Paish (for 1908–09) and by Pandit (for 1905–06), are provided in Table 2.4. Discrepancies in data, especially relating to the capital accounts, led Pandit to construct, in 1937, an indirect estimate of India's 'balance of indebtedness'.[74] Thus data on the current account for 1905–06 was utilized to construct, on a residual basis, the size of official and private capital inflows (or the, 'balance of indebtedness') which financed, *ex post*, the remaining items in the country's balance of payments. Comparing the data sources relating to the available estimates on different components of India's external payments in Table 2.4, we get the impression that the annual averages relating to capital inflows during 1899–1900 to 1908–09 were much lower in Keynes–Morison estimate than those provided by Paish (1908–09) and by Pandit (for 1905–06).

For both Keynes and Morison, the inflow of foreign capital curtailed the size of 'potential' drain to the level of the 'actual'. The authors defined the actual drain as external liabilities which remained to be met after using the capital flows for the purpose of settling the potential drain which measured the annual liabilities against home charges and other private liabilities. Incidentally, the notion of drain in Keynes or Morison had none of the political or moral overtones as was implicit in its use in the nationalist literature. As calculated by Keynes (or Morison) the size of potential drain for the decade ending in 1908–09 was at £213.4 million. This came down to an actual drain of £150.5 million with a sum of £41.9 million (official) and £21.0 million (private) borrowings abroad. The distinction drawn between actual and potential drain was probably to stress the crucial role of foreign capital inflows in financing a part of India's liabilities abroad. This position is in conflict with our observation that India was transfering, on a net basis, a substantial flow of resources to the rest of the world over the same period.

Keynes and Morison's point regarding the prevailing net inflow of capital to India was very much an accepted thesis. Pandit[75] has estimated the outstanding 'balance of indebtedness' for India, which at £16.6 million recorded the inflow of capital to the country over 1905–06. The indirect method used earlier by Viner has been used by Pandit for arriving at this estimate. Pandit's calculations, however, seems to be subject to double counting.[76] Our corrections bring the figure down to £6.1 million (a figure which was comparable to the respective sums of £8.6 million and £6.2 million obtained by Keynes and Morison as annual averages for net capital inflows for decade ending 1908–09).[77] As a point of contrast, Paish's figure of capital flows stood at £14.3 million for 1908–09, which appears as a gross overestimate (for details see Table 2.4).

The preceding account of data relating to capital inflows for India is based on the presumption that the country was receiving, on a net basis, capital from overseas. We have deliberately highlighted such positions in order to contrast them with the arguments advanced earlier in this chapter that the colonial economy was ordained, over the period, to part with resources through (unilateral) transfers abroad. Obviously, the differences between the two approaches lie in the respective characterization of the nature of claims on colonial India.

Data provided by Keynes (and Morison) for the 'Conjectural Balance of Payments of India' over 1898–1908 can be arranged in terms of the following format:

$$LTC_m^o = H + M + \Delta R - B_T - (LTC_m^p - i) \qquad ...(2)$$

where the RHS sums up the figures on home charges (H), miscellaneous payments abroad (M), accumulations of reserves in London (ΔR), and subtracts from the sum arrived at, the net balance on commodity trade plus treasure (B_T), and the gross inflows of capital on private account (LTC_m^p) less interest payments (i) on private loans. The balance is financed by gross imports of capital under official heads (LTC_m^o) as given by the LHS of the equation. Interest charges on LTC_m^o are included in the home charges and hence listed on the other side.

Before putting, in (2) above, the respective figures provided by Keynes and Morison for 1898–1908, we once again focus attention to the general impression created by the pro-British and other writings on India that the country in general was receiving net inflows of capital from abroad. Scholars including Paish (who estimated the countrywise flow of British overseas investment at end of the first decade of the present century) and Y.S. Pandit, among others, subscribed to the view. The position on net inflows of overseas capital fits in the slant in the Keynes–Morison data on India's international accounts which also matches equation (2). Net inflow of official capital (LTC_m^o) in the LHS of equation (2) thus provides the net finance for the rest of the items in India's 'conjectural balance sheet'. Keynes's data, put against the respective symbols in equation (2), appears as follows:

$$4.1 = 15.7 + 1.4 + 1.6 - 14.6 - (4.5 - 4.5) \qquad ...(3)$$

Each entry in equation (3) relates to the respective annual averages during 1898–1908 and are given in units of millions of pound sterling.

What impression do we have from equations (2) and (3) for India's international accounts over the decade 1898 to 1908–09? While gross inflows of capital in the private account (LTC_m^p) at £4.1 million annual average was netted out by the annual average for interest payments (i)—which was exactly of the same value—the merchandise and treasure balance (B_T) calculated at £14.6 million was inadequate to meet the liabilities on account of home charges (H), the miscellaneous payments (M), and the reserve accretions (ΔR). The net sum due was thus financed by inflows of long-term official capital (LTC_m^o) at £4.1 million.

In the approach to India's international accounts outlined above, all international payments are treated at par. Thus home charges, the miscellaneous payments, and the payments towards reserve accumulations are all recognized as debt entries. Expressed in present-day language, home charges are viewed as payments for ordinary (contractual) services—a perspective which was common in the imperialist historiography on India. The position, viewed from our frame of analysis, neglects the political overtone of the specific transactions in the external accounts of a country. The resulting trite and mechanistic description of a nation's international accounts does not, however, necessarily dispel the value-loaded premises. By treating home charges as ordinary invisibles, the above analysis of India's international payments did indirectly subscribe to the political context which was dominant in the imperialist perception of British India. It was thus not accidental that imports of long-term official capital were viewed by Keynes and others as net inflows of external finance in India's international accounts.

Conclusions arrived at earlier (in Section 2.3) on the identifiability of home charges as tributes from colonial India allow us to substitute the symbol for home charges (H), by that for tributes (T) in equation (2): Rearranging, we get

$$B_T = T + M + \Delta R - B_L \qquad ...(4)$$

where the net lending balance in the capital account (B_L) is defined as the sum ($LTC_m^o + LTC_m^p - i$) in equation (2), while H has been substituted by T. The remaining symbols read the same as in equation (2).

In terms of the rearranged payments balance in equation (4), the trade surplus (B_T) provides the source of net finance which meets the unilateral transfers or tributes (T), the reserve accumulations (ΔR), and payments under miscellaneous heads (M), after using, for the same purpose, the lending balance from abroad (B_L). The corresponding estimate, in units of pound millions, is:

$$14.6 = 15.7 + 1.4 + 1.6 - 4.1 \qquad ...(5)$$

where the figures are the annual averages, based on Keynes's statistics mentioned above.

Equations (4) and (5) shed new light on the pattern of utilization of India's export surpluses during the period 1898–99 to 1908–09. Surplus in commodity trade which remained after paying for the net imports of treasure seems to have been spent on settling the tributes and the acquisition of financial assets in sterling (apart from meeting the miscellaneous payments, the magnitude of which was of a smaller order). None of the major expenses (including those on reserve accumulations) had much relevance in terms of the material well-being in the national economy, as we have discussed in Section 2.3. The country's exchange receipt, from ($B_T + B_L$) in the above equations, was thus financing the sum of ($T + \Delta R$) and M, largely reflecting the obligations to the empire.

We can now cross-check the data and try to assess the magnitude of the tribute from India. In terms of the rearranged balance of payments in equations (4) and (5), the tribute seems to be roughly of the same value as that of the trade surplus on trade and treasure. Incidentally, B_T at £14.6 million was derived by Keynes after revising official trade statistics (which, according to Keynes, was an overestimate since it left out the import surpluses in India's land-borne trade.[78]) We would return to the point later in this section.

Let us look again at equation (1) where CB sales are equated to the sum of B_T and K_f. The value of CBs sold annually, as pointed out, was supposed to yield this sum. Relating the arrangement to the political processes in colonial India, the flows of remittances (in the CBs) thus seem to have sustained the flow of the imperial loot from British India, divested in forms which had very little significance from a national angle.

We now make use of equation (1) as a device to cross-check data. Let us put back the values of *CB*, B_T, and K_f from Keynes's estimates. Now the annual average relating to *CB* during 1898–1908 was at £23.2 million—a figure much larger than the sum of (B_T + K_f) at £18.2 million. How does one explain this rather serious anomaly between the two sources of statistics on remittances? Observing that the discrepancies between the *CB* and the official B_T series seem to exceed the capital inflows (K_f), we have tried to construct a new series for India's trade data. Our calculations yeild a new average for B_T in equation (5) at £17.3 million. The gap between the two sides of equation (4), however, still persists (reflecting the excess of CB sales, at £23.2 million, over remittances solicited against (B_T + K_f), the revised sum of which now stands at £21.4 million. A digression can be provided here as a plea for further research on the quality of India's trade statistics as are available for the colonial period. In our view the official statistics is found faulty on four grounds: (*a*) It excludes statistics on land-borne trade which, as a constrast to sea-borne trade, consistently showed a deficit balance for India; (*b*) it excludes purchases (imports) of official stores by the SOS in London; (*c*) it exlcudes re-exports; and finally, (*d*) the fixed rate of exchange at £1 = Rs.15 which in official statistics converts the sterling values of India's trade did not actually prevail till 1898 when the declining rupee rate in sterling finally stabilized to 1s 4d (which was equivalent to £1 = Rs.15). Keynes, incidentally, had been aware of the omission of re-exports and made a reference to the gap in the memorandum he submitted to the India Office in 1913, regarding 'inaccuracies of sea-borne trade by India'.[79] He also mentioned the 'serious discrepancies' in the declared (CIF) values for imports probably due to an under-reporting of profit margin enjoyed by foreign suppliers at the stage of entry of imports. The points raised by Keynes were, however, not all incorporated in the new series he worked out for the period 1898–1908, since the latter was adjusted for the omission of land-borne trade only.

Discrepancies in India's trade data and its inconsistency with figures for remittances (CBs) available from the India Office (which, by all means, represented a more reliable source) prepare the ground for rejecting estimates of tributes on the basis of trade data (as suggested in equation (4)). Incidentally, our pointer at the unexplained gaps between the *CB* and the B_T series, plus the capital inflows (K_f) in equation (1) sounds rather convincing as we draw attention to the controversy between Keynes and his colleagues at India office—Lionel Abrahams and James Mackay—on the same question. The observed gap between CB sales and the official series for B_T could, according to Keynes, reflect inflows of foreign capital—a route which, incidentally, we have also taken in equation (1) to indicate the links between CB and other transactions. Officials at the SOS's office, however, maintained a different position and they pointed out, in reply to Keynes's letters, the following: (*a*) Export values recorded by the customs department in India, which provided trade data, had a tendency 'to lie' since the prices reported in the value columns relating to exports tended to lag behind the actual export prices which were consistently rising during the period; (*b*) imports were, in part, paid for directly through proceeds of sterling loans raised in London. This could have exaggerated the value of imports in the official series which ignored such practices. A newspaper clipping on parliamentary questions for 1910, which was maintained by Keynes in his private papers, mentions a certain unease, prevailing in the India Office circles, on the question of CB sales in excess of home charges. (The undersecretary of state at the India office was found answering a question, put in the parliament by Rupert Gwynne, on the use of CB proceeds beyond the financing of home charges. Surprisingly enough, Keynes ignored all such issues including the limitations of trade data in his own work[80] on Indian currency and finance completed in 1913.)

Considering the reliability of the alternative sources of statistics it would be appropriate to use the annual values of CB sales (net of capital imports) as a tentative measure of the annual flows of financial transfers or tributes from colonial India. In terms of equation (1) the flow is indicated by ($CB - K_f$). Data limitations compel us to confine our attention to 1898–1908. During this period an annual average of £19.8 million (representing about 2.3 per cent of India's national income) had been the value of CB sales net of capital imports—a sum which was remitted abroad as unilateral transfer. The sum exceeded the annual averages for India's net export earnings from trade and treasure, estimated by us at £17.3 million over the same period. The transfers, however, had a wider range of a implications on the domestic economy than are captured by the quantitative magnitudes. Thus we should consider the transformations in the colonial economy which came about with rising exports and the newly opened up opportunities for expropriations of surpluses in the agrarian economy. In the present chapter we have confined our analysis to the financial aspects of export expansion. Our conclusions support the thesis on the use of colonies as sources of surplus which were appropriated by the metropolitan areas in the age of finance capital.

In terms of the prevailing financial arrangements in British India, unspent sterling reserves (R) of the SOS were regularly deposited at the Bank of England. By the policy adopted in 1905, CB sales were no longer restricted to the size of annual home charges. Thus the sale of CBs, which served as the vehicle of transfer of financial resources between India and England, could, after 1905, be utilized to finance flows of expenditure of the India Office as well as the accumulations in the India Office's reserves in London. Both, as argued in the next chapter, proved convenient to the London City. Interestingly enough, official reserves maintained in London had very little effect on expansion of currency. In fact, between 1893–98, minting of new coins was virtually suspended in India for reasons connected with the prevailing exchange policy of the government. Location of gold reserves in England was sought to be justified, in official circles, by its ready availability for silver purchases needed for India. In reality, the Bank of England was found reluctant to let the SOS take out its own deposits for purchase of silver. The rather limited options open to the India Office to use its growing reserves at the Bank of England, especially for purchase of silver in the London market soon became a sensitive

Table 2.3: Balance of trade (merchandise and treasure) and Council Bills sold (£ million)

	Council Bills sold	Official series on balance of trade	Adjusted series on balance of trade
1894–95	16.9	20.3	20.5
1895–96	17.6	20.3	20.2
1896–97	15.5	14.3	14.3
1897–98	9.5	9.5	9.5
1898–99	18.6	23.5	20.3
1899–1900	19.0	16.8	17.5
1900–01	13.3	14.7	11.6
1901–02	18.5	21.1	20.3
1902–03	18.4	22.3	20.9
1903–04	23.8	29.5	26.5
1904–05	24.4	23.9	23.0
1905–06	32.1	29.4	25.9
1906–07	33.1	31.1	17.2
1907–08	16.2	13.3	4.5
1908–09	13.9	10.0	6.0
1909–10	27.0	26.4	24.2
1910–11	26.7	31.9	29.9
1911–12	27.0	30.8	24.7
1912–13	25.7	27.5	19.9

Sources: Col.1: *RCC* (1914), p.232; Col.2: *Statistical Abstracts of British India*; Col.3: *Statistical Abstracts of British India*, adjusted as explained in note (e) of Table.2.4.

Table 2.4: Comparative estimates of selected items in India's balance of payments: 1899-1900 to 1908–09. (Figures in million £ sterling).

Sl.	Items	Keynes (annual average 1899-1900 to 1908-09)	Morison (annual average 1899-1900 to 1908-09)	Pandit (1905-1906)	Paish (1908-1909)	Official and CB trade series: (1899-1900 to 1908-09)	Official series re-estimated by another
(1)	(2)	(3)	(4)	(5)	(6)	(7)	(8)
1.	Home charges less purchase of stores in England	15.7	15.7	15.5			

(1)	(2)	(3)	(4)	(5)	(6)	(7)	(8)
2.	Private capital inflows	4.5	2.1				
3.	Private capital ouflows (including miscellaneous payments for services(f))	5.5	5.6 (net)	1.3 (16.9)	9.7 (4.7)		
4.	Official capital inflow	4.1	4.1		4.3 (5.3)		
5.	Change in official reserves held in London	1.6		1.0			
6.	Rupee debt repatriated by India (i)	0.4	0.4				
7.	Export surplus including trea-sure and offi-cial transac-tion (k)	15.0	15.0	21.8	21.2		17.3
8.	Land-borne trade (excess of imports over exports	0.4	0.8				(n)
9.	Council Bills sold in London					23.9	23.9
10.	Railway annuities			5.6			
11.	Balance of non-commercial transactions			5.7 (0.8)			
12.	Balance of indebtedness (comparable private and official capital imports)			16.6 (6.1)			

Notes and Sources: (*a*) Keynes (1911); (*b*) Morison (1911); (*c*) Pandit (1937); (*d*) Paish (1909); (*e*) The adjusted series on trade data corrects the official series for exchange rate fluctuations till 1898. Omissions in the latter for data on land-borne trade, re-exports and government purchases (stores) are corrected as well as a highly confidential issue around 1912–13. Difficulties of procuring silver from the London market even constrained the capacity of Indian treasury to honour (redeem) the Council Bills presented to it. The Bank of England on its part was interested in the overall liquidity situation of the London City which was dependent on the regular injections of the India Office's deposits. The SOS even demonstrated a conscious attempt to keep out the Indian silver merchants from the London market by denying them silver purchase contracts. Instead, the banks worked out an arrangement which favoured some London based European merchants having closer contact with the SOS. On the whole, accumulation of reserves by the SOS did have very little, if any, impact on money supply in India. Link between official gold reserves at the PCR,

in the adjusted series. *See* Table 2.3 for the discrepancy between the official and the adjusted series on trade data; (*f*) Private remittances of interest and of miscellaneous payments are recorded in Keynes's data as £4.5 million and £1.0 million respectively; (*g*) Figure in brackets refer to Pandit's estimates for home charges and freights; (*h*) Paish (1909) did not provide the details of private or official flows. His estimates for official flows, consistently larger than comparable estimates from other sources, relate to transactions for investment in railways and other types of borrowing by government and the municipalities (interest payments are recorded in brackets); (*i*) Represents additional payments by way of repatriation; (*j*) Estimates by Morison, though mentioned in text, are not used in his conjectural estimates, as pointed out by Keynes; (*k*) Official transactions include expenditure in England on stores. Imports, as ordinarily recorded, are on a CIF basis. This introduces an element of double counting in Morison's estimate, since he considers the freight separately under invisibles as well (item 3). *See* Keynes (1911) for a mention of the above point. Figures for export surplus (row 7) reported under Keynes and Morison (col.3,4) are exclusive of land-borne trade. Hence Keynes's figures for balance of trade for sea and land-borne trade (inclusive of treasure and stores) amount to £14.6 million, as pointed out in the text above; (*l*)Exclusive of freight; (*m*) Our estimates on land-borne trade are already covered by data reported under (7) which is the adjusted series. This, however, is not true of the official series which excludes, among others, data on land-borne trade which had a negative balance. Data reported in Table 2.4 may not exactly match because of rounding off; (*n*) Reported separately as net non-commercial remittances through exchange banks at £0.8 million. On a clear analysis Pandit's data includes railway annuities separately (at £5.6 million) since it is already included under home charges at £16.9 million under row (3) above. Second, it counts under the head of the balance of non-commercial transaction payments through exchange banks at £0.8 million which in reality were already covered by home charges, ordinarily transacted by exchange banks. The corrected figure relating to Pandit's balance of indebtedness is reported as £6.1 million in row (12).[81]

London branch and issue of paper money in India, though legalized in terms of the official legislation in 1905, made almost no dent on money supply because of the limited circulation of paper currency in India. While about one-third of the value of India's imports in each year comprised precious metals or gold coins, a large proportion of the treasure found its way to the unusually large hoards maintained by private individuals in India. The residual was used for new coinage at the mints. However, none of such imports contributed to the nation's capacity for current consumption or investment—a fact which also applied to India's official reserves maintained in London. We will return to these aspects of monetary transfers in the following chapter.

In this chapter we have indicated that sales of CBs during the period seem to provide an indirect estimate of the annual flows of financial resources from India to Britain. These resources were used to remit abroad the tributes (identified as home charges). In addition these also provided means of building up a stock of sterling resources at the India Office. The reserves were by and large controlled by the British financial interests. The theme of financial transfers from British India developed in the present chapter would be linked up to issues of the domestic implications in Chapters 3 and 4 which respectively deal with the financial and the real aspects of the domestic economy.

Notes

1. Raymond W. Goldsmith, *The Financial Development of India 1860–1977*, OUP, Delhi, 1983, p.6. The original figure was Rs. 18.13 billion for 1900 and we have converted it into sterling at an exchange rate of sterling at Rs. 15.
2. See K.N. Chaudhuri, 'India's International Economy in the Nineteenth Century: A Historical Survey', *Modern Asian Studies*, II, 1, 1968, pp.31–50.
3. 'As a matter of fact... it is the inflow of capital, the "drain" from England into India which drives them (prices) up'. J.M. Keynes, 'Rise in Prices 1907–09', *Economic Journal*, 1909. Editorial comments on above article appeared in *Madras Mail*, 10 April 1909.
4. Amongst the more significant writings on nationalist arguments, we include R.C. Dutt, *The Economic History of India*, Vol. II, Delhi, 1960.

D. Naoroji, *Essays, Speeches and Writings*, ed. C.L. Parekh, Bombay, 1887.

——— *Poverty and Un-British Rule in India*, London, 1901.

M.G. Ranade, *Essays on Indian Economics*, Bombay, 1898.

5. Theodore Morison, *Economic Transition in India*, London, 1911, pp. 186, 197, 202.
   J.M. Keynes, 'Review of Theodore Morison: Economic Transition in India', *Economic Journal*, 1911.
6. *See Keynes Papers* at Marshall Library, Cambridge Files IB/2 and IB/3. In a Memorandum to the India Office, dated 20.5.1913, inaccuracies of sea-borne trade data were noticed by Keynes. *Also see* J.M. Keynes, 'Notes on Sea-borne Trade of India' in supplement to *Indian Trade Journal*, 22 September 1910.
7. This includes statistics for Council Bills (or Reverse Council Bills) sold (or bought) by the India Office, the value of which measured the India Office's records on remittances between India and England.
8. Berton Stein and David Washbrook, 'Eighteenth century India: Historiography, Perspectives, and Proposition', mimeo, London, 1987.
9. See note (14) in Chapter 1.
10. *Collected Writings of John Maynard Keynes*, Vol. I, *Indian Currency and Finance*, London, 1913, p. 72.
11. Marcello de Cecco, *Money and Empire: The International Gold Standard, 1890–1914*, Oxford, 1974.
12. *See* Chapter 3. p. 130
13. *See* amongst other works on the residual approach to construct the capital accounts transactions, Jacob Viner, *Canada's Balance of International Indebtedness, 1900–1913*, Harvard University Press, Cambridge, 1924, Chapter V; Y.S. Pandit, *India's Balance of indebtedness 1898–1913*, George Allen and Unwin, London, 1937.
14. Even Vera Anstey who subscribed very little to the nationalist claims regarding a drain of wealth from British India, spoke of an 'unjust' debiting from India on political grounds which was related to military and similar other spendings. Vera Anstey, *Economic Development of India*, London, 1921, Appendix G, pp. 109–11.
15. In addition to those cited in note 4, see the following for more recent work on the subject:
    B.N. Ganguli, *Dadabhai Naoroji and the Drain Theory*, Bombay, 1965.
    Bipan Chandra, *Rise and Growth of Economic Nationalism*, People's Publishing House, New Delhi, 1966. A.K. Banerji, *Aspects of Indo-British Economic Relations*, Bombay, 1982, pp. 176–206.
16. See, for an officially accepted distinction between productive

and unproductive loans, *Final Report of Royal Commission on Expenditure of India* (under the chairmanship of Lord Welby), London, 1900, pp. 44–5.

17. Select Commitee Report to Parliament. Cited in Welby Commission, ibid. pp. 44, 45, 71.
18. Ibid.
19. Additional transfer towards debt retirement included, in 1874, cancellation of a £12 million East India Company debt, presumably through funds drawn from the revenue account of the budget.
 See also Welby Commission, pp. 44–8, 71 for statistics cited in this paragraph.
20. Raymond Goldsmith, *The Financial Development of India 1860–1977*, OUP, Delhi,1983. p. 40.
 'In 1857 there was the first world stock market crisis. It originated in a boom in USA...caused by a rapid increase in gold production and an enormous railway construction (21,000 miles were built in eight years). A large number of banks, many of them unsold, had been opened. The failure of many of these American banks and the fall in the value of railway securities (many of them held by British investors) brought the crisis to England and gave rise to heavy demands on the Bank's reserves. It was necessary to suspend the Act of 1844 and issue notes beyond the amount which could be backed by gold.' J.L. Gayler, Irene Richards, and J.A. Morris, *A Sketch-Map Economic History of Britain*, London, 1975, p. 175. *See also*, for a succint account of the Great Depression of 1873–1895, Michel Beaud, *A History of Capitalism 1500–1980*, London, 1984, pp. 117–122.
 It is not difficult to see an element of causality as well as 'financial prudence' in the Select Committee's recommendation to the British Parliament in 1874 for conversion of India government's unproductive loans to productive ones.
21. Welby Commission, Final Report, p. 71. *See also*, John and Richard Strachey, *The Finances and Public Works of India*, London, 1882.
22. Ibid., p. 259.
23. Dharma Kumar, 'The Fiscal System' in *Cambridge Economic History of India*, Dharma Kumar and Meghnad Desai ed., Vol. II, 1757–1970, Orient Longman, Delhi, 1982, pp. 934–5.
24. John and Richard Strachey, *Finances and Public Works*, p. 259.
25. Raymond Goldsmith, *Financial Development*, p. 40.
26. Welby Commission, Final Report, pp. 40-45, 47, 48.
27. Ibid. pp. 90–128.

28.

	1862–63	Annual average 1883–85
	(in Rs. million)	
Expenditure on defence and foreign affairs	16.5	19.1
Expenditure on civil charges including public works expenditure chargeable to revenue	13.0	18.8

29. India bore the entire amount of charges, both civil and military, for British administration in Aden during the period. India's share of expenses in British missions at Persia during 1891 and 1893–1895 to 1895–96 was one and half times the amount shared by the British. Similarly, a large part of expenditure on the Chinese consular establishments of Britain was borne by India. Also, India met a substantial part of charges on 'postal and telegraphic services' in Zanzibar, Mauritius, the Red Sea, the Euphrates, Tigris, and Karuph area, and consular expenses in Jeddah, Chiengmai and Surinam. Welby Commission, Final Report, p. 91.
30. Ibid., pp. 90–128, 151.
31. Ibid., p. 95.
32. Ibid., pp. 90–128.
33. Ibid., pp. 116–17.
34. Ibid., p. 81. In its memorandum to the Welby Commission, the Select Committee on Indian finance was found to be arguing that '...there is no true partnership, at any rate, no freedom of contract between England and India, that the Indian authorities have scarcely any voice at all in the adoption of military reforms; and that there is not that identity of interest in measures... which is essential for partnership.' The point was cited from an earlier despatch of the India government, dated 10 August 1883 and 25 March 1890, to the British government. Ibid. pp. 90–128.
35. Ibid., p. 151.
36. Theodore Morison, *Economic Transition in India*, London, 1911, pp. 237–41.
37. Vera Anstey, *Economic Development of India*, 1942, pp. 509–10.
38. Theodore Morison, *Economic Transition*, pp. 237–41.
39. Vera Anstey, *Economic Development.*
40. *See* note 5.
41. Mention may be made here of a few western writers of nineteenth century whose arguments support the nationalist contention.
    H.H. Wilson, 'On Tariff-free entry of Textiles', cited in J.S. Mill, *History of British India*, Vol. III.
    Montgomery Martin, *The Political, Commercial and Financial Aspects of the Anglo-East Empire in 1832.*

George Wingate, *A Few Words about the Financial Relations with India, 1859.*
Brooks Adams, *Law of Civilisation and Decay: An Essay in History*, 1896, New York, 1943.
Sources relating to nationalist literature are provided in notes (4) and (15).

42. Thomas Mun, *England's Treasure by Forraign Trade*, 1664. *See also*, amongst other mercantilist authors, Josiah Child, *Discourse of Trade*, 1775.
43. Memorandum submitted by W. Martin (App. II) to the Indian Currency Commission, 1889, *Minutes of Evidence*, Pt. III.
44. *See also* for details, B.N. Ganguli, *Naoroji and Drain Theory*, and A.K. Banerji, *Indo-British Economic Relations*, pp. 97–8.
45. *See*, for an interesting parallel drawn between 'drain of wealth' in Ireland and India and the literature thereon, B.N. Ganguli, *Naoroji and Drain Theory*, pp. 51–9.
46. 'In the first half of nineteenth century, there were seven famines, with an estimated total of one and a half million deaths from famine. In the second half of nineteenth century, there were twenty-four famines (six between 1851 and 1876, and eighteen between 1876 and 1900), with an estimated total, according to official records, of over 20 million deaths.' R.P. Dutt, *India Today*, Calcutta, 1970, p.125. *See also* William Digby, *Prosperous British India*. Interestingly enough, a British viceroy in India, Lord Northbrook, is found to have developed a remkarkable degree of complacency on the question of Indian famines by 1874, as comes out from the following statement: '...whatever means we may take to obviate or mitigate them, it must, under present circumstance, be looked upon as inevitable that famines will from time to time occur.' John Strachey, *Finances and Public Works*, p. 259.
47. Dadabhai Naoroji, *Un-British Rule*.
48. Ibid., pp. 177, 233.
49. A.K. Banerji, *Indo-British Economic Relations*, pp. 185–191.
50. *See* for example, R.C. Dutt, *Economic History*, p.xiv '...when taxes are raised and spent in a country the money circulates among the people, fructifies trades, industries, and agriculture, and in one shape or another reaches the mass of the people. But when taxes raised in a country are remitted out of it, the money is lost to the country for ever, it does not stimulate her trade or industries, or reach the people in any form'. Also R.C. Dutt, 'A plea for the spoliation of India', *JPSS*, Vol.VIII, No.3, 1885, p.17. The arguments of the nationalist echoed the following views expressed by George Wingate in his minute of evidence to the Fowler Committee on Indian currency '...taxes raised in a country and spent in another...constitute...an absolute loss and extinction of the

whole amount withdrawn from the taxed country...the cruel, crushing effect of the tribute upon India.' Memorandum submitted to the Indian Currency Committee, 1898 (App. II) by W. Martin as *Minutes of Evidence* Part III.

51. Bipan Chandra, 'Reinterpretations of Indian Economic History' in Bipan Chandra, ed. *Nationalism and Colonialism in Modern India*, Orient Longman, Delhi, 1979, pp. 28–73.
52. *See*, for a preview of the present work, Sunanda Sen, 'Trade as a Handmaiden of Colonialism: India during Late Nineteenth Century to First World War', *Studies in History*, Vol.IV, No.1 January–June, 1982.
53. Letter from Dadabhai Naoroji to Lord Hamilton dated 12 October 1900 cited by John McLane, 'The Drain of Wealth and Indian Nationalism at the Turn of the Country' in T. Roychaudhury ed. *Contributions to Indian Economic History*, Vol.II, Calcutta, 1963.
54. McLane, *Drain of Wealth*, p. 40.
55. *Bengalee*, 4 June 1903 cited in McAlpin, *Price Movements*, pp. 39–40.
56. John McLane, *Drain of Wealth*, p.28–9.
57. Vera Anstey, *Economic Development*, pp.509–10.
58. Macpherson, 'Investment in Indian Railways: 1845–75., *Economic History Review*, 1955, pp.181, 185.
59. Arun Bose, 'Foreign Capital' in V.B. Singh, ed. *Economic History of India 1857–1956*, Delhi, 1975, p. 504.
60. L.H. Jenks, 'British Experience with Foreign Investment', *Journal of Economic History*, December, 1944.
61. Henry Bearmont cited in Arun Bose in *Economic History*, p. 511.
62. Cited in Vinod Dubey, 'Railways' in V.B. Singh, *Economic History*, p.328.
63. Daniel R. Headrick, *The Tools of Empire: Technology and European Empire in the Nineteenth Century*, New York, 1983, p.182.
64. According to a recent interpretation those attacks from the later-day Marxists ignored the dialectical method of Marx, as was evident in his attempt to incorporate both the regenerative as well as the destructive role of capitalism in the colonies. Thus the charges of 'blinkered ethnocentricity' in Marx can, in terms of the study, be dispelled by recognizing the fact that '...the idea of the "cunning reason" (List der Vernunft). duly set "right way up", enabled him (Marx) to condemn capitalism and colonialism from the point of view of those who suffer them, and at the same time to consider them as important progressive forces from the point of view of objective historical movements'. See Umbretto Melotti, *Marx and the Third World*, London, 1977, p.118. *Also see* Karl Marx, 'The Future Results of the British Rule in India' in *Marx-Engels Reader*, pp.583–4, (cited in Melotti, *Marx*, p.193). Thus Marx goes to the extent of making the following statement, 'England has to fulfil a double mission in India: *one destructive, the other regenerating*—the annihilation of old Asiatic society, and the laying of the

foundations of Western society in Asia...Steam has brought India into regular and rapid communication with Europe, has connected its chief ports with those of the whole south-eastern ocean, and has revindicated it from the isolated position which was the prime cause of its stagnation', cited from Marx in *Marx-Engels*, cited in Melotti, *Marx*, p.115, (italics added).

65. See for different positions on the economic implication of railways in British India, L.H. Jenks, *The Migration of British Capital*, New York, 1927.
Daniel Thorner, *Investment in Empire*, Philadelphia, 1950.
W.J. Macpherson, 'Investment in Indian Railways'. John Hurd II, 'Railways and the Expansion of Markets in India 1861–1921', *Explorations in Economic History*, July, 1975.
See also Daniel R. Headrick. *The Tools of British Empire*.
66. *See* on the salary structure for Europeans and others during 1887–1913, A.K. Bagchi, *Private Investment in India*, 1985, p. 168.
67. *See* J.M. Keynes and Theodore Morison cited in note (5).
68. J.M. Keynes, 'Rise in Prices', 1909, cited in note (3). *See also Madras Mail*, 10 April 1909 in Keynes Papers, File IB/2 and IB/3 at Marshall Library, Cambridge.
69. Michael Barratt-Brown, *Economics of Imperialism*, Penguin, pp. 170–193, 1974, and Michaell-Barrat Brown, *Essays on Imperialism*, Spokesman Books, 1972, p. 68.
Also see Michael Barratt-Brown,. *Models in Political Economy*, Penguin, 1984, p. 88.
70. See for data on S_d, I_d, and I_f, H Feinstein, *National Income, Output and Employment in the UK*, Cambridge, 1972, p.85. For data on *i* see B.R Mitchell, *Abstract of British Historical Statistics*, Cambridge, 1962, p. 333.
71. See note (70).
72. See for statistics on tea consumption, B.R Mitchell, *Abstract of British Historical Statistics*. For the general argument on a possible rise in the standard of living of the working classes in late nineteenth century, see E. J. Hobbsbawm, *Labouring Men: Studies in the History of Labour*, London, 1964, pp. 120-5; 272-303. E.P. Thompson, *The Making of the English Working Class*, London, 1963, part II.
73. See reference cited in note (5).
74. Y.S. Pandit, *Balance of Indebtedness*.
75. Ibid.
76. In Pandit's calculations railway annuities are separately calculated as outstanding payments at £5.6 million. The sum, however, is already subsumed under home charges and estimated at £15.5 million, a fact which is ignored by Pandit as he adds the two.

Second, payments under 'non-commercial transactions' included, in Pandit's estimates, the entire flow of payments through exchange banks—an enumeration which ignores the fact that the exchange banks were instrumental, under the CB scheme, for remittances under commercial transactions (merchandise trade) as well. The above introduced an element of double counting in the figure Pandit arrived at as 'balance of indebtedness' (defined as total credits less total debits). *See* Pandit, *Balance of Indebtedness*. *See also* for other criticisms of Pandit's calculations, A.K. Banerji, *Indo-British Economic Relations*, pp. 190–4.

77. Theodore Morison, *Economic Transition*. J.M. Keynes, *Review of Economic Transitions*.
78. *Keynes Papers*, File IB/2 and IB/3 at Marshall Library, Cambridge. *See also* J.M. Keynes, 'Note on Sea-borne Trade by India', supplement to *Indian Trade Journal*, 22 September 1910, and *Times*, 9 November 1914. *See Keynes Papers*, Files IB2 and IB3.
79. Ibid.
80. J.M. Keynes, *Indian Currency and Finance*, London, 1913.
81. A handful of exchange banks, which included Chartered Bank, Delhi Bank, Specie Bank, Mercantile Bank, National Bank, and Agra Bank, had, between them, a total deposit of £21 thousand in October 1902. Keynes' 'Notes on Private Investment' in *Keynes Papers*, File No. IB/2 and IB/3.

CHAPTER 3

Colonial Transfers and Finances in the Domestic Economy

Euro-centric bias in the literature on imperialism, especially in its classical tradition, has paid little attention to colonies and the metropolitan nations. Colonial surpluses, however, have a global dimension in the context of imperialism. The present study, as mentioned in Chapter 1, draws attention to the domestic and international aspects of the colonial surpluses, focussing on the experience of British India.

We have analysed, in the present chapter, the financial implications of the transfers from British India for her domestic economy during the colonial period. Our analysis refers to the period 1890–1914 which covers the years of high finance in London City and other industrialized areas. In India links between the domestic and the international financial system became rather close during these years. With the rupee–sterling rate fixed at 1*s* 4*d* in June 1893, the prevailing monetary arrangement in India was effective to ensure a steady transfer of financial resources from the country, as we have indicated in Section 2.1. Interestingly, changes in the monetary and fiscal policies during the period reflected, in India, a distinct consolidation of the imperial rule at the level of financial management and expediency. We have sketched in this chapter, the related financial processes in India which include the fiscal-monetary mechanism for financial transfer, the quantitative dimensions of money supply and credit availability in the domestic economy, and the contrast between the official complacency and public resentments on the question of money and credit.

3.1 The changing mechanism for financial transfers and the currency policy

Financial transfers from colonial India provided a steady and growing source of finance to the London City around the turn of the last century. The India Office in London, which played the role of an intermediary in disbursing India's sterling assets, contributed to the flow of financial transactions in the City. These included the flow of its current expenses (or the entire amount of home charges) and investments in the London stock market. In addition, the sterling assets, which were held by the India Office, provided sources of liquidity and credit to the City.

The institutional set-up for financial transfers from India were tightened up, as has been pointed out earlier (*see* Section 2.1), with the closure of mints to coinage on public demand, and the announcement of a fixed rupee rate in June 1893. During the subsequent period, flows of net remittances were met through the CB network. As a consequence the India Office received a regular flow of sterling against the remittances of India's trade surplus and other sterling receipts in London (*see* equation (*1*) in Section 2.4). After 1905, the SOS was permitted to sell an unlimited value of bills in the market so long as the market was ready to purchase these at the fixed rupee rate. This led to a further swelling of CB sales in London. In terms of the network of remittances (*see* Fig. 1), a regular compensation took place which matched the sterling liabilities of the Government of India to India's claim on England against the country's export surpluses. Payments to Indian exporters in rupees were organized by exchange banks in India by presenting the bills to the Indian treasury which provided rupees. Prices of CBs were always regulated in order that the alternative route of remittances through flow of bullion was never more remunerative. While the bullion mode of remittances was open till June 1893, prices of CBs were always adjusted to the changing price of silver subject to margins which allowed for cost of remittances.

Import of treasure, however, continued even after the closure of mints in 1893. This can be explained by the (non-monetary) demand for gold and silver which was not related to the payments balance. Silver needed for coinage was an important component of these imports. In addition, demand for hoarding gold as well as silver bullion, and for gold sovereigns, kept the domestic demand for treasure imports bouyant. Annual values of imports of precious metal ranged between £4.5 million to £17.3 million over 1870–1893, and £5.5 million to £41.9 million during 1893–1914 despite silver no longer being a mode of directly settling the balance of payments after 1893. (See Table 3.1 on imports of treasure as percentage of aggregate imports over 1871–72 to 1913–14.) The relative significance of the CBs as a means of financing remittances between the two countries, however, did increase over time as (*a*) mints were closed during 1893–98, making it redundant for private traders to import silver for coinage during the period; (*b*) the volume of home charges increased over time; and (*c*) coverage of items which could be financed through sale proceeds of the CBs were no longer restricted to home charges alone—a change which permitted the SOS to add to its investible resources in England. The arrangement suited the interests of the London City by providing a steady and captive demand from the India Office for sterling assets. The practice evoked criticism from the commercial interests and the dissenting government officials in India who faced a credit shortage or other financial stringencies in the domestic economy. Assets held by the India Office in sterling soon reached a significant proportion of India government assets. The issue became a sensitive one for the City as was indicated by the Bank of England's attempts to prevent withdrawals of deposits by the India Office.

In the rest of this section we have concentrated on the actual mechanism for financial transfers from India which included the institutional arrangements involving the CB network and the transfer of gold from the paper currency and the gold standard reserves in India.

3.1.1 FROM OPEN MINT TO FIXED EXCHANGE RATE: 1870–1893

Council Bills, as has been indicated earlier, became popular as an instrument of remittance since the SOS always made it a point to sell them at a price which was consistent with the market price of silver in London and its transport cost margin. Silver, however, continued to be imported to India where it had a demand for coinage. This suited the interests of the silver producing nations which faced slump in the silver market following world-scale switchovers from bimetallism to gold currency during the last quarter of the nineteenth century. Remittances

Table 3.1: Imports of treasure and other goods: 1871–72 to 1913–14 (£ millions).

	Total imports	Treasure imports	Percentage of (2) to (1)
	(1)	(2)	(3)
1871–72	32.0	11.5	35.09
1872–73	31.8	4.5	14.1
1873–74	33.8	5.7	16.8
1874–75	36.2	8.1	22.3
1875–76	38.8	5.3	13.6
1876–77	37.7	11.4	30.2
1877–78	46.0	17.3	37.6
1878–79	42.6	7.0	16.5
1879–80	46.0	11.6	25.2
1880–81	48.5	7.4	15.2
1881–82	44.7	9.3	20.9
1882–83	46.3	11.8	25.4
1883–84	48.5	10.8	22.2
1884–85	48.7	11.6	23.8
1885–86	45.7	12.2	26.6
1886–87	47.3	8.3	17.5
1887–88	48.2	10.6	21.9
1888–89	47.3	9.4	19.8
1889–90	47.7	–	–
1890–91	–	–	–
1891–92	51.1	10.4	20.1
1892–93	43.6	10.7	24.8
1893–94	49.1	11.3	22.6
1894–95	42.5	5.5	12.9
1895–96	43.9	7.7	17.5
1896–97	48.5	8.3	17.1
1897–98	50.4	13.5	26.7
1898–99	51.7	12.3	23.7
1899–1900	54.2	14.5	26.7
1900–01	58.2	16.8	28.8
1901–02	63.7	14.2	22.2
1902–03	61.3	17.3	28.2
1903–04	66.4	26.1	39.3
1904–05	73.4	26.8	36.5
1905–06	79.1	21.8	27.3
1906–07	82.6	30.3	36.6
1907–08	96.0	28.9	30.1
1908–09	90.6	15.8	17.4
1909–10	86.5	25.8	29.8
1910–11	94.4	27.2	28.8
1911–12	102.2	36.3	35.5
1912–13	117.9	41.9	35.5
1913–14	134.7	29.7	22.0

* See footnote in p.75

Table 3.2: Seasonality in Council Bills and telegraphic transfers: 1894–95 to 1912–13 (Rupees crores)

	April-September	October-March
1894–95	15.8	15.0
1895–96	16.6	14.4
1896–97	16.4	9.3
1897–98	6.8	7.9
1898–99	12.9	15.1
1899–1900	12.2	16.2
1900–01	6.3	13.6
1901–02	9.6	18.2
1902–03	9.9	17.8
1903–04	14.2	21.2
1904–05	13.4	23.0
1905–06	15.2	32.8
1906–07	17.7	31.7
1907–08	16.1	18.1
1908–09	3.1	17.8
1909–10	15.3	25.2
1910–11	17.1	22.8
1911–12	17.1	22.4
1912–13	14.6	23.8

Source: RCC, 1914, Appendix VII, p.233

effected through direct shipments of gold sovereigns and gold/silver bullion was, however, against the interest of the SOS which was rather keen on having ready cash in London to meet its overseas commitments. The SOS was evidently successful in meeting its current expenses through sale of bills alone, the value of sales averaging at £18.6 million over 1898–99 to 1913–14—a period when the average liabilities due to home charges amounted to £17.7 million only (*see* Table 3.2 for the volume of CBs sold and Table 2.1 for the value of home charges).

Not the entire amount of inflow of bullion, before the closure of the mints in 1893, was, however, brought to the mint for coinage. Nor did the imported sovereigns widely circulate with the public since these coins had a limited acceptability even after 1898 when sovereigns attained the status of legal tender money. A portion of the precious metals coming in was

Source: Statistical Abstracts of British India. Figures include land-borne trade, government stores and re-exports. Rupee values have been converted into sterling at the prevailing exchange rates before and after 1893. Statistics for commodities other than treasure does not include land-borne trade for the years 1871–72 to 1876–77, 1888—89 and 1899–1900.

channelized into hoarding, an exact estimate of which is difficult to arrive at since there was also a tendency to melt the coins (in circulation) and earn profit.

3.1.2 REMITTANCES UNDER FIXED RATES AND THE WIDENED COVERAGE OF COUNCIL BILLS: 1893–1914

Pressures to find financial resources in the domestic budget to meet the overseas contractual obligations—which were growing with the depreciating rupee during the late nineteenth century—led the India government to reconsider its currency policy. Difficulties were also faced by the European residents. Remitting income from India became increasingly difficult for the Europeans, who were faced with the dwindling sterling equivalent of the rupee income earned from salaries or private commerce in India. The significant controlling position of the Europeans (who were primarily British in origin), both in the government and in private trade,[1] made it all the more urgent on the part of the officials to seek remedial measures. The mounting pressures were followed up with the setting up of a high powered Royal Commission on Indian Currency and Finance in 1893 (the Herschell Committee) which recommended the closure of mints (in India) to coinage on private demand, and the pegging of the rupee exchange rate at 1*s* 4*d*. Both recommendations were implemented. In order to institute the fixed sterling–rupee link, sovereigns had to be declared as legal tender money. Thus sovereigns were acceptable at the treasury at Rs. 15 as payment of revenue. But these were not made available to the public against rupee payments. In England, sales of CB on India were also fixed at the same exchange rate (1*s* 4*d*) after allowing for transport cost margin of gold sovereigns (which continued to provide an alternative form of remittance, since remittances after 1893 could no longer be effected, as mentioned earlier, through silver bullion). The set of measures guaranteed a sterling (i.e. gold) exchange standard in India—an institution which, according to Keynes, was first of its kind in the world as a whole.[2] No attempt, as pointed out above, was made to ensure a reciprocal guarantee to convert rupees into sterling. The device was introduced to support the exchange rate of the rupee in relation to sterling. It also proved useful as a support to the imperial design to centralize colonial gold reserves in London. We would return to this aspect in Section

3.1.3. Indirect support to the rupee rate in the market (which continued to deviate from the official rate till 1898) were sought to be provided through measures to implement a certain degree of demonetization (of rupee) in the domestic economy, as was suggested by the 1893 Committee. The suggested demonetization amounted to an actual melting of coins worth Rs.10 million in circulation. In addition, no coins were minted over 1893–97. These measures, according a private estimate, when implemented, amounted to a net withdrawal of Rs. 2.55 million from circulation.[3]

It was but natural that the closure of mints in 1893 was a step which immediately fuelled the demand for CBs, which became the major channel of remittance to India from London (*see* Table 3.2 for the spurt in the sale of Council Bills after 1893). Inflow of gold, both bullion and sovereigns, however, continued especially with gold sovereigns becoming acceptable at the Indian treasury. Sovereigns, accepted as revenue, often found their way to the official reserves. This practice resulted in an increase in gold as a proportion of the aggregate official reserves. The market rate of the rupee, however, continued to be lower than the official rate until a reversal took place in world gold prices which by 1898 stabilized the exchange rate at its official price of 1*s* 4*d* (*see* Table 3.3 on official gold reserves over 1898–1910).

Bills actually sold by the SOS by and large exceeded the sum earmarked as the annual budgetary estimates of CB sales (*see* Table 3.4 for discrepancy between estimated and actual sales of CBs during 1890–91 to 1912–13). As a consequence, the India Office had an immediate access to additional funds which could be accumulated in England. This sum was in addition to the current and capital account expenses of India Office which were usually covered by the sum earmarked as estimated sales of CBs. The tendency to increase the volume of bills sold was especially pronounced after 1905 when there was no longer a stipulation to limit the total sales of CBs to the value of home charges.[4]

The possibility of selling Council Bills up to the limit which could be absorbed by the market (after 1905) provided the SOS with an important tool of accumulating sterling and gold in London. The scheme was extensively utilized for purposes which included the following: (*a*) A transfer of gold reserves, located in India with the treasury and the Paper Currency

Reserve, to London. (*See* Table 3.13 and Section 3.1.3 for details and the implications of the above processes); (*b*) to provide for the sterling cost of silver procurements in England which met the demand for fresh coinage in India. This was supposed to cut back the cost of gold shipments from India which would otherwise have taken place for the purpose; (*c*) to meet, in addition, all capital expenditure of the SOS connected with purchase of railway equipment in England; (*d*) to cut down the SOS's borrowings in England; and (*e*) to finance purchase of sovereigns in transit which otherwise had to be met through supplementary sales of telegraphic transfers demanding immediate payments.[5]

Extensive use of the Council Bill scheme of remittances under its widened coverage after 1905 resulted in a marked discrepancy between the actual and the budgeted sale of Council Bills. The margin (between the actual and the sums) steeply rose from an annual average of £3.5 million to £14.8 million over the periods 1901–02 to 1903–04 and 1905–06 to 1906–07. The margin exceeded, on an average, by £7 millions during 1904–05 to 1912–13. Incidentally, sale of bills fell short of the budgeted sales during 1897–98, 1900–01, and 1907–09—years which were marked by widespread crop failure and famine (*see* Table 3.4 for the margin relating to 1890–91 and 1912–13). Bills sold in excess could add to the foreign assets of the SOS, ordinarily maintained as non-interest-bearing deposits with the Bank of England and/or as sterling securities invested in England. The arrangement eased the financial situation of the SOS and hence also took away the pressure on it to go in for fresh borrowing. The process also implied a closer link between the India Office and the London City—an aspect which would be analysed in Sections 3.3 to 3.5.

A seasonal pattern was visible in the sale of Council Bills. As was to be expected, this pattern moved with fluctuation in output and trade in India.[6] One notices, in this connection, an inconsistency between the official position and the actual practices of the India government. A memorandum, for instance, was submitted by an official from the India government to the Royal Commission on Indian Currency in 1914,[7] putting forth a claim that bills sold by the SOS were deliberately not adjusted to the seasonal trends. The step, from the official standpoint, was justified in view of the fact that official expenditure in India and in England were not necessarily linked to production

Table 3.3: Location and composition of official gold reserves: 1898–1910 (Thousands of pounds sterling)

As on last date of March	Held by Secretary of State in England	Held by Govt. of India In PCR*	Held by Govt. of India in Treasury	In GSR	Total India	Total Gold Reserves
1898	–	170	–	–	170	170
1899		2035	3	–	2038	2038
1900	1500	7500	271	–	7771	9271
1901	–	5778	136	1200	7114	7114
1902	–	7024	85	–	7109	7109
1903	–	9859	120	–	9979	9979
1904	–	10790	133	–	10923	10923
1905	–	10740	221	–	10961	10961
1906	6945	3826	295	–	4121	11066
1907	7025	3664	242	22	3928	10953
1908	3705	2713	222	–	2935	6640
1909	1500	23	69	–	92	1592
1910	2500	6202	237	–	6434	8939

Source: India Office Records L/F/29.

Note: (*a*) Figures for period after 1910 not available from the same source. (*b*) PCR and GSR indicate paper Currency Reserves and Gold Standard Reserves respectively, held in India alone.

Table 3.4: Council Bills and telegraphic transfers: 1890–1913 (£ millions)

Year	Budget Estimate	Actual Amount	Remarks
(1)	(2)	(3)	
1890–91	14.9	15.9	
1891–92	16.0	16.0	
1892–93	17.0	16.5	
1893–94	18.7	9.5	
1894–95	17.0	16.9	
1895–96	17.0	17.6	
1896–97	16.5	15.5	
1897–98	13.0	9.5	Famine in India
1898–99	16.0	18.6	
1899–1900	17.0	19.0	
1900–01	16.4	13.3	Failure of crops in 1899
1901–02	16.5	18.5	
1902–03	16.5	18.4	
1903–04	17.0	23.8	
1904–05	16.5	24.4	
1905–06	17.8	32.1	

Table 3.4 (Cont.)

(1)	(2)	(3)	
1906–07	17.8	33.1	
1907–08	18.1	16.2	Failure of monsoon 1907
1908–09	18.5	13.9	
1909–10	16.2	27.0	
1910–11	15.5	26.7	
1911–12	17.1	27.0	
1912–13	15.5	25.7	

Source : *RCC* (1914), p. 232.

Note: For the period 1872–73 to 1898–99, actual is *less* than budget estimate by £0.8 million as annual average. For 1899–1900 to 1912–13, actuals exceeded by £5 million on an average.

cycles in Indian agriculture. (The official, while approving of the general policy of investing the surplus funds in interest-bearing sterling assets, was, however, opposed to an excessive accumulation of reserves in England—a position which was consistent to the general view prevailing in India government circles on the question.)

Seasonality was rather evident in the actual sale of Council Bills. According to statistics released by the Royal Commission on Indian Currency (1914), sale of bills during the busy season of 1893–94 to 1912–13 was significantly higher (*see* Table 3.2). This was indicated at end of the statistical tables on Council Bills which read 'the amount drawn in the second half of the financial year exceeds that drawn in the first half by more than 44 per cent on the average and is almost invariably drawn at a higher rate of exchange'. The figure related to the years between 1893–94 and 1912–13.[8]

The seasonal pattern in the sale of bills by the SOS induced the Government of India to ensure a minimum level for its reserves in India during the busy season to reimburse a larger volume of bills at the treasury when need arose. The concern for a probable financial stringency resulted in a rather peculiar situation. The average level of treasury reserves at end of a busy season which was left after reimbursing the relatively larger volume of bills and other demands was often relatively large compared to what was left at end of a lean season. The paradox was pointed out in a memorandum submitted by some traders to the Royal Commission of 1898.[9] Attempts by the government to maintain larger reserves in peak seasons led to a liquidity or credit squeeze in the domestic economy during the busy season—an aspect we will discuss in Section 3.3. Explanations were provided in the official circles (*see*

Table 3.5: Average price of silver in London and rate of exchange for CB/TT on India:1872–73 to 1897–98

Year	Average price of silver per ounce in pence	Year	Rate of CB/TT per Rupee	
	(1)		(2)	
			s	d
1872–73	$60\frac{5}{16}$	1872–73	1	10.754
1873–74	$59\frac{1}{4}$	1873–74	1	10.351
1874–75	$58\frac{5}{16}$	1874–75	1	10.156
1875–76	$56\frac{7}{8}$	1875–76	1	9.626
1876–77	$52\frac{3}{4}$	1876–77	1	8.508
1877–78	$54\frac{13}{16}$	1877–78	1	8.791
1878–79	$52\frac{9}{16}$	1878–79	1	7.794
1879–80	$51\frac{1}{4}$	1879–80	1	7.961
1880–81	$52\frac{1}{4}$	1880–81	1	7.956
1881–82	$51\frac{11}{16}$	1881–82	1	7.895
1882–83	$51\frac{5}{8}$	1882–83	1	7.525
1883–84	$50\frac{9}{16}$	1883–84	1	7.536
1884–85	$50\frac{5}{8}$	1884–85	1	7.308
1885–86	$48\frac{5}{8}$	1885–86	1	6.254
1886–87	$45\frac{3}{8}$	1886–87	1	5.441
1887–88	$44\frac{5}{8}$	1887–88	1	4.898
1888–89	$42\frac{7}{8}$	1888–89	1	4.379
1889–90	$42\frac{11}{16}$	1889–90	1	4.566
1890–91	$47\frac{11}{16}$	1890–91	1	6.089
1891–92	$45\frac{1}{16}$	1891–92	1	4.733
1892–93	$39\frac{1}{16}$	1892–93	1	2.985
1893–94	$35\frac{3}{16}$	1893–94	1	2.547
1894–95	$28\frac{15}{16}$	1894–95	1	1.101
1895–96	$29\frac{7}{8}$	1895–96	1	1.638
1896–97	$30\frac{3}{4}$	1896–97	1	2.541
1897–98	$27\frac{9}{16}$	1897–98	1	3.354

Sources: 1. *Report of Indian Currency Committee*, 1899, Sessional Papers, 1899, Vol 31. 2. *Indian Currency Committee Report*, 1898, cited in A.K. Banerji, *Indo-British Economic Relations.*

Section 3.4). These, however, were often incongruous with the prevailing trends. Moreover, public reaction to such controversial questions (Section 3.3) often contested these official positions.

3.1.3 FINANCIAL TRANSFERS THROUGH OFFICIAL RESERVES

Reserves were maintained in India by the government in the treasuries and at the two currency reserves which included Gold Standard Reserve (GSR), and the Paper Currency Reserve (PCR) located in the two countries. The PCR provided 100 per cent backing to paper notes in circulation. The reserves included both gold and financial assets or securities. Fiduciary ceilings limited the maximum value of the financial assets at the paper currency reserve. The fiduciary limit, originally at Rs. 4 crores when the PCR was instituted in 1861, was later raised to Rs. 14 crores in 1912–13. Securities could be held in rupees or in sterling, depending on the location of reserves. This overall statutory ceiling on investment in securities (the fiduciary limit) related to PCR alone on its investment between the two countries. The GSR however was free from the statutory fiduciary limits, thus permitting the SOS to make use of the London branch of the GSR as a major source of its investments in the City.

Table 3.6: Location and composition of paper currency reserves: 1891–1913 (Rs. crores)

Year (last day of March)	Silver	India Gold	Securities	Gold	England Securities	Total
(1)	(2)	(3)	(4)	(5)	(6)	(7)
1891	18.6	–	6.9	–	–	25.6
	(72.65)	–	(26.95)	–	–	(100)
1892	16.0	–	8.0	–	–	24.0
	(66.66)	–	(33.33)	–	–	(100)
1893	18.4	–	8.0	–	–	26.4
	(69.69)	–	(30.3)	–	–	(100)
1894	22.4	–	8.0	–	–	30.4
	(73.68)	–	(26.31)	–	–	(100)
1895	22.7	–	8.0	–	–	30.7
	(73.94)	–	(26.05)	–	–	(100)
1896	17.9	–	8.0	–	–	25.9

Table 3.6 (Contd.)

(1)	(2)	(3)	(4)	(5)	(6)	(7)
	(69.1)	–	(30.3)	–	–	(100)
1897	13.7	–	9.9	–	–	23.7
	(57.81)	–	(41.77)	–	–	(100)
1898	14.5	25	9.9	–	–	24.7
	(58.7)	(1.01)	(40)	–	–	(100)
1899	15.10	3.0	9.9	–	–	28.2
	(53.54)	(10.64)	(35.1)	–	–	(100)
1900	5.2	11.25	9.9	2.2	–	28.7
	(18.1)	(39.0)	(34.49)	(7.66)	–	(100)
1901	11.2	8.6	9.9	–	–	29.8
	(37.58)	(28.85)	(33.22)	–	–	(100)
1902	11.1	10.5	9.9	–	–	31.6
	(35.13)	(33.23)	(31.33)	–	–	(100)
1903	10.9	14.7	9.9	–	–	35.7
	(30.53)	(41.18)	(27.73)	–	–	(100)
1904	12.0	16.1	9.9	–	–	38.2
	(31.41)	(42.15)	(25.92)	–	–	(100)
1905	13.0	16.1	9.9	–	–	39.1
	(33.25)	(41.18)	(25.32)	–	–	(100)
1906	16.3	5.7	9.9	10.5	2.0	44.6
	(36.55)	(12.82)	(22.19)	(23.54)	(4.5)	(100)
1907	18.9	5.4	9.9	10.5	2.0	46.9
	(40.3)	(11.51)	(21.11)	(22.4)	(4.26)	(100)
1908	25.2	4.0	9.9	5.5	2.0	46.8
	(53.85)	(8.55)	(21.15)	(11.75)	(4.27)	(100)
1909	31.2	0.03	9.9	2.2	2.0	45.4
	(68.72)	(0.066)	(21.81)	(4.85)	(4.41)	(100)
1910	29.3	9.3	9.9	3.7	2.0	54.4
	(53.86)	(17.09)	(18.19)	(6.80)	(3.68)	(100)
1911	26.2	9.2	9.9	7.5	2.0	54.9
	(47.72)	(16.76)	(18.03)	(13.66)	(3.64)	(100)
1912	15.5	23.3	9.9	8.5	4.0	61.3
	(25.28)	(38)	(16.15)	(13.87)	(6.53)	(100)
1913	16.4	29.3	9.9	9.1	4.0	68.9
	(23.8)	(42.53)	(14.37)	(13.21)	(5.81)	(100)

Source: *RCC* (1913), pp. 248–9

Table 3.7: Use of CB/TT proceeds in England: 1902–03 to 1911–12 (£ millions)

	General purpose (i.e.SOS's treasury)	Purchase of silver	GSR	PCR
(1)	(2)	(3)	(4)	(5)
1902–03	17.9	0.2	0.2	–
1903–04	17.6	4.0	2.2	–

Table 3.7 (Contd.)

(1)	(2)	(3)	(4)	(5)
1904–05	19.1	4.5	0.7	–
1905–06	19.1	8.1	3.5	1.3
1906–07	19.6	10.7	–	–
1907–08	13.5	1.1	0.5	–
1908–09	12.4	0.06	1.4	–
1909–10	17.8	–	8.0	1.0
1910–11	23.6	–	10.6	2.1
1911–12	25.0	–	–	1.9

Source: *Memorandum on India Office Balances*, Marshall Library, Keynes *Papers*, 53A7, item 9.

Note: The following have been excluded from the amount shown in the table: (*a*) Gold earmarked for PCR in 1905–06 amounting to £1.0 million and repaid in 1906–07; £1.0 million for 1909–10; £2.5 million for 1910–11 and £0.6 million for 1911–11; (*b*) Gold withdrawn from PCR for purchase of silver in 1907–08; (*c*) £1.0 million paid for bills sold in India during 1909–10.

The GSR had a branch in India, comprising silver ingots which could be minted into rupee coins at short notice. In London the GSR comprised gold, sterling securities, and sterling lent at short notice (deposits). There was no fixed rule regarding the absolute value or the relative share of the different financial assets in the GSR. Official reserves also included the treasury balance, a part of which was with the India Office in London.

Of the three reserves maintained by the India government, it was the London branch of the GSR which permitted the maximum investment in sterling securities since there was no upward limit. The treasury balance (of India Office) at London could not, for reasons of financial expediency, be held predominantly in a form where these were not liquid. The India Office's investments in securities also suited the financial interests of the City which had a vested interest in sustaining the flow of demand for these assets. During the fourteen years between 1899–1900 and 1912–13, accumulation in gold reserves in the Indian branch of the PCR and the treasury amounted to £46 million. Of this a sum as large as £24.4 million was actually transferred to the SOS's office in London.[10] The matter soon became a question of official concern and public controversy as could be witnessed in the long deliberations and exchange of views over the period. We have tried to document and analyse this in Sections 3.3 and 3.4. Despite large outflows of reserves to England the Indian branch of the PCR continued to possess a disproportionately

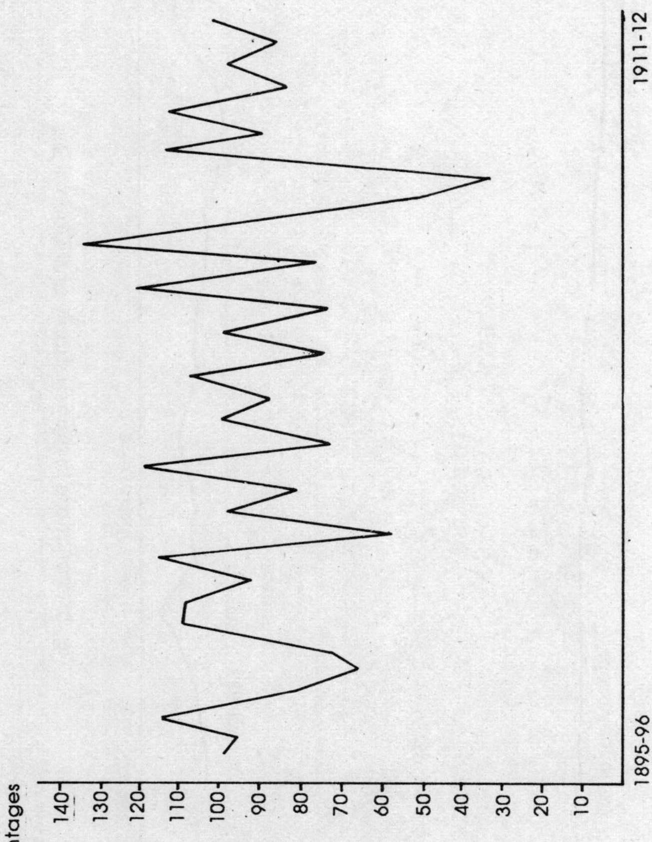

Fig. 2 Ratio of six-month averages for Council Bills sold to thirty-month moving average

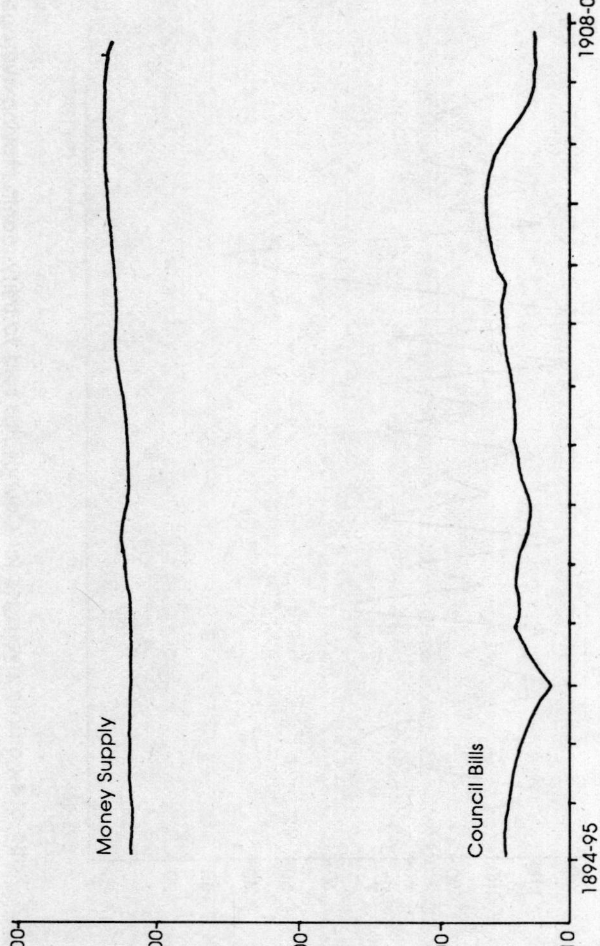

Fig. 3 Variations in money supply and Council Bills

large stock in gold, especially when contrasted to its stock of silver in coin and bullion (*see* Table 3.6). The following three, among others, could be the possible explanations:

(*a*) The official announcement in June 1893 (following recommendations of the Herschell Committee) that henceforth sovereigns were acceptable at the treasury at 1*s* 4*d*, initiated a stream of gold inflows to the treasury. The treasury, in its turn, placed a large proportion of this gold with the PCR, allowing increases in paper notes which took place during the subsequent period. Prices of gold tumbled down in international markets after 1898, heralding a development which made it attractive for private arbitrageurs to avail of the official price of gold in India (which exceeded the international price). The situation led to increased gold imports, a large part of which found their way to the treasury and then to the PCR in India.

(*b*) A net 'efflux' of rupee coins took place during the period from the Indian branch of the PCR to the public. This happened as the value of paper currency, tendered at the PCR against rupee coins in the busy season (October–March), was generally larger than the value of rupee coins which returned to the PCR in the lean seasons (April–September). This aspect is borne out by the statistics available for 1911–12 and 1912–13.[11] The fact that (rupee) coins were still popular with the public pushed out such coins from the PCR, as would be expected under Gresham's Law.

(*c*) As contrast to the rupee coin outflow, gold inflow to the PCR during both busy and lean seasons were positive, thus adding to the stock of gold held in the reserve.[12]

The proportion of silver (coin and bullion) with the PCR in India went down from 73.7 per cent in 1894–95 to 18.1 per cent and 23.9 per cent in 1900–01 and 1912–13 respectively. As was to be expected, the share of gold at the PCR in India went up, from a negligible share during 1893–94 to 47 per cent of aggregate resources at PCR in 1912–13.[13]

Accumulation of gold at the Indian branch of PCR was matched by transfer of gold between the two branches of the PCR. This was reflected (*see* Table 3.6) in the increased stock of gold at PCR (London branch) after 1905 (notwithstanding the temporary shortfalls during 1907–09.)[14] The entire process was matched, as noted earlier, by upward revisions in the statutory ceilings stipulated for the fiduciary reserves at the

PCR. (The overall limit was raised from Rs. 4 crores in 1893–94 to Rs. 12 crores by Act III of 1905–06, and once again to Rs. 14 crores by Act VII of 1910–11.) Given the dominant interest of the City in ensuring a higher rate of return for its sterling securities, upward revisions in the fiduciary limit of the PCR were permitted, allowing increases in investment in sterling securities. The new fiduciary ceiling of the PCR was at £14 millions by Act VII of 1910–11.[15]

We now discuss the official reserves in gold/sterling with the London branch of the gold standard reserve. Initially designated as Gold Reserve Fund (GRF), the account in gold was instituted in 1901 following the recommendation of the 1898 RCC (the Fowler Commission). The fund was set up through the financial resources of the government obtained through profits on minting of rupee coins in India (which could be described as seigniorage). Funds set aside in the GRF were designed (*a*) to support the official exchange rate of the rupee in terms of sterling, and (*b*) to effect an eventual switchover to gold standard in India. Recommendations of the Fowler Commission on the launching of a gold currency in India were, however, never implemented and the ambiguities connected with maintaining a gold reserve in India were rather apparent by 1906 when prospects of having a gold currency in India were deemed as remote even on part of the government. The GRF located in India was henceforth redesignated as 'Silver Branch' of the gold standard reserve. It merged with the (silver) ingot reserves (which the government had been maintaining since 1904) in order to quicken the minting of rupee coins in the country. A London branch (of the GSR) opened in the same year, however, comprised gold (bullion and sovereigns) and sterling securities—the former being deposited with the Bank of England. While gold reserves maintained with the PCR account of the India government at the Bank of England were, as could be anticipated, completely 'earmarked' (in terms of the statutory requirements on the fiduciary limits of the PCR), cash deposited under the GSR accounts with the Bank of England was freely disposable. Accumulation of gold and sovereigns accelerated at the London branch of GSR, providing the major source of finance for the SOS's investment in the London securities market. The outcome was a justified one, according to the Government of India (GOI), in terms of the judiciousness of maintaining official reserves in gold/sterling securities in London (especially with the strain on the rupee rate over 1907–08 and 1908–09).

Accumulation of gold in the PCR (India) and the flexible options to use the gold reserves at the London branch of the GSR (which were deposited with the Bank of England) encouraged further transfer of gold to England. These transfers were worked out through the sale of Council Bills, which arranged for compensation between the Indian branch of the PCR and the London branch of the GSR. The nature of the arrangement and the issues it raised were confirmed in a set of interesting correspondence between the SOS and the Finance Department of the GOI during 1906–07. Attention was drawn in these letters to the depleted ingot reserves of the PCR during the busy season of 1906–07, apparently caused by the extraordinary seasonal demand for coinage in India. A need thus was urgently felt by the India government to replenish the ingot reserves at the Indian branch of the PCR especially since the treasury balance in rupees had also dropped to a low as a consequence of no minting of coins over 1893–98.[16] The statutory ceiling on silver ingots at the GSR silver branch in India was around 300 lakh tons. In April 1906 the upper limit was revised by the SOS to 600 lakh tons, largely to ensure a smooth process of rupee coinage. Ingot reserves kept with the GSR silver branch, however, was below 600 lakh tons in March 1906.[17] The situation called for, in addition to raising the statutory limit, large scale purchases of silver in England by the SOS. The sequence of events set in motion a controversy between the Finance Department of the GOI and the India Office (the SOS) on the feasibility of the silver purchase plans. While the GOI requested the SOS to purchase 600 lakh tons of silver on 26 June 1906, the SOS suggested a rather complicated and intricate procedure which was as follows: treasury in India was to receive a temporary loan of 600 lakh tons of silver ingots from the GSR silver branch in India, at an interest rate of $3^1/_2$ per cent. To offset the above transaction, equivalent transfer in gold were to take place in London, from the treasury at India Office to the GSR London branch, both maintained by the SOS. The SOS could now invest it in gold (sterling) denominated securities earning a $4\frac{1}{2}$ per cent rate of return in London (*vide* letter from the SOS dated 24 April 1907).[18] The deal obviously was not only expedient but also profitable. Official circles in India looked upon the proposal with disfavour. It amounted, according to them, to an implicit transfer of India government revenue (as well as gold reserve) to England.

In a letter dated 21 February 1907 (No. 1078–A), the Finance Department (GOI) clearly spelt out its reservations, insisting that 'to lend money to the City is not an end in itself and the revenues in India are not raised for such a purpose'.[19] As an alternative to what was viewed as a rather cumbrous proposal, the GOI suggested a scheme whereby direct purchase of silver by the SOS was ensured on a priority basis. Specific requests were made to the India government for a purchase of silver worth Rs. 375 lakhs, while suggesting a part financing of the latter through Rs. 60 lakhs borrowed from the Maharaja of Scindia and the Russo-Chinese Bank, roughly in equal proportions. In addition, silver ingots located in the Indian branch of the PCR could also be used for providing coinage, against compensating transfers of gold in London from the GSR to the PCR. These transfers were viewed with favour by the India government which felt the need to protect the metallic base of the paper notes in circulation. In course of the same correspondence the GOI also suggested that the entire silver ingots (at 600 lakh tons) could, as a long term measure, be placed outside the PCR, preferably along with the ingot reserves at GSR silver branch in India. The suggestion was sought to be justified by the fact that the PCR, which was supposed to provide a metallic backing to the paper currency in circulation, had little, if any, potential for utilizing its own stock of silver for coinage. The GOI also suggested, in the same letter, specific targets for coining ingots, the stock of which were to reach Rs. 18 crores by October—a month which was also the beginning of the busy season. To ensure an adequate level of coined ingots as well as coins in circulation, the government suggested a steady flow of coinage averaging Rs. 150 lakh per month over the months of the lean season covering April to September in each year. The proposal was recommended as one which accommodated the interests of the trading community in India by providing for a steady flow of coins. The PCR, however, was to provide gold for the ingots since '...if...government of India is debarred from using it (the PCR) for silver purchases the silver ceases to perform its chief function'.[20]

Interestingly enough, the second part of the above proposal, which suggested the use of PCR silver in India against earmarking of gold in the London branch of the PCR, was viewed with disfavour by the Secretary of State. Evidently, the measure would have affected the SOS's control over sterling funds in

England, especially for the purpose of investment in the London City. The SOS disagreed with the GOI's position, while offering the following comments: First, with the delicate balance, as was normally maintained in the financial circles of the City, attempts to earmark gold in the PCR would affect the liquidity position as well as the financial options of the SOS. This was especially true with the immediate prospect of renewing a large number of debentures held by the SOS which were to fall due between December 1906 and February 1907.[21] The objections seemed to have their way as the India government was found to relinquish its stand by finally accepting a short-term loan of £3 million in silver ingots (equivalent at the official exchange rate to Rs. 450 lakhs) from the GSR (India) silver branch. The remaining part of the initial request for Rs. 600 lakh (or £4 million) in silver was somehow provided by the SOS which utilized £1 million of its treasury reserve to order Rs. 150 lakhs of silver. The transaction, however, was matched by transfers of gold, worth £1 million, from PCR (India) to the SOS's treasury reserve in London.[22] It is not clear as to how the PCR accounts (in India or in London) were compensated, with one possibility being that the silver coined out of the £1 million purchases were entirely placed with the PCR (India)—an aspect on which information is not traceable.

An accurate estimate of the gold transferred during the period from the Indian branch of the PCR to the SOS's treasury or the GSR in England is difficult to work out. However, one can find concrete evidences, both on such transfers and on the use of the Council Bill device to achieve such transfers. Thus during 1902–03 to 1907–08, the CB sales proceeds were utilized to deposit £6.8 million in sterling with the GSR (London). The transaction was matched by a transfer of rupees in India from GSR (silver branch) to the treasury. While the rupee sum could be used to reimburse Council Bills in India, the net effect of the transaction was the transfer of equivalent gold to England. With a similar process of transfer, £0.1 million of gold was shifted from the GSR in India to the SOS's treasury in London. During 1901–02 to 1910–11, a sum of £11.3 million in gold (which represented profits on coinage, and hence, were ordinarily to be with GSR) were actually transferred from the Indian branch of the GSR to its London branch. The institutional arrangements for the transfers were, as mentioned earlier, provided by the Council Bills. A sum of £1.1 million, representing profits on coinage, was also transferred during 1911–12, this time by directly moving the sum from the PCR in India to the GSR in London, with equivalent rupee flows in the reverse direction (i.e from the GSR silver branch to the PCR) in India. All such transfers clearly increased gold reserves at the London branch of the GSR. Unlike the funds with the London branch of the PCR or with the India Office's deposits, the GSR (London) funds were not earmarked in the Bank of England. The transfers thus permitted a greater flexibility to the SOS, by allowing it to choose its portfolio in sterling,[23]—an option which was not allowed when gold (located in London) was earmarked.

Summing up our observations on the use of the PCR and the GSR as channels of gold transfers to England during the period, we notice the following trends:

(*a*) A tendency, on the part of the SOS, to maximize the investible resources in England. This was achieved through transfers of gold (accumulated in India) to England, with explicit attempts to keep the gold non-earmarked.

(*b*) Sterling proceeds from sale of Council Bills (which were no longer limited to home charges after 1905) were used for the above purpose. The SOS often used the CB proceeds to augment gold reserves in the GSR, since, unlike the PCR or even the SOS's own treasury, gold accumulated with the GSR was not earmarked when it was deposited by the SOS with Bank of England. Compensatory transfers took place in India where silver obtained from the GSR silver branch was used for minting coins which were needed by the treasury to reimburse the Council Bills.

(*c*) Gold earmarked in London under PCR was transferred to the London branch of the GSR. Silver moved in the opposite direction in India, from GSR silver branch to the PCR, in order not to disturb the metallic reserve backing of paper currency.

The various devices to transfer gold to SOS's account in the City did help the financial climate in London. This was especially true in times of monetary stringency, as would be evident from our analysis in Section 3.3.

Contrary to what was held by some contemporary government officials, transfers of official reserves across different accounts of the government did not imply an eventual surrender of the government's current revenue to England. They did, however, imply a change in the portfolio balances with attempts to build up gold reserves maintained in London. Transfers of gold to London for the purpose of investment was considered prior to other transactions like the purchase of silver in London for coinage in India. These policies, as stressed in Sections 3.3 and 3.4, were conducive to the financial interests of the City where the SOS was functioning.

3.2 Money supply and credit situation in the domestic economy: a quantitative assessment

Mints in India were closed to the public, on the recommendation of the Herschell Committee, in June 1893. It can be established that since then the coinage of rupees in India was regulated by official discretion. Changes brought about in the currency standard in 1893 had far–reaching implications for the domestic monetary system. It was no longer possible for the public to obtain rupee coins in lieu of silver bullions, as was the case under the open-mint system. Hence private imports of silver bullion no longer proved an automatic source of monetary expansion. In terms of the measures initiated by the Herschell Committee, no fresh coins were minted between 1893–98—a step which was akin to demonetization in view of the need for expansion of currency in the economy. As mentioned earlier in Section 3.1.2, according to an unofficial estimate, the step implied a net withdrawal of Rs. 252 crore worth of coins over 1893–98.[24] While enhancing the significance of Council Bills as the chief source of remittances, the financial reforms of 1893 also encouraged imports of gold sovereign which were given a legal tender status in India. However, a high propensity to hoard (which particularly related to gold sovereigns and bullion) on part of the general public in India prevented the imports and the limited domestic circulation of sovereigns to have a dent on money supply in India. Policy announcements were issued, in June 1893 and in the next few years, on the desirability of contracting money supply (over an interim period) in order to let the rupee rate stabilize at its official parity. Open and conscious attempts to curtail money supply during 1893–98 were followed by a passive attitude of the government towards money supply, thus ignoring the need to replenish and augment the stock of money in later years. The attitude had contractionary consequences for the supply of money and credit available to the economy (*see* Section 3.4 for details of official currency policy).

Table 3.8 : Composition of money supply in India * (Rs lakhs)

Years	Paper currency in circulation (outside Presidency Banks and Treasury)	Rupee coins in active circulation (excluding hoarding)	Total active circulation of money
(1)	(2)	(3)	(4)
1893–94	1684 (10.5)	14300 (89.5)	15984
1894–95	1905 (11.6)	14500 (88.4)	16405
1895–96	2010 (11.6)	15000 (88.4)	17010
1896–97	1876 (10.9)	15300 (89.1)	17176
1897–98	1716 (10.1)	15200 (89.9)	16916
1898–99	2037 (11.9)	15000 (88.1)	17037
1899–1900	2209 (11.7)	16600 (88.3)	18809
1900–01	2191 (11.3)	17100 (88.7)	19291
1901–02	2222 (11.5)	17000 (88.5)	19222
1902–03	2480 (12.4)	17500 (87.6)	19980
1903–04	2809 (12.9)	18800 (87.1)	21609
1904–05	2845 (12.4)	20000 (87.6)	22845
1905–06	3262 (13.1)	21500 (86.9)	24762
1906–07	3644 (13.1)	24100 (86.9)	27744
1907–08	3260 (11.8)	24200 (88.2)	27460
1908–09	3495 (13.5)	22300 (86.5)	25795
1909–10	3998	n.a.	—
1910–11	4017	n.a.	—
1911–12	4461	n.a.	—

Source: *RCC*, 1914, AII, p. 250. Atkinson, 'Rupee Prices in India', *JRSS*, 1909, P. 563.

* Since gold soverigns had very little circulation we have excluded them from the definition of money supply in this table.

One can provide an indirect evidence of a shortfall in monetary expansion by contrasting the value of Council Bills sold annually in England to the annual variations in money supply (which comprised rupee coins and paper notes). The respective time series are provided in Tables 3.4 and 3.8. Data on money supply relate to 'active circulation'—a notion which runs parallel to the definition of 'active rupee coins' which was arrived at by Atkinson in 1909 by deducting hoarded (rupee) coins from total rupee coins in circulation. On a parallel basis, we have calculated the total active circulation which includes, in addition to active rupee coins, the net circulation of paper currency. The latter has been arrived at by deducting, from gross circulation, the paper money at the treasury and at presidency banks. It can be observed from Fig. 2 that the annual percentage variations in the circulation of 'active money' were virtually non-existent over the sixteen-year period between 1893–94 and 1908–09 (data beyond 1908–09 are not available since the Atkinson series on active rupee coins terminates in 1908–09). The pattern seems to be apparently incongruous with the increased volume of CB sales and the growing budgetary allocations in India under the head of 'Expenditure Abroad' (which was used to redeem the latter). Bills sold on India were essentially the instruments for remittances against the country's trade surpluses which, in absence of neutralizing forces, should have augmented the availability of cash with the public. We have plotted in Fig. 2 the relative rates of annual percentage increases in Council Bills sold and in the aggregate (active) money supply (in India) over 1893–94 to 1908–09. The figure, drawn on a semi-logarithmic scale, shows a near stationary level of aggregate money stock with the public—a phenomenon which contrasts the upward movements in the sales of CBs over most of the period barring the exceptional years during 1905–06 to 1907–08. The apparent paradox in the rather dissimilar movements in the two variables can be explained by the fact that bills in India were, in effect, reimbursed by drawing upon budgetary allocations (under the head of Expenditure Abroad)—a practice which amounted to maintaining a budgetary surplus (or net taxes) in the government account, which clearly had a constraining effect on domestic money supply and other real variables (see Chapter 1, note 14 for the possible multiplier effect of the export surplus in such situations).

Money supply in India underwent significant changes in its composition during the period. Despite the rather limited use of paper notes (the circulation of which was limited due to the currency circle system which operated till 1910[25]) and the problems experienced by the public in the use of paper notes, the share of paper currency in total money supply went up marginally as a proportion of active money in circulation. The observation confirms the basis for a hypothesis on a possible monetary stringency in India. It is important not to miss the fact that in spite of the absolute and relative increases over the period, paper notes in circulation during the period never exceeded 10–14 per cent of aggregate money supply. Viewing from the above angle, one feels justified to use 'active' rupee coins as a proxy for total monetary resources in the country. Expansions in rupee coins were problematic and limited during the period, with the legal sanctions against minting during 1893–98, and later, with the specific problems encountered by the GOI in procuring from London the silver needed to maintain the flow of new coins (*see* Sections 3.4 and 3.5).

The stationariness in money supply, indicated above, was reinforced by stringencies in the availability of credit in the domestic economy. Looking at the seasonal variations in discount rates charged by the three presidency banks in the country over 1893–94 to 1912–13, a distinct widening of the amplitude of fluctuations in the bank rate was visible, especially during the years of crop shortfalls and related famine syndromes. Since the three presidency banks and other joint-stock banks operating in India usually followed each other in fixing their discount rate, it suffices to observe the variations in the rate fixed by any one of them. Data on the seasonal variations in Bank of Bengal discount rates over 1893–94 to 1912–13 is provided in Table 3.9. The discount (or advance) rate related to potential bank loans against security of government paper or other approved collaterals submitted by borrowers. The data show a tendency for the discount rate to be subject to both an upward trend and a wider amplitude of seasonal fluctuations over the period. The strong seasonal variations over 1897–98 to 1900–01 can be related to fluctuations in agricultural output and the prevalence of famines during the period. (The busy season discount rate soared up during 1896–97 to 1897–98, and later, during 1907–08 to 1908–09—years which were marked by droughts, famines, and deficits in the balance of external trade for India.[26]) An attempt has been made in Table 3.10 to explain the annual variations in the Bank of Bengal discount rates over 1893–94 to 1908–09 on the basis of certain plausible explanatory factors which include (*a*) the 'active' money supply excluding paper money, hoards of rupee coins and official reserves, (*b*) gross money supply including private hoards of rupee coin and official reserves (at the treasury and at presidency banks), (*c*) government's expenditure abroad, earmarked in the budget, and (*d*) Council Bills sold in England. We would have liked to add as explanatory variables, the availability of cash at Bank of Bengal, and official reserves at the PCR and GSR (in India and in England). But the available data was not adequate to provide a complete time series on the last two variables. Moreover, the limited period (1893–94 to 1908–09) covered by the Atkinson series on 'active' rupee

Table 3.9 : Seasonality in Bank of Bengal discount rates: 1893–94 to 1912–13.

Year Ending March	April-September	October-March
1894	4.9	5.8
1895	5.4	4.1
1896	4.1	5.0
1897	4.8	8.7
1898	7.5	9.0
1899	7.7	6.0
1900	5.0	8.2
1901	4.0	6.1
1902	5.0	5.6
1903	4.1	5.5
1904	4.6	5.0
1905	3.7	5.9
1906	4.6	6.2
1907	5.8	8.1
1908	4.3	9.1
1909	6.0	6.7
1910	5.2	5.9
1911	4.7	6.4
1912	5.0	6.0
1913	4.3	6.5

Source: Keynes (1914), Appendix.

coins has forced us to restrict our analysis to the same time span. We have reported in Table 3.10 the results of a regression of Bank of Bengal discount rates on time series relating to the four variables listed as (*a*) to (*d*). The statistical excercise explains a very small proportion of the observed variations in the Bank of Bengal annual average discount rate. Accordingly, we need to take into account other plausible explanations, including cash reserves at presidency banks placed by the government over busy and lean seasons.

A significant tendency was observable in the data (available for a limited number of years between 1888–90 and 1892–97) on the role of the government in controlling money supply through the size of its deposits at the presidency banks. Seasonality in credit availability at the banks was bound to be aggravated since the treasury seems to have made it a practice to actually withdraw, on a net basis, part of its deposits at the presidency banks during the busy season (Table 3.11). While

Table 3.10 : Variations in Bank of Bengal discount rates: 1893–94 to 1908–09

No. of equation.	Independent variable	Intercept	Dependent variables				R^2	D-W Statistics
			CB	M_t	B_s	M'_t		
(1)	*i*	16.27	−0.01 (0.08)	0.0 (0.0)	−0.47 (0.22)		0.39	1.16
(2)	*i*	5.70	−0.04 (0.34)	0.0			0.14	1.07
(3)	*i*	7.80	−0.02 (0.03)			0.0 (0.0)	0.12	0.83
(4)	*i*	17.20		0.0 (0.0)	−0.52 (0.19)		0.37	1.17
(5)	*i*	14.61			−0.30 (0.23)	0.0 (0.0)	0.21	0.93

Symbols:
i – Bank of Bengal annual average discount ratio.
CB – Council Bills sold by secretary of state.
B_s – Budgetary surplus of GOI equivalent to item 'Expenditure Abroad' earmarked in the budget.
M_t – Total money supply excluding hoarded (non-'Active') rupee coins and paper notes.
M'_t – Total money supply including hoarded rupee coins.

Note: Data relates to the period between 1893–94 to 1908–09.
Sources (of data used in the Table):
i : J.M. Keynes, *Indian Currency and Finance*, London, 1914. Appendix.
CB : *Royal Commission on Indian Currency* (1914), Appendix II. p. 237.
B_s : As computed in Table 3.14.
M_t and M'_t : For paper notes: *RCC* (1914), Appendix II. p. 250. For rupee coins Atkinson, 'Rupee Prices in India: 1870–1908', *JRSS* 1909, p. 563 (Table 3.8).

cash available with the presidency banks got diminished as a result, liquidity maintained as official cash reserves showed relative increases during March, the 'month of acutest trade demand' (*see* note at the end of Table 3.11). This was reflected in the ratio between treasury deposits and total reserves at the three presidency banks which showed relative declines in the busy season. To look into the figures (provided for 1888–1897 in Table 3.11), 8.8 per cent of aggregate cash reserves

Table 3.11: Seasonalities in cash balances, Council Bills and bank rates

A. Seasonality in cash balances of government and of presidency banks

Month	Average cash balance: 1888–97 (Inclusive) (Rs. Lakhs)			
	Total Govt. Balance	Presidency Banks	Reserve Treasury	District Treasury
March	1713	152 (8.8)	338 (19.7)	1223 (71.3)
July	1532	164 (10.7)	358 (23.3)	1010 (65.9)
November	1050	152 (14.47)	199 (18.95)	699 (66.57)

Source : *Royal Commission on Indian Finance and Currency*, Appendices to the Interim Report, Vol. I, p. 52.

Note : '...It has been the impression for years that the Government has been sparing of their deposits with the presidency Banks during the seasons of greater pressure, with the object of stimulating exchange, and lavish with their deposits in the monsoon months when easy money has helped them to issue new loans.

In order to ascertain whether this impression has any justification in fact, the Finance Committee have had the (above) tabulated statement(s) prepared. The point to be arrived at is this. The collection of revenue, especially the land revenue, withdraws from active circulation considerable sums of money at certain seasons, and it so happens that this withdrawal of money from private hands takes place just when funds are most needed for harvest requirements. By comparing the balances in the Civil Treasuries and Reserve Treasuries with the Treasury Balances in the Presidency Banks in March, July and November of several years, a fair estimate may be formed of the revenue funds hold apart and those placed at the disposal of trade. These months are selected because, generally, March is the month of acutest trade demand and largest accumulations of revenue, July is the month of smallest trade demand, and November is the month of smallest Government revenue. (Report of the Finance Sub-Committee on Management of Treasury balances, Bengal Chamber of Commerce, quoted by W. Parsons, Secretary, Bengal Chamber of Commerce in *Memorandum for Committee*, 17 December, 1898), ibid., p. 51.

B. Cash balance of presidency banks (Rs. Lakhs)

	Total		Government Deposits	
	April–Sept.	Oct.–March	April–Sept.	Oct.–March
1888–89	316.1	258.5	110.0	90.5
			(34.79)	(35.0)
1889–90	262.6	222.5	136.3	98.7
			(51.9)	(44.35)
1890–91	392.3	678.7	94.3	100.2
			(24.00)	(14.76)
1891–92	630.9	476.1	94.5	86.8
			(14.97)	(18.20)
1892–93	482.2	472.9	91.1	92.3
			(18.8)	(19.5)

Source: *RCC* (1898) p. 150.

Table 3.12: Official treasury reserves in India and in England: 1892–93 to 1912–13 (£ millions).

	India	England	Total
1892–93	10.1	2.2	12.4
1893–94	17.0	1.3	18.3
1894–95	15.0	2.5	17.5
1895–96	11.0	3.3	14.3
1896–97	9.2	2.8	12.0
1897–98	10.6	2.5	13.1
1898–99	11.1	3.1	14.3
1899–1900	8.4	3.3	11.7
1900–01	10.5	4.0	14.6
1901–02	11.8	6.6	18.5
1902–03	12.0	5.7	17.8
1903–04	11.8	7.2	19.1
1904–05	10.7	10.2	21.0
1905–06	11.7	8.4	20.2
1906–07	10.3	5.6	15.9
1907–08	12.8	5.7	18.5
1908–09	10.3	8.4	18.6
1909–10	12.2	15.8	28.1
1910–11	13.5	18.1	31.7
1911–12	12.3	18.3	30.6
1912–13	19.2	8.7	27.9

Source: Statistical Abstracts of British India.

at presidency banks were accounted for by government deposits in March—the month when trade demand was most 'acute' and revenue collections at their maximum. The ratio rose to 10.7 per cent in July—the month of smallest trade demand. In September—the month of smallest government revenue—the proportion rose further to 14.4 per cent. The movements in the ratio clearly indicate an official design to maintain liquidity at the treasury in order that it was adequate to reimburse the Council Bills which came in larger volumes in the busy season. (Bills sold in the busy season were about 44 per cent higher than those sold during the lean months of 1894–95 to 1912–13, as can be seen from Tables 3.2.) Moreover, it was common on part of the GOI to collect its land revenue at end of each harvesting season—a practice which probably also curtailed a sizeable part of the purchasing power in the economy during busy season (which included March–September period). Both practices, while augmenting the flow of cash at the treasury, were at the cost of a residual reduction in cash available to the public over the busy season, and was a matter which obviously was of no concern to the government. The presidency banks were forced to restrict or ration the credit they could advance during the months of high trade demand, through higher costs attached to bank borrowings. Thus interest charges on credit advance (which could be treated as a supply price) necessarily had to move up steeply in busy seasons. The contractionary effects of official monetary policy on the organized money market had strong repercussions on the internal credit market, controlled by the indigenous money-lenders (or *shroffs*) in the country. As a contrast to the export business, which was controlled by the European joint-stock banks, local trade was handled by *banias* (the indigenous merchants) who had to depend on the rediscounting of trade bills, and on *hundies* (informal letters of credit) for finance. A great degree of reluctance and reservation (the details of which have been given in Section 3.4) marked the attitude of the presidency banks in lending directly to the public. The view was shared by Keynes who sought to justify the prevailing monetary practices in India in his notion of an implicit automaticity in the gold exchange standard system in the country. An argument was also advanced by Keynes and, later, by Tomlinson[27] that monetary stringencies in colonial India were specific to particular sectors of the 'disjoint credit market'. Both, arguments are open to

Table 3.13: Imports of silver, net silver coinage, hoards/dishoards, change in reserves, change in rupee coinage available with the public: 1894–95 to 1912–13 (Rupees lakhs)

	Imports of silver bullion	Net silver coinage	Hoards/ dishoards by public	Change in reserve held with PCR/GSR	Change in official reserve at treasury and presidency bank	Net sum with-drawn/released by government	Net change in silver coinage with public
(1)	(2)	(3)	(4=2−3)	(5)	(6)	(7=5+6)	(8=3−7)
1894–95	633	3.0	603	29	1029	1058	–1055
1895–96	658	0.2	658	–473	–304	–777	777.2
1896–97	585	–6.8	601	422	–593	–1015	1021.8
1897–98	847	37.8	810	76	262	–186	223.8
1898–99	398	37.2	361	64	250	314	–276.8
1899–1900	358	132.0	226	–991	78	–913	1048.1
1901–02	951	1693.6	–742	418	–408	10	1683.6
1902–03	696	324.9	372	–20	322	177	147.9
1903–04	1365	1115.5	250	56	25	81	1034.5
1904–05	1326	781.2	545	–13	–32	–45	826.2
1905–06	1572	1687.6	–115	222	–168	–54	1633

Table 3.13 (Contd.)

(1)	(2)	(3)	(4=2−3)	(5)	(6)	(7=5+6)	(8=3−7)
1906–07	1401	2337.8	64	612	155	767	1570
1907–08	1947	1569.1	378	1148	–219	929	640
1908–09	1207	24.5	1183	1582	380	1962	–1938
1909–10	945	11.3	934	–1392	–393	–1785	1796
1910–11	863	19.9	844	–412	309	–103	–83
1911–12	534	–	534	1066	192	1258	–1258*
1912–13	1720	1575.0	145	415	–192	223	1352

* Figure for net coinage not available.

Sources: *RCC* (1914), Appendix II, p. 254. RBI, *BMS*, p. 981.

question. The fact that fluctuations in the presidency bank discount rates synchronized with the general production cycles in agriculture was rather evident in the systematic deviations between the busy and the lean season rates. The above, in our view, provides an indirect evidence of the possible links between the working of the organized money market and the general seasonalities in internal trade and agriculture in India.

Table 3.14: Assets held by the GOI: 31 March 1913 (£ millions)

	India	England	Total
1. *General treasury balance*	19.2	9.2	28.4
2. *Paper currency reserve*	37.0	8.7	45.7
Gold	19.6	6.1	25.7
Silver (rupees)	10.8	–	10.8
Sterling security	–	2.0	2.6
Rupee security	6.6	–	6.6
3. *Gold standard reserve*	4.0	18.5	22.5
Silver (at Indian branch)	4.0	–	4.0
Gold (at Bank of England)	–	1.6	1.6
Sterling securities	–	15.9	15.9
Sterling lent at short notice	–	1.0	1.0
4. *Total*	60.2	36.4	96.6

Source: RCC (1914), Appendix II p. 248. *Statistical Abstracts of British India* 1914–16, LXXVII, p. 87. and *Benthal Papers* at South Asian Studies, Cambridge University.

Inadequacy of credit and money supply in the economy stood in sharp contrast to the growing financial reserves of the government maintained between the treasury, the PCR, and the GSR[28] (*see also* Section 3.1.3 on transfers through official reserves). With the exception of the PCR, reserves situated in London showed a common tendency to grow at a relatively faster pace. We have provided, in Table 3.12, the annual figures relating to treasury balances maintained in India and England during March 1892 to March 1913. But for the sharp rise during 1912–13 the data clearly show a pattern where reserves maintained in India grew at a rather nominal rate. As a contrast, treasury balances maintained by the SOS in London rose sharply over the same period. This was matched by a similar growth in the level of GSR reserves in London (barring the silver branch in India, GSR reserves were all maintained in London). The overall picture relating to the relative magnitudes of official reserves held in its three accounts and located between India and England at end of March 1913 are provided in Table 3.14.

Despite the rather irregular pattern of treasury balances at the end of 1912–13, which included the unusual dip in the proportion and the absolute size of treasury balance located in England, the magnitude of other official assets maintained in England was substantial. Treasury balances held in London fell from £18.3 million in 1911–12 to £8.7 million in 1912–13 (*see* Table 3.12). The above was matched by £18.3 millions of investment in sterling securities during 1912–13—a sum which was rather substantial compared to the meagre sum of £6.6 million invested during the year in rupee securities (Table 3.14). Assets maintained with the PCR, however, continued to be relatively large in India for reasons analysed in Section 3.1.3. Inclinations to transfer assets from the PCR to the GCR were quite prominent.[29] This was explained by the possibilities of utilizing most of the GSR for purchase of sterling securities in London—a prospect which was not open to the metallic reserve requirements and fiduciary limits with the PCR. Holding most of the assets in India as backing to paper currency was unattractive; the different heads in which official assets were held can be seen from Table 3.14. Interestingly enough, cash reserves at the Indian branch of the PCR, held in the form of gold, was larger than the value held in silver in March 1913. (We have provided, earlier, the forces explaining such tendencies.) Since silver in the PCR comprised rupee coins (or ingots), the disproportionate balance in gold curtailed the capacity of PCR to convert the paper money (into rupee coins). According to the estimates of the RCC (1914), share of silver in the PCR cash reserve which was 69.7 per cent in March 1893 fell to 30.6 per cent, and then to 23.9 per cent in the respective financial years ending in March 1903 and March 1913.[30] (Shortfall in rupee demand caused by the 1907–09 famines explain the short-lived reversals in the otherwise steady fall in silver as a proportion to total PCR assets over the period). The relative abundance of gold in PCR (India) prompted the SOS to transfer them to London where these could be invested. We have already indicated in Section 3.1.3 the mode of transfer and compensation of funds between the PCR, GSR, and the SOS's treasury reserves in London in order to achieve this goal.

The continuous transfer of reserves to England was a practice which was difficult to justify in the context of the rather stringent money and credit situation in India.

We can now sum up the relatively significant aspects of official policy on holdings of reserves in colonial India during the period of our study in the following way:

(*a*) Reserves maintained by the India government at the treasury, the PCR, and the GSR were all subject to significant expansions over the two decades preceding the First World War. The balances maintained with the PCR went up by 160 per cent as it rose from £17.6 million at the end of March 1893 to £45.9 million by the end of March 1913. The treasury reserves also went up by 125 per cent, rising from £12.4 million to £27.9 million between 1892–93 and 1912–13. Finally, the GSR, which was instituted out of the profits on rupee coinage in 1900, showed remarkable accumulation with £22.5 million reserve at the end of 1912–13 (*see* Tables 3.6, 3.12 and 3.14). Aggregating the components, official reserves seem to have expanded by at least 200 per cent over 1893–1913—a pace which contrasts the rather stationary trend in the supply of active rupee coins or in paper notes (*see* Table 3.8).

(*b*) A systematic tendency was there during the period to transfer the official reserves to London where these were maintained as cash with the SOS's treasury, the PCR, or the GSR (preferably the latter where no ceiling existed on their investment in sterling securities). After 1905, sales of CBs could be geared to achieve these transfers, often effected though compensatory flows between the various reserves.

(*c*) Official reserves held at the end of March 1913 recorded £96.6 million. Of these the PCR held the bulk (about £45.7 million). Reserves held in London were about 31 per cent of the total. Excluding the PCR, official reserves in London were about 55 per cent of the total. Of these the GSR alone had £18.5 million which was more than 50 per cent of the London-based reserves. Incidentally reserves at GSR at the end of March 1913 was nearly the same as the average treasury (SOS's) balances over the previous two years. (Capital treasury reserves in London at the end of 1912–13 was unusually low. *See* Table 3.12 and 3.14.)

(*d*) Reserves with the GSR in London were almost entirely (about 85.9 per cent in March 1913) invested in sterling securities; between the PCR and GSR in London around 50 per cent was invested in (sterling) securities. This proportion was certainly rather high when one considers the alternate use of reserves, especially in supporting the domestic monetary base in India or in support of the exchange value of the domestic currency (Table 3.14).

(e) Currency and bank credit expansion in the domestic economy had a direct link to the PCR. Moreover, as we have indicated in the next section, official currency policy in India discouraged the use of treasury reserves for credit expansion within the country. As for the PCR, its metallic base was a component of its 100 per cent backing against paper notes in circulation. Hence silver or gold maintained with the PCR could not be used to mint rupee coins, which was the dominant form of money demand in India during the period. Nor could it be used, even when located in London, to procure a prompt supply of silver for coinage of rupees in India. (Paper notes, the circulation of which moved up by 164.9 per cent over 1893–94 to 1911–12, were still 13.5 per cent of total active money supply in 1908–9. *See* Table 3.8 for details.)

(*f*) As for the credit flows which originated from the network of banks in India, reserves maintained by the government in the three presidency banks often moved in a contraseasonal fashion by withdrawing funds from the banking system in the busy season. The probable contractionary effects of such practices on supply of credit in the busy season have been pointed out earlier in this section.

3.3 Public resentment in India on official policy concerning money supply, credit availabilities, and reserves

Closure of mints in June 1893 and the official policy of witholding new coins over 1893–1900[31] created, by 1900, a situation of financial stringency in the economy. Attention was drawn, by resenting merchants and commercial community in India, towards the steady decline in both cash and credit available to the public. The related stringencies, as pointed out, further aggravated during busy seasons. The situation led to discontent among the public, especially since cash reserves and sterling securities were mounting with the India Office in London. The issue was viewed with an entirely different perspective by the India government. It was using, after 1905, the CB sales of the SOS to transfer reserves from the PCR and the treasury in India to the India office and the GSR in London.

A forum was found by Indian traders and merchants to lodge their protests against the financial policies of the colonial government, as evidences on monetary questions were collected by the Royal Commission on Indian Currency (The Fowler Committee) in 1898. The Royal Commission on Currency and Exchange (also known as Chamberlain Committee) of 1914 collected, at an interval of nearly sixteen years, a fresh set of evidences from private merchants, traders, and bankers. We offer, in this section, a commentary on public attitude relating to the question of monetary stringency in India, drawing on the evidences offered to the two royal commissions on Indian currency.

Attention was drawn in 1898 by some leading merchants, in their evidence to the Fowler Committee, to shortage of currency and credit in India. Closure of mints in 1893 and the follow-up measures had, by 1898, stirred public opinion and the tightness of the loan market was a subject of discussion even for the European or Anglo-Indian merchants. Prominent amongst them were Sir J.L. Mackay (ex-Secretary, Bengal Chamber of Commerce), Allan Arthur (President, Bengal Chamber of Commerce), John Littlewood Symmons (Chairman, Bombay Chamber of Commerce), and Stephen Augustus Ralli (of the oldest import-export agency in India). Four of them including Allan Arthur, Stephen Ralli, J. L. Mackay and Littlewood Symmons cited in common a particular situation where loans were withheld by the Bank of Bombay to a client even when the rate of interest offered equalled the market rate of 18 per cent and securities offered as collaterals were government papers.[32] (Official rate of discount announced by the Bank of Bengal in the busy season of 1898 was much lower, at 9.0 per cent. See Table 3.9). Market rates charged in the interior areas were even higher, and a range of 20–30 per cent was observed in the upcountry, according to the witness provided by Sir J. L. Mackay. Both Allan Arthur and Stephen Ralli confirmed this argument by narrating their impressions on the considerably higher interest rates in the interior areas. The prevailing attitude of these Anglo-Indian or European merchants on the question of the credit squeeze is reflected in the following extracts which are documented from evidences submitted to the 1898 commission on currency:[33]

> 'Trade of India is very much handicapped owing to want of loanable capital in this country.' (Sir J. L. Mackay)
> 'Discount rates were never as high in last 20 years. The busy season when such rates are higher seem to be much longer since mints were closed in 1893.' (Frank Forbes Adam)
> 'Stringency of money is a terrible tax on the trade and industries of the country and on this point everyone is agreed, e.g. jute and other manufacturers pay 12–14 per cent to carry stocks of raw material while Dundee and Lancashire carry theirs at 4–5 per cent.' (Allan Arthur)

Monetary stringency which was rather pronounced around 1898 could be related, according to merchants in the country, to a number of factors including the closure of mints since July 1893, and the fixing of the rupee rate at 1*s* 4*d*. Incentives provided to Europeans in major commercial and government positions in India to remit their earnings home and to repatriate capital (at the guaranteed official exchange rate which was higher than the prevailing market rates), according to these merchants, could cause stringency of credit. (Repatriation of capital by Europeans, however, was common even before 1893 when the anticipated decline in the rupee rate provoked a large number of European managers at different exchange banks in India to send home a part of their banking capital in India. The steps were taken in order to arrest further declines in the sterling value of their assets.) Evidences adduced by Sir Allan Arthur, the ex-president, Bengal Chamber of Commerce,[34] to the Fowler Commission indicated that the above pattern of behaviour was common with a number of exchange banks in India around 1893. Flight of capital to England, however, continued after 1893 because of a persistent disbelief among European capitalists in India that the rupee could ever be relied upon as a store of value. Mention here may be made of Charles Stuart Fox, a leading merchant and broker operating in India, who subscribed to the above view.[35] J.L. Mackay, ex-secretary of the Bengal Chamber of Commerce, even revealed that a specific banking company had actually remitted its entire capital to England, even when the rupee rate was close to 1*s* 4*d* (in fact the rate was at 1*s* $3\frac{1}{8}$ *d*).[36]

Decision of the monetary authorities to cut back money supply during 1893–98 was held as unjust by merchants operating in India, especially in view of the shortage of credit in the market. Augustus Ralli (of the import-export agency) was unhappy over the monetary policy with shortages of what he described as 'loanable funds'. Charles Stuart Fox questioned the prudence of the policy with the bank rate going up to 14 per cent. Arguments advanced by the government that fiscal difficulties led to the closure of mints were questioned by Allan Arthur who also drew attention to the surpluses in the fiscal budget.[37] (*See* Table 3.14 for data on the budget and the concept of the budgetary surplus from a national angle.)

By 1914, when a fresh round of evidences were submitted by the private commercial community in India to the Royal Commission set up under the chairmanship of J.A. Chamberlain, public resentment on monetary policy had shifted ground. Centred earlier on demonetization as the factor held responsible for the overall credit shortages in the domestic economy, arguments put forth in 1914 by merchants drew attention to accumulations of official reserves in England. Indeed, the steady transfer of financial resources through official arrangements over the decade and half between 1893 and 1914 aroused strong public sentiment against the official practices which, according to them, related to issues on 'size, location and use' of official reserves—a subject which drew a lot of concern in the set of evidences advanced to the 1914 Chamberlain Commission.[38] Interestingly, in India the government started resenting the fact that the SOS's reserves were disproportionately large. A major element of the criticism was the surveillance exercised by the Bank of England over the India Office, on matters concerning SOS's capacity to disburse its own cash balances which were normally deposited with the Bank. Intervention on the part of the Bank of England was deemed as inconvenient (if not unjust) by the government and the commercial community alike in India. The coincidence evoked sharp attacks from several merchants and bankers who submitted evidences to the Royal Commission of 1914 (*see* Section 3.4 on official positions relating to financial stringency in India).

Around 1914 the most vociferous of the resenting merchants included Montagu de P. Webb of the Karachi Chamber of Commerce. In a memorandum submitted to Chamberlain Commission he attacked the prevailing monetary policy of the government. Webb questioned, in particular, the prudence of maintaining large official balances in London: '...the best use of the balance... would have been to place money at the disposal of the Indian money market', as put by him. Webb's arguments opened up a heated controversy between the India government and the mercantile community in India on the advisability of tendering official funds for commercial purposes. In evidence submitted to the RCC (1914) Webb expressed concern that instead of lending the government's surplus funds in India to the commercial public (in the country) these were transferred to London where the SOS was actually disposing them off in the London market at interest rates lower than the market rate which prevailed in the City.[39] Webb had a considerable following amongst his fellow merchants in India, a large number of whom had been experiencing credit constraints because of the prevailing financial stringencies. Alexander McRobert (who represented the Upper India Chamber of Commerce) actually suggested that the GOI should make it a practice to lend to the presidency banks and exchange banks in India whenever market rates of interest in the economy tended to exceed 6 percent per annum.[40] An extreme suggestion was put forward by Daniel Hamilton, the secretary to the Bengal Chamber of Commerce, who demanded that the entire amount of official balance (at least at the treasury) should immediately be lent out to the presidency and exchange banks without any stipulation regarding security.[41]

It is interesting that even as early as in 1898 the bankers, working as senior officials in the (virtually state controlled) presidency banks, were resenting the prevailing attitude of the GOI on the supply of credit to the Indian money market. Thus Alexander Martin Lindsay (governor of the Bank of Bengal) stressed in his evidence to the RCC (1898)[42] that funds at the disposal of the bank was rather inadequate to meet public demand in busy season. He also drew attention to what was viewed as a rather paradoxical situation of the relatively higher level of the treasury balance in busy season. (We have already pointed out in the note to Table 3.11 A these aspects of official reserves.) Drawing attention to the Bank of Bengal discount rates over 1888 to 1897, Lindsay stressed that the rate had reached an all time high of 7.9 per cent in 1897, which indicated a state of financial stringency. (Figures in Table 3.9 indicate the average rate during busy season of 1897–98 even higher at 8.7 per cent.) The bank governor, however, could not, for obvious reasons, hold official policy as solely responsible for the rather unprecedented increases in the bank rate. Thus he offered an explanation of the high rate in terms of

Table 3.15 : Expenditure and revenue of the Government of India (£ million)

Year	Gross revenue		Expenditure charged to revenue		Net revenue expenditure		Capital outlay not charged to Revenue	
	India	England	India	England	India	England	India	England
1892–93	59.8	0.2	44.3	16.3	15.5	(–) 16.1	1.5	1.0
1893–94	60.0	0.1	45.4	15.8	14.6	(–) 15.6	1.6	0.7
1894–95	63.0	0.2	47.0	15.7	15.9	(–) 15.5	2.0	0.7
1895–96	65.1	0.2	48.7	15.6	16.4	(–) 15.3	1.9	0.6
1896–97	62.2	0.3	47.9	15.7	14.3	(–) 15.4	2.0	1.1
1897–98	64.0	1.9	51.6	16.1	12.4	(–) 16.0	2.0	0.8
1898–99	67.3	0.2	48.6	16.3	18.7	(–) 16.0	2.4	0.7
1899–1900	68.3	0.2	49.4	16.3	18.9	(–) 16.1	2.3	0.6
1900–01	75.0	0.2	56.4	17.2	18.6	(–) 16.9	1.2	0.6
1901–02	15.8	0.4	54.0	17.3	21.8	(–) 16.8	3.1	0.8
1902–03	76.7	0.6	56.0	18.3	20.7	(–) 17.6	3.5	1.2
1903–04	70.2	0.7	49.8	18.1	20.3	(–) 17.3	3.8	1.3
1904–05	70.4	0.6	48.1	19.4	22.2	(–) 18.8	4.7	1.5
1905–06	69.8	0.9	50.1	18.6	19.7	(–) 17.7	7.8	2.0
1906–07	72.7	0.8	52.3	19.2	19.9	(–) 18.3	6.0	2.5
1907–08	70.2	0.7	52.2	18.4	18.0	(–) 17.7	8.8	2.4
1908–09	69.1	0.6	54.5	18.4	14.5	(–) 18.3	7.0	3.4
1909–10	73.8	0.7	54.8	19.1	19.0	(–) 18.4	5.2	2.0
1910–11	79.7	0.9	57.1	19.5	22.5	(–) 18.6	8.1	1.8
1911–12	81.7	0.1	58.9	-	22.8	(–) 18.7	6.2	2.1
1912–13	85.8	0.9	63.4	20.2	22.4	(–) 19.3	2.0	2.4

Source: *Statistical Abstracts of British India.*

Table 3.16 : Budgetary allocations: Net revenue raised in India* (Rs. lakhs)

Year	Amount
1893–94	240.0
1894–95	291.2
1895–96	289.4
1896–97	238.3
1897–98	193.2
1898–99	282.2
1899–1900	283.5
1900–01	279.0
1901–02	327.0
1902–03	310.1
1903–04	304.5
1904–05	333.0
1905–06	295.5
1906–07	298.5
1907–08	270.0
1908–09	217.5
1909–10	285.5
1910–11	337.5
1911–12	342.0
1912–13	336.0

* Net revenue from India = gross revenue from India less expenditure in India

where gross revenue = revenue from India + revenue from England
and gross expenditure = expenditure in India
= expenditure in England

Since the net revenue from India was consistently positive it indicated the size of budgetary surplus from the point of view of the domestic economy (i.e. excess of domestic revenue over expenditure).

Source: *Statistical Abstracts of British India.*

Figures originally given in starting are converted to rupees at the exchange rate prevailing in each year. Figures for rupee-sterling rate are from the *Royal Commission on Indian Currency (1914).*

'famines'. The contractionary effects of the continual financial transfers accelerated over 1893–1914.. The inexpediency of government policies was fairly obvious as another senior official, this time within the government (and not in banks), attacked the prevailing practices where funds initially earmarked for famine relief were regularly withdrawn for 'military operations in the frontier' and for 'railway constructions in the interior'.

Such acts, according to James Edward O' Connor (the director-general of Statistics), was responsible for a net withdrawal of credit from the commercial centres—a link which he did not, however, spell out. Sale of rupee securities by the government was also held by O'Connor as a further cause of net withdrawals from the money market. Like the Bank of Bengal governor (Lindsay), the director-general of Statistics (O'Connor) was reluctant to come out with an open attack on official policies. Thus his evidence concluded with a rather non-committal position that there remained '...no evidence of a contraction of currency' in India,[43]—a position which does not tally with his other observations pointed out earlier.

3.4 Official positions on money supply, credit availabilities, and growing reserves

Issues arising in the context of financial and monetary policy during the period were complex enough to generate tendencies, on part of the policy-makers, to react to the changing circumstances. This often entailed a shift in their respective stand to accommodate the changing situations. Contrasted to the 1890s, when a near unanimity prevailed between the Government of India and the SOS's office, on decisions affecting the supply of money and credit in India, reactions of the two wings of the India government, viz. the GOI and the SOS, on similar issues tended to diverge over the next decade. Some of the ongoing debates and controversy were brought to the fore in 1913 by the Chamberlain Committee Report on Indian Currency and Finance. The issues debated centred around the size of the India Office balances and their use in London.

We have documented in this section the state of the above controversy and the issues which concerned the Government of India and its London office (the SOS's office). We have drawn attention to the shifts in the official position, during 1893–1914, on issues which include (*a*) supply of rupee coins, (*b*) feasibility of gold currency in India, (*c*) availability of credit in local money markets and possible use of official reserves for lending to the public, (*d*) use of official reserves to purchase silver for coinage, (*e*) transfer of funds from the PCR and treasury to GSR in London (for investment in sterling assets), and (*f*) accumulation of reserves at the India Office. The period starts with the closure of mints in 1890s.

Supply of rupee coins soon became a sensitive issue to the

India government as mints were closed to unlimited rupee coinage in June 1893. Explicit in the official move was the goal, as mentioned earlier, of stabilizing the market value of the rupee at the officially announced rate of 1*s* 4*d*. It is interesting to note that despite application of all the contractionary official devices on money supply in the domestic economy, officials were convinced that supply of money in India continued to remain responsive, even after 1893, to expansions in the net trade demand and to the inward remittances of the CBs. However, policies implemented to demonetize the rupee during 1893–98, as indicated in the last two sections, were evidently instrumental in contracting the flow of currency in circulation. On the whole, the closure of mints in 1893 (to private requests for coinage) established an effective state control over money supply in India—a position which remained either unnoticed or unacceptable both with contemporary public officials and in the analysis which followed later. It is necessary to point out that fresh coinage, which was introduced after 1898, was strictly regulated by official decisions to import silver in order to mint them.[44] Similarly circulation of paper money was guided by limits set on the latter in terms of the 100 per cent (metallic plus fiduciary) reserve requirements which had to be held in the PCR as backing to paper currency (*see* Table 3.6). While encashment of Council Bills at the treasury did generate new money income and supply of currency to exporters, the macro-level expansionary effect on the economy as a whole was partly offset by the leakages via the budgetary practices—a matter we have already brought to notice in Chapters 1 and 2.

The urge felt by the India government and its officials to ensure an arrangement which could protect the sterling value of all remittances from India was explicit in the official note of David Barbour who happened to be a member to the Finance Council of the GOI to the Herschell Committee of 1893.[45] Barbour's proposals were in part incorporated in the recommendations of the 1893 Committee. He suggested (*a*) closing of the mint for private purposes, and (*b*) the fixing of the rupee rate at 1*s* 4*d*. However, David Barbour also suggested introduction of gold currency in India—a proposal which was never implemented. Drawing attention to the prevailing financial situation in the economy and its unfavourable consequences, he mentioned, first, the continuous increase in both the rate and in the coverage of taxes in India since the year 1882 when remissions were last sanctioned. (He also hinted at the adverse repercussions on income distribution, especially affecting the ryots under land systems with permanent settlement.) Second, Barbour referred to the terms of trade losses which the country experienced from an observed lag between prices of exports and imports. Finally, he pointed out that the '...Anglo-Indian government has attracted...(to India)...a depreciating metal (silver) purchased at a much higher cost. This factor enhanced the exchange risks or losses for both the commercial classes and potential investors in India.' Most of the above problems, according to Barbour, could be remedied by the introduction of a gold currency in India—a proposal which was not acceptable to the government. However, other proposals of David Barbour were accepted by the Herschell Committee and later implemented by the government. (We may here recall that a telegram was sent by the India government on 23 June 1893 to the SOS, announcing both the formal closure of mints, and the fixing of the rupee rate at 1s 4*d*. Also, sovereigns were given a legal tender status within the country with their value fixed at Rs. 15 per unit.) However, these steps were far removed from an actual introduction of gold currency in India, as was clear from the very limited circulation of sovereigns in the country. The Fowler Commission report on currency, which was submitted in 1898, provided an *ex post* justification for the measures introduced during 1893–98. An explanation was also offered by James Fairburn Finlay, secretary to the Finance department of the GOI, who submitted a note in his official capacity to the RCC of 1898.[46] Thus implementation of the Herschell Committee's proposal on an actual melting of coins worth Rs.10 crores was a step, according to Fairburn, to reduce the relative 'redundancy' of rupee coins in India, obviously to ensure the rupee rate to settle at 1s 4*d*. In a despatch of 3 March 1898, the GOI officially accepted the rationalization, stressing that the measure was designed to 'revive' confidence in the rupee since '...holders of capital are afraid to send it out (to India) as long as currency is on a silver basis, and it is in such an amount that a turn of the scale, whether by cessation of activity in trade or in any other way, will send down the rate of exchange.' Clearly the government was wanting to '...get over this transition stage.'[47]

Introduction of gold currency in India, while accepted in principle in terms of the Fowler Committee recommendations, was never implemented by the government. (We had picked up this point earlier, showing even David Barbour, a member to the Finance Council of the SOS, was counselling, as early as 1893, for a gold coin for India.) Ambivalence on the part of the government on this question during 1893–98 was followed by a second round of proposals with the Fowler Committee recommendations for a gold currency in India. In a statement submitted to the latter, Fairburn suggested a three-stage sequence for an eventual introduction of gold currency. These included (*a*) imports of gold worth £5 million by the SOS, purchase of which could be financed by additional borrowing in London; (*b*) official sale of silver bullion against gold (the silver could be obtained through approved melting of rupee coins); (*c*) gold obtained through above two sources could be kept as the 'core of gold reserves' in India.[48] The proposal was adopted in principle by the Fowler Committee, with its suggestion that a gold reserve fund (GRF) be set up in India which could eventually initiate gold standard in the country. However, during the interim period the reserve was to cater to maintaining of the rupee rate only at the official rate of 1*s* 4*d*.[49]

The longer-run target (of having a gold currency in India), however, became rather remote as the proposal experienced rough weather in the official circles. We refer here to the controversies between Sir John Law of the government's Finance department and Sir J. Waterfield of the India Office in the financial despatches around 1900. A shift in the GOI's attitude on gold currency was rather apparent with John Law questioning whether the public's high propensities to hoard in India would eventually make the launching of gold currency a feasible proposition. As an indirect evidence (of the propensity to hoard gold in the economy), Law mentioned the return flow of gold to banks and post offices in India and also to the prevailing premium rates of 12.5 per cent or above fetched by sovereigns in commercial centres like Kanpur (even when they were virtually of no purpose as a medium of exchange). An official exchange of sovereigns against rupees would have, according to Law, depleted the officially held stock of gold—an outcome which might eventually have endangered the basis of the gold exchange standard in India. (The exchange value of rupee in sterling at the fixed exchange rate of 1*s* 4*d* and the one-way convertibility of sterling in terms of rupees were the essence of the gold exchange standard.) The official view as it prevailed in 1900 on the introduction of a gold currency was summed up by John Law as he concluded that '...it will take a very long time before essentially conservative habits are overcome and gold naturally finds its way to circulation.' It was but logical that gold transfers to England were considered the '...safe course to build up a reserve in gold...(and) the government has remitted to England £1 million from its stock of gold and will continue to do so.'[50] Interestingly, the trend in the physical transfers of gold reserves from India to England (*see* Table 3.17) was rather prominent till 1905-06. Later, the policy was one of retaining gold in London through CB sales which had no upper limit after 1905 with compensating accounting transfers in India or England. The changing circumstances eventually brought in a rift between the GOI and India Office on the desirability of maintaining balances in London, discussed later in this section.

Money supply was closely linked to the adequacy of bank credit in the domestic economy. We have already drawn attention to some typical reactions, around 1900, to the shortage of credit experienced in the economy. Stringency was clearly experienced around 1898 with government officials like Martin Lindsay of the Bank of Bengal reacting to the financial policies of the government. Questions of credit shortage, however, came up in a big way over the next decade as large scale transfers of funds to England were evident, especially with the use of the GSR for sterling investment and the accounting transfers and compensations between the treasury, the PCR, and the GSR maintained between the two countries. By the year 1913–14 issues which were prominent in government deliberations included credit shortage, difficulties of procuring silver for coinage, large scale transfers of funds to GSR (and their investment) in England, and finally, 'excessive' accumulation of official reserve in England. One identifies, in official policies, a consistent design to use the financial surpluses from the colony to further accumulations at the financial centre in London City. By early twentieth century, issues like the introduction of gold currency in India or the extent of demonetization had clearly receded to the background as less important.

The rigid stand of the government on proposals for lending money to the public was not new at the turn of the century. We can refer back to an official note, prepared by Sir James

Table 3.17 : A. Transfers of gold:1899–1900 to 1912–13 (£ million)

	Net Receipt of gold in PCR and treasuries in India (excluding transactions with SOS)	Net withdrawal of gold to SOS's account	Net receipt of gold including transactions with SOS
(1)	(2)	(3)	(4)
1899–1900	5.7	nil	5.7
1900–01	3.8	4.5	−0.7
1901–02	3.8	2.0	1.8
1902–03	3.5	0.5	2.0
1903–04	5.1	4.2	0.9
1904–05	5.5	5.4	0.1
1905–06	0.3	5.3	−5.0
1906–07	−0.1	nil	−0.1
1907–08	−1.0	nil	−1.0
1908–09	−2.7	0.2	−2.9
1909–10	6.3	nil	6.3
1910–11	0.02	nil	0.02
1911–12	9.4	nil	9.4
1912–13	6.5	2.3	4.2

B. Seasonal pattern in gold transfers (£ million)

	(1)	(2)	(3)
1911–12 (Apr-Sept)	0.01	nil	0.01
(Oct-March)	9.3	nil	9.3
1912–13 (Apr-Sept)	0.7	nil	0.7
(Oct-March)	5.8	2.3	3.5

Source: *RCC* (1914), Appendix VIII, pp. 251–3.

Westfield, the finance minister, in 1889. It was perfectly justifiable, according to the finance minister, that the Bank of England should lend its deposits, which included the SOS's treasury balance with the latter. The practice was not, according to Westfield, in conflict with the official sanctions in India against the use of official reserves in the three presidency banks for advances in the money market. Monetary stringency, if at all prevalent, was not, according to Westfield, caused by official policy in India, which only '...places at the SOS's disposal, for drawings, everything that they could spare subject to the condition of about eight crores remaining in the cash balances, as the minimum...Moreover in times of difficulty special legislation was taken (December 1886) to add to the cash balances two crores of rupees out of the (Paper) Currency Reserve...*In this there is ample evidence that the policy of the government throughout is the very opposite of seeking to raise exchange by causing stringency*' (italics added). Attempts had been made, as was pointed out '... to place at the disposal of the market every rupee that they can spare, obviously at the London market'.[51] Arguments used above to avoid direct lending of official funds to commercial public in India continued to dominate thinking in the official circles, as was evident in similar policies pursued by future generations of officials over the next two decades. Evidently, the Government of India maintained a double standard on the question of lending public funds, with regular sanctions provided to the SOS to lend through the London money market.

More instances are available which indicate that the government was consistently hostile towards proposals to lend official balances to money market in India. In an early correspondence with the Bombay Chamber of Commerce around 1898-99, the finance secretary to the India government explained the official reluctance to keep the entire balance with presidency banks. '...If the whole of the surplus cash was kept in the presidency banks, trade would rely on the permanence of the reserves thus supplied to it, and that, in case of a sudden demand for cash the government of India would either be forced to abandon its right to reduce its balance in the presidency banks or risk producing a financial crisis by suddenly and largely reducing the reserves of these banks.'[52,53]

Facilities for advances in the money market seemed to have been considerably strained by 1913 when a large number of indigenous banks collapsed under financial duress. While Sydney de P. Webb, the Karachi merchant, was claiming that '...the best use of the surplus balance would have been to place money at the disposal of the Indian money market,'[54] sanctions were solicited at long last from the SOS by India government for permitting the presidency banks to lend official deposits, presumably to ease the prevailing conditions of stringency in the domestic money market. Suggestions were thus solicitated to offer a lending rate which was lower than the market rate by 2 per cent.[55] In reply to the above request from W.S. Meyer, member of the GOI's Finance department,

Lionel Abrahams of the SOS's office expressed an element of scepticism towards the idea of concessional or other lendings. The India government official mentioned, in his letter of 23 September 1913, the case of Bank of Bengal which had requested the SOS for an advance of Rs. 50 lakhs at an interest rate which was 1 per cent less than the prevailing bank rate (a demand which was justified by the brisk jute trade anticipated in Bengal). Considerable deliberations took place before the final consent could be obtained from the SOS.[56] Another request, around 1913–14 from the Indian Specie Bank (which also handled silver trade) for a short-term credit of Rs. 50 lakhs from the SOS met with an outright disapproval.[57] The incident was also significant in connection with official policy on silver purchase in London—a matter discussed later in this section. Loan advances as well as silver purchase contracts were denied to Choonilal Saraiya, the manager of the Indian Specie Bank, under circumstances which clearly indicated an element of imperial discrimination against the indigenous merchants and financiers. The Indian Specie Bank (along with its subsidiary firm which was handling silver trade) was liquidated in November 1913.[58] A large number of other Indian banks which were similarly liquidated over 1913–14 included the People's Bank, the Oriental Bank, and the Bank of Upper India—all of which were managed by Indians.[59] Even a liquidation of the Oriental Bank, which was managed by Europeans, could not arrest the general run on banks over the period. In a typically complacent mood W.S. Meyer of the government's Finance department remarked in September 1913, that '... the rotten institutions had gotten rid of.'[60] In India the government was thus rather oblivious of the consequences of the rather stringent monetary policies (pursued over the preceding decade and half) for the Indian money market. It naturally suited the ruling interests, both in India and in London, to ignore altogether the possible consequences for local trade and industry.[61]

The GOI was more or less unanimous with the SOS that official balances transferred to London were not to be advanced as credit to the commercial public in India. However, both offices of the government were aware of an embarrassment while justifying their positions. This became especially evident with the wide-ranging discretions enjoyed by the SOS over the mounting reserves at its disposal. As was to be expected, differences soon cropped up between the GOI and the India Office on questions of administrative expediency, with the former experiencing problems of managing its finance in the face of the continual flow of funds to England. It was gradually realized by the government officials in India that the SOS's office was given discretionary powers in deciding financial matters concerning India. Exchanges between the India office and the GOI gradually took the form of sharp queries and reticent explanations on vital problems like the accumulation and final use of GSR funds in England, use of the India Office balance for silver purchases in England, and finally, the legitimacy of further accumulation of financial resources at the India Office.

The India government was probably providing a precedence to the SOS when it deliberately took a rather solicitous stand in one of its directives issued in 1913. This allowed direct lending of treasury funds (in India) during busy seasons on a short-term basis. Sums lent out ought not, according to the rather cautiously framed directive, to exceed Rs. 4.5 crores at a time and for durations which exceeded 4 months. Sums lent over the busy season could thus be expected to return to the treasury before the onset of the next busy season. Interest charged on such loans were to be lower than the presidency bank rate by 1 to 1.9 per cent.[62] The set of suggestions clearly implied a departure in GOI's policy from its earlier stand, which was in broad accord with the SOS's dictum regarding the inadvisability of lending official reserves below the presidency bank rates.[63] Pressures generated by the GOI led the SOS to allow, after much deliberations, the India government to advance money directly to the market in 1914. The lendings could be at an interest rate which was lower than the bank rate by a maximum of 2 per cent. Great reservations were shown on the matter by Keynes, the distinguished India Office official, who held that '...unless great care is taken, government loans may become a substitute for, not an addition to, private deposits'. Moreover, '...in order that banks do not prefer government loans to private deposits, rate of interest ought not to be too low compared to that in the market.'[64] Clearly, the rules of the game were very different when it related to the SOS's lending policy in England. Thus short-term loans were regularly advanced from the SOS's reserves at interest rates which could be lower than the prevailing bank rate by 1 per cent. Questions were raised in the British parliament, attacking the SOS for the above discriminatory practice. In reply, Lord Asquith of the India Office gave an explanation in terms of the SOS's need to lend short-term advances in order to ensure that funds would be forthcoming for a renewal of its floating debts.[65] The issue, however, continued to be a matter of public discussion, as was evident in the editorial comment of a leading Indian daily '...the practice leaves impression that the real explanation of the balances... has not been divulged.'[66] While the SOS's office was on the defensive regarding its reservations on lending the official balances in India to the commercial public, the position was no longer acceptable by 1913 even to the India government. It was, however, important to the GOI that it should somehow put up with its initial stand and stay away from money market in India. At the same time it was somewhat unacceptable to the officials in India that the SOS should continue to utilize its official balances for the purpose of short- and long-term investment in London, and at interest rates which subsidized this market.[67]

There was a distinct tone of disapproval in the India government's deliberations over the GSR reserves, which were concentrating in London. Revising its earlier ambivalent attitude (of 1898) towards the gold currency question, the GOI had requested, in a letter written to the SOS on 14 May 1908, for imports of sovereigns to India and for their introduction as gold currency. A prompt reply was sent on 19 June 1908 by the SOS who insisted that the proposal would only provide '...more convenient supply of gold for ornaments or even a better material for currency in India, instead of husbanding these resources as two of the chief safeguards of our solvency'; the safeguards referred to the use of gold as support to exchange, and as a potential for an eventual change-over to gold currency.[68] Divergence of opinion on the question of the location and use of the GSR widened over the next few years and in 1910 one more government official in India suggested imports of sovereign in order to meet their (unfulfilled) demand in India as a means of exchange. An insistence by the GOI ultimately led the SOS's office to partly concede as it agreed to a proposal to introduce half-sovereigns as a medium of circulation in India. These coins could either be imported directly or minted in India through imports of bullion from abroad. [69]

Purchase of silver for rupee coinage in India was an exclusive monopoly of the India Office in England. The matter opened up one more area of discord between the India government officials who worked in India and those who were with the SOS's office in London. Purchase of silver out of India Office's reserves opened up, even as early as 1906–07, an area of disagreement, prompting the GOI to question and rule out the SOS's practices. These included its strictures on silver ingots at the Indian branch of GSR and also on silver earmarked with the London branch of the PCR. As an alternative the SOS suggested a scheme in terms of which the GOI was empowered to borrow silver at 3.5 per cent interest from the GSR silver branch and pay it back through transfer of gold to the London branch of the GSR (where it could be invested at 4.5 per cent interest rate).[70] While the SOS was entrusted, since the early years of British rule, with the India government's silver procurements from London, the SOS had already entered into a six-year contract with the Bank of England in 1906, which effectively delegated the entire responsibility on the matter to the Bank. The contract was to expire by 1912 and the matter became an area of concern, especially with the rather attractive rates of brokerage and insurance premium prevailing in London on silver deals. These were in the nature of cuts and were shared by the bullion dealers as well as the Bank. In general, absolute secrecy was maintained in silver deals, as informally agreed upon in the interest of avoiding adverse speculations in the market. Despite precautions adopted, India Office's silver purchase programmes drew attention in the London market, probably with the disproportionate size of the deals as a single source of demand. Often to the detriment of the terms of purchases, the market developments led the Finance Committee of the GOI to persuade the SOS to enter into forward contracts in silver in 1910–11. Sir James Mackay, the SOS, instructed Lionel Abrahams, the under-secretary, to employ a different bullion dealer, Samuel Montague and Co., as sole agents for the purpose.[71] The decision of forward market intervention, however, was reverted as a member of the India government's finance council advised the SOS to stay away from the forward market since 'the government ought not to play in hands of speculators which forward speculators do', as it was strongly put in a letter of 2 February 1911.[72] Objections had also been raised earlier on the clauses of the silver purchase contract of 1906. In a note placed by Lionel Abrahams to the SOS's council on 2 April 1910, a point was raised by

E.L Franklin of Montague Company, the silver dealer, that it was undesirable for the SOS to place most of its silver contracts with Mocatta and Goldsmith, a second silver dealer in the City. Lionel Abrahams at this stage even hinted at a possibility that the SOS may actually go in for a contract in 1912 with the Montague Company. A note was placed, in the mean time, by the Accountant General's department at India Office, which relied on recent information received for deals during 5 March to 16 March 1912. It was pointed out that the SOS had actually purchased silver at prices which were higher than the respective market quotations on each such day.[73] In a letter addressed to the SOS (dated 25 August 1912) the GOI in its turn requested the SOS for permission to enter into a direct silver purchase contract with an exchange bank located at Shanghai. Such requests, as could be anticipated, were turned down by the SOS, on the ground that direct deals on part of India government with exchange banks would violate the preconditions relating to secrecy, ordinarily maintained by it on the matter. The message was conveyed in a telegram from the SOS dated 28 August 1912, marked 'very confidential'.[74]

Silver trade in the City was handled by four bullion dealing agencies (or business houses) in 1912–13. These included Mocatta-Goldsmith and Sharps-Wilkins which got, between them, the entire contract for the India Office's silver purchases under the old arrangement. It was but natural for firms which were left out to try for a share in this big deal in silver (India Office's purchases, arranged through its agent, the Bank of England, was the chief source of demand for silver in the London market). Under these situations Samuel Montague Co., the largest bullion trader in the City, started manoeuvring with the SOS's office in London for a contract. Contents of the SOS's silver purchase deals, as mentioned above, were kept a closely guarded secret by the SOS in order to avoid adverse speculations which could affect the India government's finances by pushing up silver prices in London. The veil of secrecy was exploited by the Montague Co. which eventually succeeded in 1912 to influence the SOS and win a silver purchase contract. The company, as viewed by the India office, was an influential business house in the City which was instrumental in marketing a large sum of GOI's railway debentures. The Bank of England, the intermediary to silver purchases (of the SOS), had, however, been extremely reluctant to terminate the contract.[75] It is interesting that the Bank of England even indicated a strong desire continue with the prevailing arrangement of silver purchases with its right to subcontract in the market, one which obviously suited the Bank's interests. Disputes between the India Office and the Bank of England were referred to a legal arbitrator who settled the matter in SOS's favour by allowing it to place an order directly for the purchase of £5 million worth of silver on 4 March 1912.[76] Secrecy continued to be maintained on such transactions. It is interesting, at this point, to reveal the contents of an unofficial correspondence (marked 'Secret'), dated 9 January 1912, between Sir Felix Schuster of the India Office and the Montague Company. The letter clearly indicated that the Montague Company was optimistic about the possibility of getting the contract—an expectation which was rather contrary to what was officially disclosed by the SOS on the question. In a bid to maintain absolute secrecy, the Montague Company was proposing, in the same letter, a purchase of £50 million worth of silver from the market in each week and also to informally place the bullion at the SOS's account with the Bank of England. To avoid the possibility of a leakage, the whereabouts of the silver deposits were not revealed to any third party (which included the Bank of England).[77] That the level of confidentiality crossed the limit of normal business ethics was very clear from the following excerpts from the letter: '.... in order not to allow our deliveries to the Bank of England to synchronize with your payments we have already started depositing bars with them... and we shall endeavour to avoid any time depositing bars to the approximate value of the money we claim of you on the same day...' Further points were raised on the *modus operandi* of the transaction, which add to the conspiratorial tone of the letter. Thus, it reads. '... how would you like us to hand in your deposit receipts? Shall we send them up to your office on the morning of the pay days by a confidential messenger who is not in our bullion department?... Shall I call on your office one evening on my return from the City?' The letter also conveyed the impression that Samuel Montague of the aforesaid company was actually a close relation of Edwin Montague of the SOS's council, something which was considered to be a sensitive issue. '... We particularly do not care about approaching Edwin Montague on this matter for reasons that must be obvious to you'.[78] As expected, the India Office's dealings with the Montague Company was open to public criticism and censure in London, especially in view of the Bank of England's hostility and its influence in the City. In a letter written by the SOS on 8 November 1912, the SOS was alluding to a point which apparently was already raised in the British House of Commons. The matter concerned the legal status of the Montague Company in terms of the contract renewed in March 1912. Informations were sought in the Parliament as to whether the Montague Company was operating in the London market in the capacity of a broker or simply as a dealer of the SOS. The company justified its reluctance to disclose by the secrecy clause in the agreement on sources of its silver purchases. The company even expressed its displeasure at such queries, making it explicit that '... if the object of the question is to imply that we are engaged in a conspiracy to pile up large stocks of silver and sell them to you at an enhanced price we protest most indignantly against such an imputation.'[79] However, the state of alliance between the Montague Company and the SOS's office in London indicated the level of the ongoing collusion between the influential business houses and the imperial government (of which the SOS was an organ). The pattern of such collusion was an evolving one, as was indicated by the dominance of other firms (Mocatta-Goldsmith in particular) in earlier contracts, a pattern which prevailed during the decade when the Bank of England (rather than the SOS) was empowered to take a final decision on the mode of purchase.

Consistent with the overall designs of an imperial oligarchy which controlled Indian finance, the SOS made it certain that the silver purchase contract was never given out to any Indian firm. Mocatta-Goldsmith, the firm providing silver till 1906, was categorically asked, by the SOS, to explain the exact nature of their links to the 'native' dealers.[80] References in particular were made to Choonilal Saraiya (an Indian silver dealer mentioned earlier, who also was the director of the Indian Specie Bank) who was described in the local press in India as '... the moving spirit behind the Bombay silver ring.'[81] The adversities impinged on by the imperialist government and its agents forced Saraiya to the worst possible calamities which included a state of financial insolvency, liquidation of the Indian Specie Bank (and the company), and eventual suicide on his part. In November 1913, Saraiya had offered to sell Rs. 2 lakh worth of silver at $25\frac{1}{2}$ *d* per ounce to the SOS and also asked for a temporary loan of Rs. 50 lakhs from the SOS's balances in London.[82] Both requests were rejected by the SOS. A very clear instance was hence provided of a systematic discrimination against Indian merchants and financial institutions—an attitude which was consistent with the general tenor of the imperialist policy. We reproduce, as an indirect evidence of the prevailing official attitude, an extract from Saraiya's statement which came out in a local newspaper: 'While the SOS is freely selling Council Bills as mentioned by him in the interest of trade, and the cash balance of the government of India are but lent freely to London bankers, at comparatively cheap rate of interest, the rate of interest of all Presidency Banks in India stands at seven per cent with certain chances of higher rates if the Government of India does not advance. I thought this was the proper time to approach the Government of India, if they can see their way to lend their balances to India. I have offered the security of their $3\frac{1}{2}$ per cent promissory notes so that the government may not have any cause for refusing the loan on the score of security. If the government balances are lent in India during the busy season they are sure to assist Indian trade and industries.'[83] This sums up the view the indigenous merchants held against the current official policies of the imperial government, which incidentally, was very little affected by such protests. Public protests and parliamentary questions[84] concerning the Indian Specie Bank did not deter the government from finally rejecting, in December 1912, all proposals put forward by the Bank. The matter drew public attention both in India and in England as questions were raised in the British parliament on 12 November 1912, regarding the appropriateness of denying the silver contract to Choonilal Saraiya, especially when prices offered by him were lower than the market quotations.[85] Market prices in January 1912 were higher than the quotation of the Indian Specie Bank at $25\frac{1}{2}$ *d* per ounce, which was rejected by government.[86] The SOS's bid to keep out the Indian Specie Bank from silver trade in London was eventually successful as '...the bank was liquidated in November 1913,' as reported in a local newspaper, '...due to the operations of Mr. C. Saraiya, the bank manager in the silver market' (*Times of India*, 22 November 1913).[87]

Differences also cropped up between the government officials in India and at the India Office on the final use of the government's sterling denominated assets. This led the SOS to submit a memorandum to the Chamberlain Commission of 1913 on a controversial issue of the day, concerning the 'size, location, and use' of India Office balances. The SOS was trying to project a separate identity of its own in terms of its interests over financial management of the country, something which was differentiated from the policy directives of the resident officials in India. In London it was no secret that the financial management at the India Office had far-reaching repercussions on the pace of financial intermediations in the City as a whole. This created a tendency for Bank of England—the custodian of high finance in that age of imperialism—to try out its power over the SOS by withholding the use of India Office funds at its own disposal. The growing treasury reserves of the IndiaOffice, the unspent balances of which were regularly maintained at the Bank of England, were often a source of major controversies between the SOS and the Bank officials.

We now review in the rest of this section, the India Office's memorandum to the Chamberlain Commission on 'size, location, and use of India Office balances' in 1913 and the deliberation (during 1905–06 to 1912–13) between the India government and the India Office on investment policies of the SOS in London. The important and detailed memorandum was submitted by Lionel Abrahams, the under-secretary of state at the India Office to provide an explanation of its treasury balances and other sterling assets which were growing in England. Pointing at the continuous excesses of the 'actuals' over the budgeted sales of CBs over 1909–10 to 1912–13,[88] which were often described as 'surplus' funds, the memorandum revealed that the SOS's balance was maintained in a non-interest-bearing account with the Bank of England. The remainder, however, was lent to an 'approved' set of stockbrokers, banks, and discount houses in the City through the intermediation of the SOS's official broker. The money lent was for a short period. The above aspects were indicated in a separate memorandum by Walter Badock who mentioned the case of brokers who were regularly depositing funds at select London banks—a practice which was evidently facilitated by the disposability of surplus funds at the India Office.[89] The growing reserves at the India Office were justified, in terms of the SOS's memorandum, by the rising financial liabilities of the SOS in London during the period. Justifying the investment in sterling securities by the SOS, which at £15.9 million was more than half of the total sterling assets and about twice the treasury balance of the SOS in London in the year 1913, the memorandum appreciated the financial prudence implicit in the procedure. Incidentally, this reflected the official line of thinking at the SOS's office over the entire period of heavy sterling investment, with criticisms faced by the earlier secretaries of state. Opposing the demands in India for placing the India Office's sterling funds at the disposal of the local commercial community in India, the memorandum stressed the need to keep them in London. Public demands in India included, for example, the proposal by Thackersay in the Legislative Council of India on 22 March 1912. Placing India Office's reserves at the money market in India would, according to Badock's memorandum, have encouraged additional hoards of gold currency while proportionately reducing the investment income of the SOS from the sterling investments. Moreover, if sterling funds were located in India, an execution of purchase orders of silver in England would have meant a delay of at least three weeks of time (which is ordinarily taken by an average consignment) and also, additional costs to physically transfer the sterling to England. The memorandum thus advocated the location of gold reserves in England for reasons which also included expediency in silver purchase arrangements. The argument sounded rather paradoxical, especially with the mutual allegations and controversies between the two branches of the government in India and England, and also between the SOS and the Bank of England, on the practices governing silver purchase contracts.

Differences between the GOI and the India Office on the question of sterling investment, however, seem to have started in 1907 when the India government suggested a ceiling for investment out of the GSR funds. Funds at the GSR had increased rapidly during 1906–13. Thus from £7.6 million at the end of January 1906, the stock of sterling securities with the GSR steadily rose to £12.5 million and £15.9 million respectively by the end of February and March 1913.[90] Disputes between the GOI and the SOS on the mode of sterling investment in London can also be traced back to the SOS's proposal of 1906–07 that an additional £20 thousand be invested out of the cash reserves at the London branch of the GSR in consols or in War Loan bonds. The GOI did oppose the move on grounds of the prevailing monetary stringency in the domestic economy. The SOS, however, was insistent in maintaining the GSR as a separate account as originally suggested under the recommendations of the RCC (1898). As a step to implement its proposals, the SOS's accountant-general ordered a purchase of stocks worth £1 million, distributed equally between $2\frac{1}{2}$ per cent British government consols and the Transvaal and Irish stocks. Implementation of the order raised the size of sterling investment to £13.01 million in March 1907 (of which about 60 per cent were British consols).[91] Much later, and at end of substantial sterling investments in the meantime by the SOS, a question was raised (on 22 march of 1912) in the Indian Legislative Council on the possible losses from sterling investments under the GSR. The SOS replied in response to a query from the GOI (letter of 29 February 1912)[92] admitting that actual shortfalls in market value of securities below their cost prices did, in fact, account for losses to the SOS. A sum of £80 thousand was sacrificed, according to information provided by the SOS, as a result of depreciations in sterling assets held with the GSR in April 1912. Wide-ranging depreciation in the value of consols (each unit of which fell by 16 per cent) led to larger losses in GSR sterling investments, the value of which was stated to be £7 million by March 1913.[93] According to the SOS's estimates, about 80 per cent of this was due to depreciation in consols alone.[94] The circumstances clearly called for a review of the SOS's policies. In March 1913 the SOS agreed to a proposal suggested earlier by the India government to set aside, as cash reserves, £5 million of the GSR funds every six months. This was arranged in view of the dearth of investible securities and the probable capital losses. Earlier, in December 1912, the SOS had already accepted the changes in its portfolio as it sold £5 million worth of consols at a depreciated rate and reinvested the sum in treasury bills, London Country bills, and Exchange bonds.[95] In a despatch dated 30 September 1909, GOI had also suggested a ceiling of £25–30 million for PCR and GSR gold reserves of the SOS put together in England. It was suggested that the value of silver stocks at the two reserves were respectively to be Rs. 15 crores and Rs. 3 crores. In addition, a minimum treasury reserve was proposed in India with Rs. 18 crores in silver at the beginning of each busy season.[96] In a despatch dated 18 February 1910, the SOS disagreed with the above proposals and reiterated the need and desirability of maximizing gold reserves in England. The GOI's insistence that the need to maintain the cash content of the GSR was '...independent of the money market' finally persuaded the SOS to accept, in February 1912, the £25 million ceiling on GSR sterling investment.[97]

A ceiling was also suggested, in the same letter, on cash balances which could be maintained as treasury reserves by the SOS. The upper limit was fixed at £27 million by the SOS. If exceeded, the balance was to be spent on capital outlays in England which included expenditure on irrigation and railways.[98] While commercial circles in India were critical of the contra-seasonal oscillation in the government's treasury balance, the situation in England was similar in terms of the movements in the treasury balances of the SOS. (The SOS admitted, in an official note, that its cash balance was higher in busy season.) As an explanation (or justification), the SOS mentioned that (*a*) its borrowing programmes were more active in the lean season, and that (*b*) the cash obtained through the actual sale of Council Bills often exceeded the sum budgeted in the busy season.[99] In a memorandum submitted by Walter Badock, the accountant-general of India Office, it was clearly confirmed that the SOS was regularly lending, around 1913, a part of its cash balances in the busy season, to bankers, discount houses, and brokers of 'high standing' in the City. In addition, considerable sums were already invested in long dated sterling securities. By 1913 the India Office had already achieved a special position in London City in terms of its potentials for investment and commercial purchases. This made the SOS an active player in the undercurrents of the money game in the City—a situation which was contrary to the notion of a neutral state machinery in the context of the colonial economy, highlighted by the imperialist historians.[100]

The changing official position on matters concerning the supply of money and credit, the expediency of gold currency in India, and the growing sterling assets at the India Office documented in this section narrate a story of an emerging pattern of conflicts, and concentration of economic power in India under colonial rule. While the India government was reluctant to concede to the demands of the resident European merchants and some prominent bankers for easy credit and money supply in India, problems of financial management was evidently becoming acute for the resident India government officials. Hence it was logical that the officials in India came to disputes with those in India Office on matters concerning the options left for the use of India Office balances. In London the SOS's active involvement in the financial circles created another source of conflict. By 1913 the sterling investments of the SOS became a sensitive issue in the City with the Bank of England taking an active interest in preventing the SOS from withdrawals. Evidently the India Office was drifting to a position where it had to confront the powerful financial interests in the City. The shifting and conflicting positions of the different authorities (which included the India government departments, the India Office, and the financial magnates including banks and silver merchants in London) were in accord with the changing scenario regarding the role of the empire in the consolidation of finance capital in London City, a general discussion of which will follow in Chapter 5.

3.5 The colonial currency system in India under gold exchange standard: 'Automatic Adjustment' or a tool for financial transfer?

Official complacency on currency policies in India around 1913 was echoed in Keynes's work on Indian currency which was published in 1913. The book can be regarded as an analytical supplement to the report of the Chamberlain Commission on Indian currency, of which Keynes himself was a member. Problems relating to the functioning of the Indian currency system were completely ignored by Keynes who was highly appreciative of what he described as a 'very efficient' application of the principles of gold exchange standard in India.

Official complacency on currency policies in British India thus had its analogue in the analysis of the 'gold exchange standard', offered by Keynes, the bare 'essentials' of which included, according to him, 'the use of a local currency mainly not of gold, some degree of unwillingness to supply gold locally in exchange for the local currency, but a high degree of willingness to sell foreign exchange for payment in local currency at a certain maximum rate, and to use foreign credits in order to do this.'[101] India, according to Keynes, was '...the first to adopt it (gold exchange standard) in a complete form'. Keynes was aware of the significance of his analytical construct as he stressed, '...speaking as a theorist, I believe that it contains an essential element—the use of a cheap local currency artificially maintained at par with the international currency or standard of value.'[102]

Keynes was aware of the ethos amongst his contemporaries on the infallibility of the market. He also was probably conscious of the ongoing debates, especially within official circles, on problems experienced by the government and by commercial circles in India under gold exchange standard. It was thus necessary for him to attack the position that the Indian currency practices entailed a 'managed system'. As a counter-argument he mentioned the 'promptness and certainty with which at all times it can meet its international engagements'—an aspect which according to him was a 'measure of financial strength'.[103] Money supply under the system was fairly 'automatic', according to Keynes. The Council Bills provided, as per Keynes, the requisite remittances that fell due from England, on account of the favourable trade balances which India earned *vis-a-vis* the rest of world. He mentioned four probable situations to establish his point: (*a*) One where CB sales were larger than the value of trade surplus. Rupees advanced against the CBs were then procured not only from the treasury but also from the branches of the PCR and the GSR in India. In London the two reserves (PCR and GSR) had compensatory deposits of sterling from SOS's balances; (*b*) CB sales were less than the trade surplus, when gold inflows supplemented the former while paper currency could be issued against the gold reserves; (*c*) Proceeds of CB sales in London were utilized to purchase silver for coinage in India. While this led to a rise in rupee stock in India, equivalent coins were demanded by the exchange banks who presented CBs to the treasury. Simultaneously, profits on coinage were vested with the GSR; (*d*) CB sales were regulated to prevent a fall in exchange rate of the rupee to its gold import point—a process designed to ultimately permit the same amount of rupees in circulation as would have happened when the alternative route of gold imports and their subsequent use for purchase of silver was adopted. For Keynes, situations (*a*) and (*b*) indicated that the supply of money (especially of rupee coins) remained fairly automatic and it adjusted to the level of remittances as were needed to settle the trade balances. With situation (*c*), gold was sold in England in order to purchase silver for coinage (in India). This did not, in

Keynes's logic, disturb the money supply (potential increases in which were always guaranteed by the availability of gold reserves located in India or England). Finally, the last possibility (*d*) related to short-term contractions in the supply of rupees in India, which essentially were related to contractions in the trade balance.

The central argument offered by Keynes on the Indian currency system related to the principle of an automatic adjustment. The government's role was recognized as a 'dealer' in foreign currency. On part of Keynes there was thus no reason to suspect a discretionary control of money supply by the state. We may recall the whole network of compensations between the two countries operating to settle payments in opposite directions, i.e. in the direction of India for her net exports, and towards England for the home charges and other disbursements of the SOS (including the adjustments in its reserves at the Bank of England). Looking at the transactions as a whole, we have noticed that the country's net export income earnings was only an offset to the net revenue raised from the country when the latter was earmarked as expenditure overseas. It is difficult to assess to what extent a resulting cut-back in demand[104] was actually contributing to a shortfall in output in the domestic economy. (This was so since the stagnation in output, as has been argued in Chapters 1 and 5, was also linked to the process of surplus extraction which came up with commercialization of the economy.) It would be too simplistic to offer a pure Keynesian type of demand-based explanation for the shortfall in income and output during the period. In other words, it was not just the curtailing of demand for domestic output, but also the changing mix of the latter and the related changes in the pattern of expropriation and utilization of surplus which provide a fuller explanation of the prevailing stagnation in the agrarian economy of India. However, the pattern of the financial flows in the economy were certainly restrictive and the pace of the curtailing devices was set by the volume of CBs sold—one on which the SOS had gained perfect manoeuvrability by 1905.

Stringencies experienced in the domestic credit markets in India were explained by Keynes in terms of shortages which were entirely sector-specific. He saw no reason to expect that money supply including credits would fail to respond to the expansions in demand as were bound to result from the net exports earned by the country. Keynes's explanation of credit shortages relied on (*a*) the disjoint credit markets (between rural and urban centres), and (*b*) the high cost of remitting funds from abroad, relative to the incentives in the form of interest rate differentials. Both, in terms of present-day vocabulary, were instances of market distortions. The different principles of operation of the submarkets were evident in the movement of the presidency bank rates which, according to Keynes 'follows the market', and in the active role of exchange banks in providing funds for financing trade in London. (Both the presidency and the exchange banks originated from the European-managed joint-stock sector which controlled the export trade. The above was a contrast to local trade which was handled by *banias*). The solution to credit shortages, according to Keynes, was through wider access to funds which could be provided by setting up an imperial bank in the country.[105]

Supply of money could, by no stretch of imagination, be labelled as automatic during 1893–98. While Keynes could slight such deviations by confining attention to gold exchange standard (which, according to him, started functioning after 1898), his predecessor, Alfred Marshall, found it a little more precarious to label the system as automatic. Marshall's evidence to the Fowler Committee (of 1898) shows an awareness of having to put up as a matter of policy in India, high discount rates and shortages of money and credit in order to prevent declines in the rupee exchange rate. Marshall, however, supported the contraction in money supply after the closure of mints in 1893. The discount rate, according to Marshall, was a reflection of 'business' which depended on what he viewed as 'real capital'. Supply of money (or 'money capital') could only indirectly influence the discount rate by making business more 'fluid'.[106] Implicit in the argument was the promise of a dichotomy between the real and the monetary factors, and the functioning of the real variables at the level of full capacity utilization. Shortages of money and credit, as noticed earlier, drew a lot of attention in the deliberations of the RCC 1898. Witnesses drew attention to the 'power being placed in the hands of the Government to close mints to the public, while retaining to itself the power to coin rupees' while the Commission members continued to deny that the steps introduced had impaired the automaticity of currency. As for the India government's practice of accepting gold in lieu of rupees, the step, according to the Commission, in effect, prevented deviations of the rupee from its mint parity. A continuous inflow of gold, triggered off by upward variations in exchange rate in the direction of gold import points would, as believed by the Committee, eventually turn the system to a pure gold standard—a currency arrangement which was actually advocated by the Fowler Committee.[107] Sceptics of the official view included government servants like Martin Lindsay who offered direct evidence of stringency in cash and credit availability during busy season—a point which has been mentioned earlier. Commenting on the gold export and import points (reckoned as safety valves for the fixed mint parity under gold (exchange) standard, Lindsay noticed that neither were operative in India. While the gold import point was never approached, the system 'lacked elasticity' to maintain outflow of gold at the export point. No adjustment, again, was foreseeable, according to Lindsay, through the capital account since flows of capital were remarkably shy because of high risk premium in India.

The myth of a self-correcting adjustment mechanism underlying the Indian currency system continued to dominate the thinking of the majority of statesmen and public figures over 1898–1914, as is evident from our earlier discussions in this chapter. Such a complacent attitude regarding the Indian currency system, however, permeates even to some recent researches on the subject. In a recent work, Tomlinson[108] openly puts a disclaimer to what he views as a 'conspiracy theory of Imperialism'—to explain official economic policy in India before 1914. Rather, such policies were, according to him, 'mainly concerned with the day to day running of its own business' to meet 'short-term expediencies'. Tomlinson seems to follow Keynes in his rejection of the argument that gold exchange standard in India was a managed currency system. His study claims to refute the 'fanciful' descriptions in the available literature[109] on the 'deliberate attempts to benefit the London capital market at the expense of the Indian one.' As a concrete illustration he draws attention to the £16 million sterling investment out of GSR (the largest source of sterling funds at India Office) at the end of 1912—a sum which was considered small when compared to the £600 million aggregate British debt at the time.[110] Tomlinson also follows Keynes's study on Indian currency in his analysis of interest rate structure and its variations, none of which, according to him, resulted from deliberate state policies. Thus the three layers of sub-sectors of the money market comprised the presidency banks (lending against government securities), *shroffs* (lending against trade bills and *hundies*), and village money-lenders or *mahajans* (who would even combine the operations of a landlord and a money-lender while lending to peasants in distress against collaterals). These agents operated, according to Tomlinson, in separate spheres of activities. His arguments on the disjoint credit market in India, traceable to the aforementioned study of Keynes, was evidently faulty as can be judged by the strong seasonal pattern in presidency bank discount rates, which matched the agricultural production cycles. Operation of the indigenous money-lenders was reinforcing, in terms of the strong seasonal tendencies, by advancing money to their clientele (which comprised the *banias* who obtained the funds on the basis of trade bills and *hundis*, while advancing such funds to the peasant cultivators or landless labourers). It is thus difficult to subscribe to the view that in India the money market was a completely fragmented one and that the scarcity/abundance in one or more of them was only relative and not an absolute one.

What, then, remains of the much-adhered doctrine of a self-correcting process of adjustment under gold standard or gold exchange standards? Standard interpretations offered in text-books on international economics on the processes thus seem to be flawed as explanations.[111] In India the system implied, in addition, a clear conditioning of official policy in terms of the interest of the ruling alliances or the oligarchy. The latter included, apart from the British government, government officials in India and at the India Office, and also the mercantile and financial lobby controlled by the Europeans and Anglo-Indians in India. The essence of the process, however, was that all the financial matters were inevitably guided by the dominant interests. This left very little to be settled, as could be anticipated, through an impersonal, automatic market adjustment process. In this chapter we have documented and analysed the various processes which range from strict control, often discriminatory, over supply of money and credit, discriminatory purchases of silver in England for coinage in India, use of official machinery to transfer reserves to England for purposes of sterling investment (even at risk of an implicit capital depreciation), transfers of funds from other reserves to GSR (London) to achieve the same purpose, and a disposal of India Office's cash reserves in a manner which furthered the interests of London-based financiers and brokers. We have also commented on the growing significance of the India Office in the City. India Office affairs, especially on financial matters, attracted public attention in both England and India around 1912–13. The Bank of England, which was the chief custodian of finance capital in the City, often wielded the authority to openly intervene and to stop India Office from embarking on specific actions. (Recall again the silver purchase contracts of the SOS in the City, its sterling investment and the portfolio distribution and eventual disbursement of the treasury reserves maintained at the Bank of England as interest-free deposits.) The India Office's treasury balances were even directly lent to the City on attractive terms—a matter which was raised and discussed in the Indian Legislative Council.[112] While the SOS in England was convinced that its lendings had beneficial effects in the City (by 'lowering the general commercial rate' and related advantage to trade in London generally, and to Indian trade incidentally), individual members of Council objected to the practice. This was more because the SOS's broker was lending the India Office funds at charges (brokerages) which were lower by at least $\frac{1}{4}$ per cent than the comparable rates charged by the Bank of England's brokers.[113] It was a rather vexed question as to whether the India Office could justify its sterling assets and the lending policies in London, especially with its opposition to release such reserves for the purpose of lending, in the considerably squeezed domestic credit markets of India. Felix Schuster, the influential member of the India Office Council was found to support the SOS as it stopped the GOI from lending official funds to the public (in India) at concessional rates (which were lower than the presidency bank rates by $1\frac{1}{2}$ to 2 per cent). As it was held by the SOS's office, lendings in the City provided relative ease in the credit market, which even improved the prospects of future borrowings by the India Office. The arguments were clearly in line with those of the financial wizards in the City, as endorsed by Sir Felix Schuster.[114]

On the whole, the state of dissent, public protests, veil of secrecy, and underhand dealings, as seem to have prevailed on the question of currency policy in India, provide adequate grounds, in our judgement, to dispel the automaticity argument in the official financial and exchange policy over the period. It is difficult to accept that this policy was only '...providing the rupees to satisfy the demand for Indian goods', and that the distance between the official administration and the rest of the economy defied a description of the prevailing gold exchange standard as a 'managed currency system'.[115] We have sought to establish, through an analysis of both qualitative and quantitative evidence, a distinct process of deliberate intervention that was identifiable in the monetary sphere of the domestic economy. Much of it was initiated by imperial designs of Britain on the older colonies like India which provided potentials for an intricate system of expropriation through tributes, investment income, profits on trade, and access to international reserves. We have noticed the emergence of conflicting views on specific monetary and fiscal issues which culminated in serious controversies. These included, among others, issues relating to the use of official reserves for domestic credit. Exigencies of administration prompted the resident India government officials to protest the fact that India Office was determined not to let India government use its funds for such purposes. Hierarchy in financial administration was fairly complete under British rule with the India Office often having the final decision on the debated issues. Similarly, matters of dispute between the India Office and the Bank of England were most often settled in favour of the latter (the exception probably relates to the silver contract obtained by the Montague Co. in 1913). At the local level, pressures put forth by the private commercial community were similarly dismissed by the India government which even refused to concede the dissenting voices of its own officials like Martin Lindsay. The conflicting positions only indicated the innate contradictions emerging within the broad sphere of finance capital in relation to the colonies. Incidentally, the financial worth of India in the empire, and specifically, of the India Office in terms of its contribution to finances in the City was certainly not measurable by India government's share in aggregate sterling investments in London. The issue, rather, has to be settled by bringing into focus a much wider range of transactions, communications, and arrangements between the various agents operating within the system. The discourses offered in this chapter aim to fill in the gaps in the literature on these aspects.

Notes

1. It may be recalled that external trade and banking in India were mostly controlled by Europeans during the period. Internal (domestic) trade and the indigenous money market, however, were controlled by their Indian counterparts—the *beparis, baias, mahajans,* and *shroffs* in the country. *See* on evidence relating to the dominance of Europeans, arounnd 1893, *RCC* (1893), pp. 441, 494, 503. Also, Despatch from the India Government, 21 June 1892 and Proposals of David Barbour of the Finance Department, Government of India (henceforth GOI), *RCC* (1893).
2. J.M. Keynes, *Indian Currency and Finance.*
3. *RCC* (1914), Appendix to the Interim Report, Vol. I, Appendix VIII, pp. 240, 503.
4. See Table 3.2.
5. H.F. Howard, *India and the Gold Standard,* Calcutta, 1911, pp. 5–21; H.L. Chhablani, *Indian Currency and Exchange,* Madras, 1925, pp. 16–19, 62.
6. April–September is the lean season while October–March represents the busy season in Indian agriculture.
7. *RCC* (1914), Appendix II, p. 235.
8. *RCC* (1914), Appendix II, p. 233.
9. *RCC* (1898)
10. *RCC* (1914), Appendix VIII, pp. 251–3. *See also* Table 3.16.
11. *RCC* (1914), Appendix VIII, pp. 251–3.
12. Average inflow of gold to the PCR over the lean seasons of 1911–12 and 1912–13 amounted to £7.5 million per season (April–September). The inflow continued to be positive at £2.3 million over October–March, the busy season of the period. Transfer of gold from the Indian to the overseas branch of the PCR amounted to £2.3 million over the period. *RCC* (1914), Appenix VIII, pp. 251–3.
13. RCC (1914), Appendices to the Interim Report of the Commissioners, Vol. I, Appendix VIII, p. 239–42 and Appenix II, pp. 248–9.
14. Ibid.
15. Ibid.
16. GOI, *Reports of Currency Committees,* Calcutta, 1931, p. 107.
17. *See* for details IOR/L/F/5, *Letter from the Finance Department, GOI, to the SOS,* No. 144, dated 26 April 1906.
18. Ibid.
19. IOR/L/F/5/4.
20. Ibid.
21. IOR/L/F/5, SOS's letters dated 24 April 1907 and 25 June 1907.
22. *RCC* (1914), Appendix III, pp. 145–6.
23. While the official argument in support of the GSR included its usefulness as a support to the rupee rate, not much was done to actually put it in use for such purposes. It was only during

1908–09, when the India government sold RCBs on the SOS (given the adverse trade conditions) that a sum of £8 million was paid out by the SOS, met entirely through the GSR in London.

24. Estimate by Sir J.L. Mackay, president of the Bengal Chamber of Commerce, submitted to the RCC (1898). *See* also note (3).
25. Before 1910, paper currency standard rested on seven circles of origin. Legal tender status of individual paper currencies remainedd confined to the respective circles or their origin. GOI, *Reports of Currency Committees*, Calcutta, 1931, pp. 134–5.
26. *See RCC* (1914), Appendix VII, p. 232 for records of an official announcement tha 1898–99, 1900–01, 1907–08, and 1908–09 were famine years.
27. J.M. Keynes, *Indian Currency and Finance*. For a recent interpretation, see B. R. Tomlinson, *The Political Economy of the British Raj*, Cambridge, 1978.
28. *RCC* (1914), Appendix II, p. 248; *Statistical Abstracts of British India*, 1914–16, Vol. 77, p. 87, and *Benthal Papers*, South Asian Studies, Cambridge.
29. *RCC* (1914).
30. Instituted in 1861, the PCR was supposed to provide a 100 per cent backing to paper currency circulating in the country. Comprising of rupee coins (designated as silver), gold, and securities, fiduciary limits were placed on the form and absolute size of the reserve. The ceilings for total investment were revised upwards to Rs.12 crores by Act II of 1905, and to Rs. 14 crores by Act VII of 1911. Ceilings relating to gold-based (sterling) securities were also raised upwards, to Rs. 2 crores (1905) and Rs 4 crores (1911). None of these stipulations were present with the GSR in England the major part of which was invested in gold securities. *See RCC* (1914).
31. GOI, *Reports of Currency Committees*, p. 111.
32. Evidence of Sir J. L. Mackay, Allan Arthur, and Stephen Augustus Ralli, given to the Fowler Committee quoting a letter of John Littlewood Symmons of Bombay Chamber of Commerce, *RCC (1898)*, pp. 499, 552–4.
33. Ibid., pp. 494, 776.
34. Evidence by Allan Arthur, quoting extracts from the 53rd Report of the Directorate to the National Bank of India, dated 27 February 1894. *See RCC* (1898), p. 552.
35. Ibid., p. 664.
36. Ibid., pp. 510–11.
37. Ibid., p. 554.
38. See Section 3.4.
39. *RRC* (1914), Vol. II (cmd. 4956–5017).
40. Ibid., (cmd. 3928–3956).
41. Ibid., (cmd. 8468–8498).
42. *RCC* (1898), p. 592.

43. Ibid., pp. 519–25.
44. This, of course, excluded the private demand for silver imports, a large part of which was hoarded. *See* Table 3.13 for an argument that net coinage of silver was but a fraction of total silver imports, especially till 1900.
45. Official note by David Barbour submitted on 21 June 1893 to the RCC (1893).
46. *RCC* (1898), Accounts and Papers, Vol. 61, C. 9037. p. 544.
47. Ibid., p. 332.
48. *RCC* (1898), Accounts and Papers, Vol. 61, C. 9037, p. 544.
49. Ibid.
50. IOR/L/F/5/29. (File marked miscellaneous on gold and silver), Sir John Law's demiofficial note to Sir J. Waterfield of India Office in 1900.
51. *RCC* (1898).
52. *RCC* (1898), p. 46. Letter dated 12 January 1889, No. 234.
53. The practice of maintaining a specified part of official reserves at presidency banks can be traced back to 1861. A decision was taken by the government to maintain such funds as a compensation offered to the presidency banks for the services rendered in districts which did not have an official treasury. Also the measure was a step to give back the presidency banks some control over government funds in lieu of their earlier command over paper currency which was terminated with the Paper Currency Act of 1861. No interest was to be paid by the presidency banks on the agreed level of official reserves deposited with them. Rather the governments paid, in terms of the arrangement, interest on the shortfalls, if any, from the agreed minimum of deposits at the Banks.
54. Memorandum submitted by Montagu de P. Webb, president of Karachi Chamber of Commerce, *RCC* (1914), Vol. 2 (cmd. XIX), (cmd. 4956–5017).
55. IOR/L/F/7/224, Collection 24. Letter dated 2 October 1914 from GOI to SOS.
56. IOR/Eur/Mss/F 136/14, *Meston Papers*.
57. IOR/L/F/7/214, Financial Collections, No. 24, File 1–7.
58. IOR/L/F/7/214, Financial Collection 24, *Capital*, 2 January 1913. Also *Times of India*, 22 November 1913.
59. *Meston Papers*.
60. Ibid. Letter dated 23 September 1913.
61. *See*, for an analysis of similar discriminations over the banking sector and the advances of credit, A.K. Bagchi, 'Anglo-Indian Banking in British India: From the Paper Pound to the Gold Standard', *Journal of Imperial and Commonwealth History*, May 1985.
62. IOR/L/F/7/220, GOI's letters to SOS dated 25 April 1913.

63. See, for example, George Hamilton, the SOS's letter of 9 may 1888. IOR/L/F/7/220 Financial No. 87.
64. Letter from J. M. Keynes dated 17 October 1913, IOR/L/F/220 Collection 24.
65. *See, The Times*, 24 February 1913, in *Benthal Papers*.
66. *Times of India*, 13 March 1913. Also note the following comments in the 6 September 1913 issue of the same newspaper: '...the country finds the government is not at the back of the Presidency Banks and consequently that banks are not at the back of the discount market.' Again '...the merchants ask why agony should be caused to the trade and industries of the country when by immediately increasing the Exchequer with the Head Offices of the Presidency Banks the situation could be automatically cured and bumper harvest comfortably financed.' *See Benthal Papers.*
67. According to E.C. Harrison, the comptroller-general of the GOI, the SOS's lending policy deprived exchange banks in India of all possibilities of access to official funds. The situation was considered as paradoxical and discriminatory when such banks were able to borrow the SOS's funds through their head offices in London. *RCC* (1913), Minutes of Evidence, Vol. II. Evidence submitted by E.C. Harrison, comptroller-general, Government of India.
68. Letters dated 14 May 1908, No. 2826–A from GOI and reply dated 19 June 1908 from SOS, IOR/L/F/5/29.
69. Ibid. Letter from Lionel Abrahams, assistant under-secretary of state, dated 4 January 1910.
70. IOR/L/F/5/4, letter from SOS, Financial, No. 131, 20 September 1907.
71. Ibid. Letter from Sir James Mackay, dated 25 November 1910.
72. Ibid. Letter dated 2 February 1911.
73. Market prices were based on the quotations relating to next day, reported in *The Times*. IOR/L/F/7/422, Note by AG. Reference Paper F. 527, 1913, mentioned in the letter from the financial secretary of the SOS, dated 29 January 1913.
74. Ibid.
75. IOR/L/F/7/442, Collection 42, File 2, Letters from Sir James Mackay, SOS, to Bank of England, Dated 26 March 1906.
76. L/F/4/7/220 and L/F/5/4.
77. *Keynes Papers*, Marshall Library, Cambridge (Box 53A7, Item 8).
78. Ibid. Unofficial letter between Felix Schuster of the India Office and Samuel Montague and Co., dated 9 January 1912.
79. Ibid. Letter from Samuel Montague and Co., 13 November 1912.
80. L/F/7/421, Financial Department, Collection 42, Letter from Messrs Mocatta and Goldsmith, dated 29 August 1912.
81. Ibid., *Capital*, 2 January 1913.

82. IOR/L/F/7/214, Financial Collection No. 24, File 1–7, *Capital*, 2 January 1913.
83. Ibid., *Times of India*, 28 December 1912.
84. Ibid.
85. Ibid. Question raised in British parliament by Mr Gwynne.
86. IOR/L/F/7/442, Collection 42, File 2.
87. IOR/L/F/220, Collection 24. On 25 November 1913, the *Times of India* reported '...A run on banking firms and Marwaris who found it difficult to renew their hundies due to lack of funds.'
88. *RCC* (1914). Appendices to the Interim Report, Appendix III, p. 93.
89. IOR/L/F/5/4. Statement of Walter Badock, accountant-general of GSR, 16 April 1912. *See RCC* (1913), Vol. I, Appendix XI, pp. 309–10. *Also see* letter dated 27 November 1913 from Bank of England to SOS. *Benthal Papers* (Box 20, File 1) Cambridge. Statistics presented in Table 3.14 in the text indicate a short-term lending of India Office's balance in March 1913 amounting to £1 million. This was against the GSR, and hence, in addition to the above-mentioned short-term loans from the SOS's treasury reserve.
90. IOR/L/F/5/4, GOI's letters No. 66 (26.2.1907), No. 144 (26.4.1906), SOS's letter No. 131 (20.9.1907) (Financial). Also IOR/L/F/7/214 Financial Collection 24, *Times of India*, 28 December 1913.
91. IOR/L/F/5/4, Minute of SOS on investment of GRF, dated 27 March 1906 (No. F 1863 and No. 1667)
92. IOR//L/F/7/214, Financial Collection No. 24, File 1–7. IOR/L/F/7/442, Collection 42. See Walter Badock's statement on GSR dated 16 April 1912.
93. IOR/L/F/7/214, Financial Collection 24.
94. Ibid.
95. Ibid. SOS's note dated 22 December 1912.
96. RCC (1914), Appendix II, Despatch No. 236, p. 180. Also IOR/L/F/5/7.
97. IOR/L/F/5/7, Letter from the SOS to GOI, dated 29 February 1912.
98. Ibid.
99. *Keynes Papers*, Marshall Library, Cambridge, Box 53 A7, Item 9. Also *RCC* (1914).
100. See in particular Keynes, *Indian Currency*. *See also* despatch dated 28 June 1912, *RCC* (1914) Appendix II, pp. 201–2.
101. J.M. Keynes, *Indian Currency*, p. 20.
102. Ibid., p. 25.
103. Ibid., p. 178.
104. *See also* Chapter 1, Note 14 for a fuller exposition of the argument.
105. J.M Keynes, *Indian Currency*.
106. Alfred Marshall, *Official Papers*, Macmillan, London, 1926, pp. 280, 322.
107. *Reports of Currency Committee*, Government of India, Calcutta, 1931, p. 38.

108. B.R. Tomlinson, *Political Economy*, pp. 22, 25.
109. Refers to Marcello de Cecco, *Money and Empire*.
110. B.R. Tomlinson, *Political Economy of the Raj*, pp. 22, 25.
111. *See* Robert Triffin, 'The Myth and Realities of Gold Standard' in R.N. Cooper, ed., *International Finance*, Penguin, 1976.
112. In a question raised in the Indian Legislative Council on 22 March 1912, it was revealed that two-third of the cash at the GSR in London was advanced to approved borrowers of the SOS against securities. The reminder (one-third of the total) was advanced to seven leading banks in the City who were not supposed to lodge securities. IOR/L/F/5/4/SOS, Minutes of Finance Department.
113. *RCC* (1913), Minutes of Evidence, Vol. II.
114. Ibid.
115. B.R. Tomlinson, *Political Economy*, p. 21.

CHAPTER 4

Pace of Real Transfers from India: Export Surpluses and Spoliations in the Domestic Economy

Monetary aspects of a drain or a financial transfer from British India fit in well with the picture of a corresponding real transfer from the country. Attention is directed in this chapter to the pace of such real transfers for the years 1890–1914—a period when the British rule in India was consolidated enough to yield a steady flow of returns from the country. We have discussed in preceding chapters the essence of the mechanism which arranged for remitting the financial transfers from India on a regular basis through the proceeds of the export surpluses which were common during the period. It may be recalled that net export earnings (which remained at the end of payments for imports of commodities, gold, and silver) were regularly retained in England and disbursed by the India Office on home charges. The residual, if any, constituted the India Office's accumulation of sterling denominated assets in London. From an accounting angle, export surpluses earned by India during the period were thus utilized to meet the home charges (identified earlier as unilateral transfers), and to add to India Office's sterling assets in London which took the form of deposits with the Bank of England and/or investments in sterling denominated securities. None of the above contributed to the current flow of income in the domestic economy, as argued earlier in Chapter 2.

It thus appears appropriate to identify the export surplus as a measure of real transfers from India, providing the finance towards unilateral transfers and the externally held assets. The structural implications of the process of remitting the real transfers would be explored in the present chapter, revealing a pattern of spoliation in the domestic economy with stagnating trends in output.[1] This is in contrast with the picture of an apparent buoyancy in the economy, reflected in the general uptrend in prices and the rising export volume and/or revenue during the period. The overall picture was thus one of an apparent paradox—one where the rise in prices and exports failed to stimulate growth in the exporting country.

Export expansion in India during the period of our study was accompanied by at least three significant developments in the domestic economy. First, the changes in the composition of output which included, by 1900, a large share for cash crops or other foodgrains, most of which catered to the external market. Relative and absolute expansions/contractions in acreage under exportable/home consumption crops indicated a switch in the cropping pattern. Decline, in particular, in the trend rates of change in the area under cultivation of inferior grains (jowar, bajra, ragi) was prominent. This was in contrast to the respective expansions in acreage under rice, wheat, and other cash crops (jute, cotton), all of which experienced a boom in the export market.

The second aspect of the export expansion relates to the sectoral shifts in the internal prices of different crops. Price indices for exportables as well as for inferior grains (both unweighted) were both in the upward direction. Price indices (unweigthed) relating to agricultural goods rose faster than those for nonagricultural goods, while the unweighted indices relating to the inland prices of exportables (FOB) rose faster than the CIF prices of importables. On the whole the trend in most of the prices in India were in the upward direction during the period.

The third significant aspect relates to the pattern of distribution and utilization of surpluses in the domestic economy which resulted from the organization of production and trade of the major export crops. The typical pattern in the extraction and distribution of surpluses from agriculture, which emerged during this period, pre-empted, as indicated later in this chapter, the possibilities of further investment in agriculture. Organization of production and marketing of crops under 'forced commerce' often gained prominence under rising exports, operating as a major causal factor behind the above processes. The outcome was a tendency for stagnation in agricultural performance, evident in the data on aggregate output and in the yield performances. The drag in the major performing sector of the economy, viz. agriculture, was prominent enough to bring in tendencies for a deceleration and stagnation in the economy as a whole. These three aspects will be documented in the following sections of the present chapter.

Analysis offered in this chapter, on the implications of export expansion in the domestic economy, lead to conclusions which are strikingly different from those often derived in the literature dealing with developments during the period. Mention may be made here of some studies which relate to price movements in India during this time. Often the analysis has relied on quantity-theoretic arguments which largely dwell on money supply as a major explanatory factor. This prevented such literature from looking into other plausible explanations concerning the output variations and related aspects.[2] There remains, in the literature, a second approach to price movements during the period—one which relates the short-term fluctuations in output to the short-term movements in prices, thus leaning on the steady uptrends in export prices as the factor behind the long-run expansion in export crops.[3] Variations in output as well as prices over the long-term are thus related to export expansions. This in terms of the above explanation brought the gains of specialization to the domestic economy.

Section 4.1 of this chapter dwells on the output trends in the aggregate and its sectoral pattern during the period. Section 4.2 analyses the price movements—both aggregate and sectoral. In this section we have also examined some explanations offered in the available literature on price variations which, as mentioned above, are mainly in a quantity-theoretic framework. Section 4.3 considers the argument that both price and output movements in the period were symptomatic of a major dynamism imparted by the export boom. It also offers our own analysis of the tendencies observed (in the first two sections) on output and price variations and questions the universality of the arguments advanced regarding an international sharing of gains under free trade. The analysis of the structural changes in the domestic economy are continued in Section 4.4, which offers a study of the pattern which has been typical in the prevailing surplus expropriation and utilization. The documented facts and their analysis are intended to provide an explanation of the overall stagnation in the economy. The spurt in export activities obviously did not prove to be a propelling factor in the context of the colonial economy, which was sharing very little of the gains from international specialization. The qualitative and the quantitative evidences adduced in this section have been primarily based on information relating to Bombay and Bengal presidencies which were high export regions. The selection of the regions strengthens, in our judgement, the conclusion arrived at in this chapter on the international integration and its impact on the Indian economy during the period.

4.1 Output trends in the economy

A marked sluggishness can be observed in the trend rate of changes in agricultural output over 1891–1916 (Table 4.1). Foodgrain production showed worst performance with nominal rate of change at an annual 0.01 per cent over 1896–1906, an average which underplays the more serious crop shortfalls during the 1896–98 famine. An improvement, to 0.30 per cent (per annum) over the next ten years (1906–16) was evidently other than significant. Using different sub-periods (Table 4.2), both all-crop and foodgrain output seem to be subject to negative annual per cent growth rates over 1900–01 to 1905–06 and 1910–11 to 1913–14. None of the intervals, it is significant to note, covered the officially announced famine years which included 1897–98, 1899–1900 and 1907–08. Both all-crop and foodgrain production, once again, showed a negative annual growth rate over 1910–11 to 1913–14.

Disaggregating the overall trends in crop output into variations in area and yield per acre, both food and non-food crops did seem to register small negative movements in terms of the annual average yield per acre during the quinquennium ending in 1908-09 compared to the preceding quinquennium (Table 4.3). The position was different in the next quinquennium when yield per acre improved in general. Annual averages relating to area under cultivation, however, recorded continuous increases over 1900–01 to 1913–14. Understandably, variations in yield swamped the effect of acreage changes on output variations.

The above picture, however, conceals the cropwise variations. To assess the impact of export expansions (which consisted of both food and non-food crops) on agricultural performance, it is important to highlight the variations in the individual cropping pattern in the economy. Of the five major export crops, viz. jute, cotton, oilseeds, wheat, and rice (which together comprised about 46 per cent of the export value in 1910) only two (rice and wheat) featured under foodgrains. However, unlike wheat, rice was used more for domestic consumption. (Important differences, however, remained in the quality of grains since the rice consumed in bulk within the country largely consisted of the inferior varieties. We could not construct a series, because of data inadequacy, where the different varieties of rice production are systematically shown.)

Commenting on the cropwise distribution of acreage and yield variations in the major crops produced in the country, acreages for most of the exportables (wheat, jute, and cotton) showed increases in terms of the annual trend values over 1896–1906 (Table 4.4). The pattern was not necessarily followed in regard to crops meant for local consumption, e.g. jowar, ragi and even for rice—a point which needs mention and emphasis. During the next decennial, spanning 1906-1916, trend rates of change in acreage, even for exportables, were less spectacular. However, most of them (other than jute) compared favourably with the consistently negative trend rates of acreage for the local consumption crops (jowar, bajra, and ragi) which are normally described as inferior grains. On the whole, the export crops showed a tendency to move up in terms of expansion in acreage as one compares the similar performance of those meant for home consumption.

The relatively superior record of performance of exportables in terms of area cultivated was, however, not matched by better yields per acre. Individual cash crops (e.g. jute, wheat, rice, and cotton) showed a tendency to be subject to the constraints of diminishing of stationary yield values over the period. The same was true of the three inferior crops, jowar, bajra, and ragi, none of which had export markets. It is thus evident that availability of external markets could not initiate innovations in production methods so as to overcome the prevailing tendencies towards lower yields in the economy (see Table 4.4 for data). Barring sugarcane, which showed an improved performance in terms of productivity per acre, improvements in land productivity were not typical for most of the other export crops (Table 4.5). The above resulted in low or negative growth rate of output during the period which has been documented in Tables 4.1 to 4.3. The pattern was matched by sharp annual variation in crop returns, often around a stationary trend. Production of rice (which was half of total foodgrains output and one-third of all-crop output in India over 1891–1897)[4] fell below the preceding year's

Table 4.1: Trend rates of change in output: crop aggregates (percent per year) 1891–1916

Reference decade	Foodgrains	Non-foodgrains	All crops
1891–1901	0.88	1.28	0.97
1896–1906	0.01	1.90	0.35
1901–1911	1.24	1.51	1.34
1906–1916	0.30	1.96	0.69

Source: George Blyn, *Agricultural Trends*, p. 327.

Table 4.2: Trend in agricultural products: 1891–1914

Period (Year ended 30 June)	Average annual per cent rate of growth of all crop production.	Average annual per cent rate of growth of foodgrains production
1891–92 to 1895–96	5.3	5.0
1895–96 to 1900–01	0.9	0.8
1900–01 to 1905–06	–0.8	–1.2
1905–06 to 1910–11	5.1	5.8
1910–11 to 1913–14	–4.6	–5.5

Source: George Blyn, *Agricultural Trends*, p. 349. Cited in A.J. Latham, *The International Economy and the Underdeveloped World 1865–1914*, Croom Helm, London, 1978, p. 130.

crop returns in 13 out of the 23 years between 1891 and 1914. Indices relating to both annual crop data for foodgrains as a whole, and for the all-crop average registered a drop in 11 out of the 20 year period between 1893–94 and 1913–14. Again, the annual drop in the all-crop average was 32 per cent over 1896, 16 per cent over 1911 (which, unlike 1896, 1899 or 1907, was not a famine year).[5] On the whole, the stagnation in the growth rate in foodgrains contributed to the rather stationary level of agricultural production as a whole, given the large weightage of foodgrains in the latter. Expansion in acreage alone for non-food output (cash crops)—largely in response to the export opportunities—could not push up average performance in agriculture as indicated by the overall output or acreage of crops in general. Nor did the export expansions help augment the yield of land, either under cash crops or under foodgrains. Later in this chapter we have brought in some further implications of the process in terms of, first, the distributional share (rent, interest, profit, or wages) of different agents involved in the production or marketing of agricultural output, and second, in terms of the impact on the real income enjoyed by the cultivators (indicated by the changes in per capita output available for consumption).

Table 4.3: Annual averages for area and yield per acre for principal crops in British India: 1900–1914 (yield measured in rupees at 1924–29 prices; area in million acres)

	All crops			Foodgrains			Non-food crops		
	A	O	Y	A	O	Y	A	O	Y
1900–04	182	965	53.0	151	739	48.9	31	226	73.0
1905–09	188	955	50.8	153	718	46.9	35	237	67.8
1910–14	193	1059	54.8	156	787	50.5	37	271	72.9

Note: *A* = area, *O* = output, *Y* = yield per acre. Foodgrains include rice, wheat, jowar, bajra, barley, maize and gram. Non-food crops include linseed, sesame, groundnut, rape, mustard, sugarcane, cotton, jute, tea and tobacco.

Source: George Blyn, *Agricultural Trends*, cited in N.K. Chandra, 'Long Term Stagnation,' 1983.

Table 4.4: Trend rates of change in selected crops: output, acreage and yield (per cent per year)

	1891–1901	1896–1906	1901–1911	1906–1916
Output				
Rice	0.37	–0.37	0.49	1.12
Wheat	1.63	2.35	2.03	1.56
Jowar*	1.48	–0.17	–0.42	1.09
Bajra*	2.47	1.96	1.74	0.46
Maize	2.20	1.31	1.05	1.63
Ragi*	1.17	0.25	–0.16	–0.30
Cotton	2.17	4.85	2.90	1.43
Jute	2.61	4.03	1.07	0.81
Acreage				
Rice	–0.21	–0.36	0.31	0.38
Wheat	–0.26	2.29	0.60	0.88
Jowar*	0.70	–0.17	–0.76	–0.17
Bajra*	1.82	1.94	1.52	–0.18
Maize	1.72	0.73	0.13	0.10
Ragi*	0.15	–0.12	0.09	–0.50
Cotton	–0.33	4.25	3.11	0.57
Jute	–0.55	5.49	2.16	–1.85
Yield per acre				
Rice	0.52	0.07	0.21	0.74
Wheat	2.53	0.34	1.35	0.76
Jowar*	0.80	0.16	0.41	1.17
Bajra*	0.78	–0.26	0.22	0.64
Maize	0.46	0.63	0.91	–1.52
Ragi*	1.25	0.40	–0.26	–0.23
Cotton	2.44	0.87	–0.35	0.95
Jute	3.22	–1.05	–1.40	2.61

*Indicates inferior grains from the point of view of consumption.
Source: G. Blyn, *Agricultural Trends*, pp. 327–9.

Table 4.5: Productivity per acre of selected crops in India: (Rs. per acre at 1938–39 prices)

Annual average over the period	Rice	Cotton	Sugarcane	Wheat	Jute
1900–01 to 1904–05	42.4	15.0	137.3	22.9	83.2
1905–06 to 1909–10	37.6	14.6	132.3	22.4	68.3
1910–11 to 1914–15	40.4	14.6	152.6	23.9	81.8

Source: Computations done by Bagchi on the basis of data given by Sivasubramonian's estimates of gross value of agricultures. A.K. Bagchi, *Private Investment*, p. 96.

Table 4.6: Record of price variations in India: 1890–1914 (base 1873 = 100)

	Unweighted series			Weighted series		
	Exports	Imports	All commodities	Agricultural goods	Non-agricultural goods	All goods
	(1)	(2)	(3)	(4)	(5)	(6)
1890	104	91	101	127	98	117
1895	111	85	104	124	100	120
1900	134	96	110	147	96	143
1905	116	96	110	135	108	135
1910	127	109	122	148	116	150
1914	160	114	147	210	134	187

Sources: Columns 1,4,5,6 K.L. Datta, *Indian Prices*, columns 2,3 Thingalaya, cited in McAlpin 1983, Price Movements, pp. 903–4.

Table 4.7: Percentage of acreage and output of non-food grains to all crops in British India: 1901–02 to 1913–14

	Percentage of area	Percentage of output (at current prices)
1901–02	16.26	24.54
1906–07	18.81	26.32
1913–14	19.73	27.18

Source: A.K. Bagchi, *Private Investment*, p. 109

Table 4.8: Percentage of output of non-food crops to total value of crops at 1938–39 prices

1901–01 to 1904–05	36.2
1905–06 to 1909–10	37.7
1910–11 to 1914–15	37.1

Source: A.K. Bagchi, *Private Investment*, p. 95

Table 4.9: Exports from India: commodity composition (percentages)

	Foodgrains	Non-foodgrains	
		Cotton and jute products	Others
1890–91	19.5	12.0	68.5
1900–01	13.1	13.7	73.2
1910–11	18.4	14.1	67.5

Source: *Statistical Abstract of British India*, quoted in K.N. Chaudhuri, *Foreign Trade*, 1983, p. 844.

4.2 The price movements

Upward movements in prices, prominent by the 1880s,[6] clearly became a cause for concern to the India government. A committee was appointed, in 1914, to enquire into the 'Causes relating to the rise in Prices'.[7] The committee, led by K. L. Dutta, observed systematic variation in sectoral prices. Prices of inferior grains were found to rise faster than those relating to other foodgrains.[8] Foodgrain prices, on the whole, showed a systematic upward movement over the period. Comparing the relative changes in the sectoral price series (unweighted) provided in the K.L. Dutta Committee Report, exportables seem to register the highest unit value increases compared to those for imports (CIF unit value) or the all commodity averages. Since the all commodity average included non-traded goods, export products were evidently subject to steeper price rise. At this point we feel it necessary to stress that the coverage of exportables was subject to changes over the period. Inclusion of commodities which experienced sharper upward movements in price (typically the high value products) might have lent an upward bias to the price indices (unweighted) for exportables over the period. (Prominent among exportables around 1910 were rice at 11.8 per cent of total value of exports, raw cotton at 14.4, oilseeds 10.8, raw jute at 9.9, and jute manufactures at 8.8 per cent. The respective shares were much lower in 1870 with rice at 7.1 per cent, raw cotton at 0.1, oilseeds at 4.6, raw jute at 4.3, and jute manufactures at 0.4 per cent.) The series relating to weighted price indices, decomposed into agricultural and non-agricultural products, showed a pattern where the increases in the former were pronounced (Table 4.6). The K.L. Dutta Committee Report (1914) on Indian prices emphasized the beneficiary role of exports to cultivators in India.[9] This was preceded, in 1909, by a paper[10] by F.J. Atkinson, the director-general of statistics of the India government, who wrote several papers on 'Rupees Prices'. Price increases in India during 1870–1908 could, acccording to Atkinson, be explained by the (*a*) increases in money supply, (*b*) scanty rainfall, and (*c*) increases in the propensity to hoard amongst the public.[11] According to his argument, while money supply had a direct impact on domestic prices, rainfall and hoarding propensities (especially of foodgrains by traders) had their respective second round effects via temporary shortfalls in output and additions to profit margins. Tendencies to hoard silver (as jewellery and for precautionary purposes) reflected the consumption habits of the rich, and in particular, of zamindars living in areas under permanent settlement. Such propensities led to a proportionate reduction, according to Atkinson, in 'active' money supply and a consequent dampening effect on prices. (Official figures relating to coins and currency in circulation was naturally larger than active money supply.) Atkinson's paper pointed at the observed increases in active money supply during 1870–1908 and at its causal impact on the generally rising prices in the economy.[12]

The above argument had an implicit quantity-theoretic bias which was by and large in conformity with the theoretical premises accepted in the contemporary literature. Interestingly enough, Atkinson's thesis has been revived in a recent paper, written jointly by Adams and Craig in 1979.[13] The time series on price variations in India over 1861–95 has been regressed on (*a*) variations in active money supply, (*b*) rainfall, *a la* Atkinson, and in addition, on (*c*) railroad mileage, and (*d*) silver imports relating to the same period. Results based on a linear regression analysis led to the observation that the coefficients relating to the first three variables were each significant and together capable of explaining 46 per cent of total variation in prices. Regarding rainfall, the authors argued (in line with Alkinson) that increases (or declines) in the variable would influence prices in the opposite direction.

Additions to railroad mileage (which the authors interpreted as an index of commercialization) had a similar negative effect on domestic prices, presumably through a scaling down of the transport cost margin and the related dampening effect on prices.[14] As for the effect of silver imports on prices, while it was possible to explain a greater proportion (51 per cent) of the total variation in price when the variable was incorporated as an additional explanatory factor, the relation, according to Adams and Craig, was a tenuous one since levels of hoarding had presumably increased (along with increases in the level of prosperity amongst the upper income classes) during the period, as was observed earlier by Atkinson. Thus both prices and the level of hoarding, while independent of each other, might have increased over time, which ruled out a possible causation between additional hoarding and price increases.[15]

Emphasis laid in the above-mentioned literature on variation in money supply as an explanation of price movements ignores, in our view, the fact that the simultaneity in the movement of the two variables might as well be incidental (especially when both are subject to upward increases over time). Based on a quantity-theoretic reasoning, explanation of price changes in terms of variations in money supply alone clearly tends to underplay the role of supply factors. Interestingly, the latter was subsumed in the emphasis on the effects of rainfall on prices, which ostensibly could arise through variations in output alone.

4.3 Rising exports and the structural changes in the domestic economy: sharing of international division of labour and the domestic economy in India

What, then, can one assess regarding the economic implications of rising exports on the level of output as well as standard of living in colonial India during the period of our study? Moreover, if exports from India during the period served as the chief instrument of arranging transfers abroad in real terms (as pointed out earlier), what remained of the role of exports in the context of the benefits from an increased international division of labour? What, in particular, were the distributional effects of the rise in export volumes and in their prices on the domestic economy? We will address some of these crucial questions in this section.

Foreign trade evidently had become important in the Indian economy after the opening of the Suez Canal and the extension of the railway network in the domestic economy. Annual compound growth rates of exports went up by 6.31 per cent over the decade at the end of the 1860–61 which, incidentally, was an all-time high during 1830–1930.[16] The rising pace in exports continued except during the war years, till the collapse of world markets in the 1920s.

Growth of exports in general and the higher level of production (as well as exports) of cash crops, according to views held, benefited the domestic economy in more than one way. In a cropwise study of price variations in British India over 1860–1947, McAlpin[17] has differentiated the short-term fluctuations in output from its long-term trend, especially for the years since the mid-1880s, when the upward trend was more pronounced. Short-run fluctuations in prices of rice and jowar (both of which catered more to the home market) as observed by McAlpin, were determined, subject to one-year lag, by fluctuations in per acre yield relating to the two crops. Fluctuations (short-run) in prices of wheat, cotton, and jute, (the three major export crops) were, however, influenced very little by similar fluctuations in yield per acre. Instead, their prices, according to McAlpin, were predetermined by the long-run uptrend in prices set in by forces of international demand. In an attempt to lay stress on both trade and transport as forces opening up the economy, McAlpin mentioned the beneficial effects of railroad network in the country, the foundations of which were already laid by 1860s. The 'pull' factor, which could provide a demand-based explanation of price variations in India could not, however, be substantiated in the paper in absence of detailed cropwise observations on export trends in world market and India's share in it. Moreover, the (international) demand-based explanation of the rise in prices in India neglects the role of switches in cultivation amongst different crops, a reference to which has been made earlier.

McAlpin's analysis led her to conclude that there was a generally beneficial effect of trade and improved transport for the domestic economy. The position may best be subsumed through the following quotation:

> Increasing integration of Indian markets for some products with world markets explain some of the variations in prices not explained by yields per acre for crops traded internationally. The overall upward trend in agricultural prices for the early 1880s to 1915 was due to increased demand from Europe for India's agricultural products. The demand was made efficient by falling inland and ocean transport costs. The dwindling

> value of the rupee led to rising prices in India for those goods in demand in the world market (and their close substitutes, i.e. jowar and bajra, followed by wheat prices). *The overall effects of such rising demand on the agricultural sector* was to provide new and improved markets for the sale of produce probably *to raise real incomes and to stimulate cultivation.* (Italics added).[18]

We quote, in full, a similar argument which was advanced by K.N. Chaudhuri:

> ...expansion of commercial crops for export was a *dynamic process* which increasingly drew the subsistence sector into the commercial or monetary sector and converted the peasant producers into market-oriented farmers; raw cotton and raw jute, along with foodgrains and oilseeds, were India's principal exports, the production of which was in the hands of peasant small holders...(and)...there is *little doubt that exports of jute brought a substantial degree* of prosperity to the peasants of Bengal. (Italics added).[19]

Arguments cited above rest on the conviction that in India the opening up of trade opportunities imparted a distinct dynamism to the domestic economy, and that it was pervasive enough to usher in improvements in real income. Our preceding observations (in Sections 4.1 and 4.2) provide little reason to accept the view that trade was instrumental in ushering in dynamism, growth, and real income gains to the domestic economy. Our position on the matter, which runs contrary to the view held, among others, by McAlpin and Chaudhury is strengthened further by the following observations, some of which have already been mentioned earlier:

(*a*) Aggregate growth rate of domestic output around 1900 was dominated by variations in agricultural performance. Sectoral share of secondary output was at an annual average of 11.8 per cent only during 1900–01 to 1904–05 and at 12.9 per cent during 1910–11 to 1914–15, both measured at constant 1960–61 prices. The share for the tertiary sector in net domestic product was more than double the share of the secondary sector, indicating a discrepancy between the net domestic product and the net material product. Thus primary goods comprised more than 80 per cent of the net material product.[20] These observations indicate the dominance of primary goods (and especially of foodgrains) in total output.[21] These also highlight the significance of the near stationariness of primary product output (and of foodgrains in particular) over the period (Tables 4.1 to 4.5).

(*b*) Movements in yield per acre remained an important component as an explanation of the slow and stationary growth rate in agriculture over the period. The all-crop average relating to yield fell from Rs. 27.6 to Rs. 25.9; later rising to Rs. 26.6 for the respective five-yearly periods ending in 1904–05, 1909–10, and 1914–15. The figures, measured at 1938–39 prices, evidently indicate a stationary picture.[22]

(*c*) Disaggregate data on yield and acreage variations over the period dispel the belief that export expansion, of cash crops and other high value foodgrains, were able to initiate widespread yield-raising operations in agriculture for exportables or for other crops. Declines in trend rates of yield could be observed for rice, wheat, cotton, jute, and sugarcane during the decennium ending in 1910–11 by comparing the similar rates during the previous decennium (Table 4.4). As indicated in Table 4.5, yield per acre at constant prices registered a drop for most of cash crops during the quinquennia ending 1904–05 and 1909–10. The relatively different picture for the next five years is related to the data sources which are different from that used in Table 4.4.

Isolated instances of output expansion for individual cash crops were thus necessarily related to acreage rather than yield improvements. Examples include cotton crop, the production of which expanded, despite drop in yield rates during 1896–1906 and 1901–11 (Table 4.4). Expansions in acreage were marked in the Bombay-Sind area which experienced the cotton boom.[23] The above has at times been interpreted in the literature as agricultural prosperity in the Bombay region. It is not difficult to refute the basis of such interpretations.[24] For jute, however, acreage during 1906–16 fell while the yield was relatively higher as compared to the previous decade. Output responded unfavourably to such changes, as revealed by the considerably lower trend rate of change in jute production during 1906–16. (The same pattern in yield for jute can be observed from Table 4.5). In general, for cash crop production as a whole, the acreage expansions, if any, were often inadequate to offset the declines in yield per acre, resulting in less than proportionate increases in output, as we have observed earlier in this chapter.

(*d*) Composition of agricultural output changed over the period with absolute and relative expansions in the area cultivated under the non-food varieties. Figures available indicate an increase in share of non-food crops in total agricultural output, valued at current prices, over 1901–02 to 1913–14. The above was accompanied by similar increases in percentage share of the non-food crops in total cultivated area (*see* Table 4.7). Proportion of these crops in total value of output, when calculated, however, remained more or less unchanged over the same period at constant prices—a fact which indicates a relative rise in their prices.[25] As already stressed above (*also see* Table 4.3), shortfalls in yield per acre were more than balanced by expansion in acreage in the case of non-food crops, thus making possible an increase in the volume of output, measured at constant prices. From the preceding account one can confirm the basis for observed 'switches' in cultivation from foodgrain to cash crops, as it happened in the Bengal presidency, with a shift in the cultivated area from rice to jute production. It is possible to adduce additional evidence to switchovers documented by economic historians.[26]

(e) A steady and uninterrupted flow of foodgrain exports, which took place from India over the period reduced the availability of grains within the economy, especially during years of severe crop shortfall. In as many as thirteen out of the twenty-one years between 1891–92 and 1912–13, net availability of foodgrains declined in greater Bengal—a major exporting area—as a consequence of international trade. Given the population growth, per capita net availability fell during twelve out of the twenty-one year period in greater Bengal. Trend rate of change in population for India as a whole, estimated at 0.42 per cent per annum over 1896–1906, exceeded the annual foodgrain trend rate, estimated at 0.01 per cent over the same period. Similar was the scenario over 1906–1916 when annual average trend rate for population was at 0.49 per cent while foodgrains had a 0.3 per cent trend rate per year.[27] It is not difficult to expect that per capita output of foodgrains in the country as a whole fell over 1896–1916. Coming back to data on availability of foodgrains, the trend rates of change recorded decline in British India over the reference decade of 1896–97 to 1906–07, while for greater Bengal such declines took place over 1896–97 to 1906–07, 1901–02 and during 1911–12 as well. Interestingly, while exports of foodgrains reduced their domestic availability, little respite was offered by imports which primarily comprised cotton yarn and textiles, sugar, silk, and woollens (the four items accounted for more than 50 per cent of India's imports in 1900).[28] A negative or near-stationary trend rate of change was obtained for most foodcrops output other than wheat, as indicated in Table 4.4. The above, was matched by a similar or even worse picture relating to availability of foodgrains as a result of trade.

Above observations run counter to the thesis—referred to at the beginning of this section—on the growth-inducing effects in India of specialization in crops having an export market. Nor does it lend credence to an argument on the positive real income effects of free trade in the domestic economy. The general picture relating to stagnation or deceleration of domestic output and the lack of consumption availabilities thus corroborates the theme we advanced in Chapter 2 that, from a macro-economic angle, export earnings failed to generate real income flows within India during the colonial period.

4.4 Surpluses and their utilization in the exporting economy: an explanation of stagnation

Forces inhibiting growth in colonial India were largely endemic in the process of export expansion itself. A fuller understanding of this outcome demands an unfolding of the distributional implications of international trade in the domestic economy, dwelling on the trade-inflicted pace of income transfers. As would be indicated in this section, these transfers had negative repercussions on investment potentials in the agrarian economy of colonial India, especially in the wake of commercialization of agriculture in the country. Drawing illustrations from two high-export-growth regions where increased level of trade and commercialization could presumably have a relatively greater impact on growth, we now focus our attention to an understanding and an analysis of the forces of economic retardation in colonial India.

We find it instructive to lay bare the factors which presumably held back cultivating units in colonial India from initiating productivity advances. Some of the aspects we have highlighted below include evidence relating to the immediate effects of introduction of cash crops, especially, on investment in land, the pattern of land system and the economic status of the tenant/owner-cultivator in the economy, the appropriation of surplus from agriculture (as land-rent, profit on grain trade, or as interest on loans advanced), and finally, the effects of above on net investment on land and its yield. An attempt has also been made to relate the above aspects to the depressed level of living for the 'lower classes of population'—a subject widely discussed amongst contemporaries in late nineteenth century India. The analysis makes it amply evident that none of the surpluses appropriated from agricultural production were reinvested on land. Nor was it possible for the cultivators to make use of the residual output (which consisted of their subsistence) to initiate yield-augmenting investments. The role of the state, which, by any criterion, had been far from neutral in terms of the actual developments, has also been highlighted in order not to miss out the implications of the imperialist designs implicit under British rule in India.

Attention has been drawn, earlier in this chapter, to the fact that export expansions from India during the period of our study were matched by simultaneous increases in the production of cash crops in the economy, and that, this was largely made possible through extension of acreage. We now draw attention to the possible increase in marketed surplus in agriculture (which was a logical concommitant to the increased level of exchanges during the period). Incidentally, while growth in demand (especially external) for the commercial crops induced expansion in their acreage, the crop selection could be 'induced' or 'forced' by traders' advances (*dadans*)[29] towards high profit cash crops (and not, as argued by McAlpin and others, as a response to favourable market conditions).[30] Introduction of cash crops led, as one of the immediate consequences, to a rise in the marketed surplus for the cultivator who was now forced to participate in the market even for subsistence. Growth in marketed surplus (relative to output), however, was not confined to cash crops alone since the rising level of trade (both internal and external) elicited increases in the marketed surplus for foodgrains as well. For most of the crops, output sold in the market was largely determined by the need, on the part of the cultivator, to obtain cash. The need to service old debt or to meet revenue demand in cash often explained the compelling circumstances where marketed agricultural surpluses, both for food and non-food output, was no longer determined by market incentives. Thus output was often hypothecated before the harvest against advances from moneylenders, grain dealers, or even from the landlords (economic functions of these three agents were often combined).[31] The exact terms of contract for the above-mentioned transactions naturally had a significant effect on the portion of output the cultivator was forced to part with. Thus no guarantee was there that the residual, left as disposable surplus, was at all adequate to meet the needs of subsistence, and the financing of working capital as well as fixed capital which were needed by the cultivator.

Organization of production in agriculture can never, under private property relations, remain independent of the legal and economic status of the actual cultivator. In Bengal presidency, which contributed the major share of exports from the country since the middle of the century, a wide-ranging differentiation of peasantry provided the background for the Act of 1859. The legislation sought to define the rights of occupancy ryots against rent enhancements and eviction with an implicit object of instilling a spirit of co-proprietorship in the agrarian sector. The step, however, proved self-defeating with uneven power relations in the countryside especially with the power enjoyed by the landlords on matters concerning litigation and extra-legal practice. No effective protection was provided to the ryot by the act, and an increasing differentiation of peasantry continued to prevail, as was observed later by the Rent Law Commission of Bengal in 1880. In the meantime rise in jute prices had brought into prominence the category of 'substantial ryots' in the jute growing belt—the intermediaries who could get perpetual lease from landlords by paying them bonus.[32] Contrary to what probably was anticipated by the government in terms of its ideas on co-proprietorship for ryots, very little was contributed by such peasants to 'dynamic enterprise'.[33] Describing the prosperous ryots who acquired a fortune through jute price increases, the Dacca Divisional Report of 1872–73 noted, with concern, '...a great many ryots have money to put by, though unfortunately instead of being invested, it is for the most part buried.'[34] In the Pabna Revolt of 1873–75, one notices a very clear instance of the growing power of the substantial ryots—intermediaries who could organize themselves against the landlords.[35] A relative prosperity for this class came with an intensification of subinfeudation in land resulting in a numerical increase and a material worsening of the 'under ryots'.[36] As could be anticipated, the pro-ryot stance of the 1859 act and the 1880 Rent Law Commission were virtually set aside in the 1885 act, removing the existing limits on rent enhancement and on the rights of occupancy ryots to sell land. The balance in land legislation thus tilted back, both in letter and spirit, towards a doctrine of 'high landlordism', with little realization that landlords or the intermediaries had, under the given circumstances, very little interest in improvement of cultivated land.[37]

In Bombay presidency, which represented the other high export region in India during the period, a similar pattern was evident, both in regard to differentiation of peasantry and the failure on the part of the richer sections to pioneer productive investment. Widespread indebtedness amongst the differentiated peasantry in the region was a cause of concern to the Deccan Riots Commission of 1875. Unlike the substantial peasant in the permanently settled areas of Bengal, the 'rich peasant' of the ryotwari region in Bombay presidency was not an intermediary. Instead he wielded legal land titles, vested on him by the state. Differentiation of peasantry in Bombay presidency led, by late nineteenth century, to the rise of the typical rich peasant who held, according to Charlesworth, the 'key to economic position', with independence and autonomy in the 'credit relationships as well as command over resources'.[38] 'Commercial activity' of the rich peasants also resulted in higher land prices, increased land transfers, and growth of cash crop cultivation in Maharashtra. These changes, according to Charlesworth, reflected a higher index of prosperity in the region.[39] The interpretation, in our view, ignores the very crucial distinction between commercial (or exchange) and production processes in the economy. Production visibly was at a low key, in spite of the increased level of commercial activity by rich peasants. This was evident in the stationary land yield for food and non-food crops alike in the Bombay-Sind area during 1890–1912—a mention of which has been made earlier.

It has been suggested that the changing economic scenario in Maharashtra countryside during late nineteenth century generated a financial climate which rendered money-lending or trading relatively more lucrative than productive investment in land. The situation curtailed the economic strength of the rich peasant relative to that wielded by the merchant moneylender, the Gujarati *vani* or the Marwaris.[40] It is, in our view, rather disputable whether the identity of the rich peasant was one which was separate from that of the money-lender or that of the trader. The amount of surplus earned was rather conveniently maximized by agents who had access to all three activities, and thus enjoyed a commanding status, for historical reasons, over poorer sections of the peasantry. It is thus possible to explain why the growing prosperity of landlords or the rise of the substantial ryots had very little effect on the level of agricultural productivity in the Bengal countryside. Indications of the prevailing rate of return on land transfers and on loan transactions are available, which reflect sharp increase in land prices (titles of land) in a growing land market and a steep upward movement in the rate of interest charged in the rural credit market. Purchase/subletting of land also became prestigious, with social status attached to land ownership in the rural society.[41]

In the rural economy of India, lending offered a lucrative channel for procuring the surpluses earned from agriculture. A common practice was to lend grains at prices suitably adjusted to the convenience of the lender. Paddy advances were offered in Bengal villages, at interest rates ranging from 150 to 312 per cent in the prosperous district of Jessore during the 1870s, while repayment in grain used to take place in the post harvest months when their prices were the lowest.[42] Cash was advanced at interest rates varying between 24 and 37 per cent in the Nadia district of Bengal, as observed in the famous Duffrin Report of 1888.[43] 'Small loans offered without security commanded 30–37 per cent interest in Bengal, as observed by the Famine Enquiry Commission (FEC) of 1881.[44] In the Bankura district of Bengal, the rate of interest was observed to vary between 9 and 36 per cent in 1908, depending on the nature of security advanced as collateral.[45] Evidences were submitted, to the Industrial Commission of 1916–18, on the prevailing interest rates, the monthly rate of which was as high as 10 annas per rupee in Bengal.[46] Prospects of money-lending turned out to be all the more lucrative under the prevailing legal system. Thus '...by facilitating the recovery of debts and by making bonds, mortgages and negotiable instruments as secure as gold, the law established an atmosphere of trust and confidence which permitted a quick allocation of resources to every type of business which showed some signs of promise'. Every bond under the system of ex-parte decree was as good as a writ and '...the debtor condemned himself if he did not honour it'.[47]

Profits on trade relating to grain or cash crop provided, as mentioned earlier, an alternative source of income to those engaged in commodity trade. Attention may be drawn to records of prices especially of foodgrains, the movements in which provided ample opportunities to sell at a profit during years of scarcity. Retail price for rice went up in the Bilaspore district of Central Provinces as rice, sold at 80 *seers* per rupee in 1863, fell to 8 *seers* per rupee by 1898. Between 1895 and 1898 rice sold per rupee fell from 18 to 7$\frac{1}{2}$ seers in the same district.[48] It is not difficult to prove that grain dealers enjoyed higher profit rates as foodgrain prices went up by steeper margins in the interior areas, especially during the famine years.[49] Export agencies, controlled by Europeans, were in collaboration with indigenous grain dealers in the 'up country', sharing the 'loot' which came about through price increases.[50] It was admitted by grain dealers in Bengal that profits in grain trade were much higher during the 1896–98 famine, with expansions in the level of stocks with indigenous dealers.[51] Extension of railway network in the country led to higher profits in grain trade, as pointed out by Rev. J. J. Lohr, a North American Missionary, in his evidence to the FEC of 1898.[52] The level of profits was considerably protected by monopoly of traders, as admitted by traders themselves.[53] In terms of the data furnished by James Edward O'Connor, the director-general of statistics in India, food prices rose by more than 100 per cent during the famine of 1896–98.[54] Fluctuations in prices provided, in general, an opportunity to earn high profits on part of traders, rendering speculation more profitable than before. Thus both usury and trade (in agricultural crops) provided profitable channels of investment, reducing the prospects of further investment in land. (The latter by definition included yield-raising expenditure only. Purchases of land titles, which, as indicated in the record of land transfers, were considerable during the period, cannot, thus, be treated as investment in land. We do not enter into the details of these land transfers which, in our view, constitutes one more dimension of the process of commercialization in agriculture.)[55]

If landlords, the intermediaries, or the rich peasants were not inclined towards investment in land, logically it fell entirely on the cultivators to initiate the process. It is not difficult to conclude, looking at the various claims on the produce of the cultivator (which included rent, profit margin of traders, and interest on advances) that options left to him were not too many. One can cite some instances of the exhorbitant land rent on the peasant, both in the ryotwari and the permanent settlement areas, during the second half of nineteenth century. Layers of surpluses, extracted as rent, were appropriated by the intermediaries on land who were numerically larger in the relatively prosperous areas. Thus, in the Backergunj district of East Bengal, as many as twenty categories of intermediaries are reported in a recent study.[56] In Rangpur—one of the relatively prosperous districts of Bengal—20 per cent of the value of rice harvested in 1874 was used by the peasant to meet cost of rent alone, as pointed out in a contemporary's report.[57] Another contemporary, writing on the same region pointed out, '...when the jotedar pays Rs. 100, he collects Rs. 200 from actual cultivators', thus making the intermediary margin exactly 100 per cent of the revenue paid.[58] While revenue paid was officially fixed, under the permanent settlement at 9/10 of rental, in practice it be came a much smaller proportion of local land rent exacted. Sharing of output between the tenant cultivator and the landlord or the intermediaries was dependent on the economic status of the former. In Bengal, around 1880, the share going to the peasant varied between 25–50 per cent of output under the *auggaira*, *adhihali*, or *barga* system of tenurial relations.[59] By 1911 concentration in land is observed to be rather high in the region, with the number of owner-cultivators and tenants more than 20 times the number of rent receivers, as estimated in the census data. As is expected, the official records on rent collected understated the actual amount extracted by the landlords and the intermediaries by using legal as well as extra-legal channels. Data on produce rent in Bengal[60] around 1910 indicated a general picture where 50 to 75 per cent share of produce was reserved for the superior land holders, with the exact share depending on the terms of contract.[61] Several researchers pointed out that rent paid in cash, while similarly high, induced additional burdens on the cultivator as he was brought into the cash nexus.[62]

Economic conditions of the 'Lower classes of population', reflecting the status of an average ryot, became a subject of concern in the different official and private enquiries by

Table 4.10: Cost of Living index for 'Lower Classes of Population in Bengal': 1885–1913.

Year	Total expenses*	Index (Base-Average expense 1880–84)
1885	3.54	117.76
1886	3.36	111.77
1887	2.80	93.14
1888	2.97	98.80
1889	3.81	126.74
1890	3.87	128.74
1891	3.54	117.76
1892	4.27	142.04
1893	4.43	143.37
1894	4.49	149.36
1895	3.49	116.10
1896	4.25	149.70
1897	5.66	188.29
1898	4.45	148.03
1899	3.66	121.75
1900	4.14	137.72
1901	4.51	150.03
1902	4.68	155.80
1903	3.98	132.40
1904	3.89	129.40
1905	3.88	129.07
1906	4.78	159.01
1907	7.10	236.19
1908	7.17	238.52
1909	6.59	219.22
1910	4.51	150.03
1911	4.68	155.68
1912	5.96	181.63

* Expenses include the rupee cost of 1 *maund* of rice (equivalent to 82 3/7 lbs.) and 10 *seers* (1 20 3/5 lbs.) of grams. The above is assumed to reflect the monthly expenses of two average adults and one child.

Source: Price data relate to unit prices of Ballam rice quoted in Calcutta and the national average for grams—*Statistical Abstracts of British India*. Data on average rice consumption per adult: 'Report on the Lower Classes of Population in Bengal' Calcutta 1888, submitted by P. Nolan, Secretary, Govt. of Bengal to Secretary, Revenue and Agriculture Department, Government of India.

contemporaries. In a report submitted in 1888 by P. Nolan, secretary, Government of Bengal, it was pointed out that the minimum annual expenses for an average ryot family (two adults and one child) could be met through the average returns from an eleven acre holding.[63] The estimates were based on a survey of four villages in West Bengal, where the average size of land holdings was between 4 $\frac{1}{2}$ and 6 acres—a fact which clearly indicates a sub-subsistence level of existence for the poorer ryots. The report points to a letter, written by a government official in Bengal which goes as follows: '...of the poorer cultivators and labouring classes, ...it does not appear that they have been able to do much more than live even in good years, and there can be no doubt that they have no reserve to fall back upon in bad years.'[64] It is thus not surprising that a private memorandum was submitted to the government pointing at the deteriorating condition of an average ryot in 1892.[65] Decline in average level of living during the period also gets reflected in the observed decline in real wages of agricultural workers between late nineteenth century and the First World War.[66] Using official data on retail prices of commodities, we have constructed a weighted cost-of-living index for an average poor family surviving during the period (Table 4.10). There took place, over the period, a steady decline in the standard of living of an average family consisting of two adults and one child, as indicated in the rising cost of their standard consumption basket per month computed in Table 4.10. Price data available at the district level have been used to compute the rising cost of the consumption basket, comprising 1 *maund* of rice and 10 *seers* of gram for each adult. No commensurate increase, as can be comprehended from the general impression, took place in money wages of unskilled workers during the period.

In the report submitted by Nolan, the different claims on output contributed by an average ryot on a five-acre holding were documented as follows:

Total annuual value of produce on farm land	Rs.	252	*annas* 8
Plus female income	Rs.	12	
Less expenditure on food and other necessities which includes 2lbs of rice and 20 gms of gram per day and fuel, salt, oil	Rs.	120	
Less clothing	Rs.	15	
Less outgoings on wages of farm labour and rent	Rs.	47	
Net income	Rs.	82	*annas* 8

Given the various contractual obligations the cultivator normally had to meet on account of past debt,[67] the situation amounted to one where the cushion left for the cultivator was too thin to allow even subsistence, and definitely far short of a capacity to invest. Putting together the different claims on the peasant's income, one can think of a stylized situation where a typical ryot had to pay 70 out of a total of 100 units of output produced as rent and other expenses. Of the remaining 30, a large share went to money-lenders, as the ryot was forced to borrow at interest rates which were higher than rental rates. It might further be incumbent on the ryot to repay old debt with fresh borrowings in each period. This left a margin for the cultivator which was not large enough for his own consumption, let alone investment. As pointed out in a study, under the typical conditions which prevailed during the period, even a bumper crop provided little relief to the cultivator who often was forced to sell at post-harvest prices. (Thus a bumper crop actually depressed the prices, reducing crop revenue.)[68]

Our analysis of the growth-inhibiting forces and a lack of material improvement for the peasantry in colonial India would remain incomplete if we do not bring into the picture the influence of the ruling state, the role of which was certainly far from neutral. As it has already been pointed out, it was far beyond the immediate priorities of the ruling state to implement a land system in India which would have removed the obstacles to investment in land. The Act of 1859 of Bengal presidency, later incorporated as Tenancy Act VIII of 1885, did very little beyond providing a legal definition of the occupancy ryot. Thus '...the legal status of the occupancy ryot was not necessarily connected with the act of cultivation' as was observed by the Rent Law Commission of 1880.[69] Rather the legislation, according to observers, provided security to the money-lenders against the loans advanced.[70] Land legislation, as noted earlier, tilted in favour of zamindars with the Bengal Tenancy Act of 1885. A passive attitude of the state towards initiating and implementing progressive land legislation was coupled by a similar official stance on the question of indebtedness amongst the peasantry. We may mention in the above context, the Alienation of Land Act and the annual reports on it for 1901–03. However, legal clauses on the right of pre-emption, alienation of the peasantry, and the number of land transfers could not control the tendency, prevalent amongst money-lenders and the 'richer agriculturists' to throw out the indebted peasants from their landholdings.[71]

While increase in foodgrain prices (especially in inferior varieties) brought in hardship and economic distress, the government was keen on maintaining an apparent neutrality on questions of trade. Thus virtually no restrictions were imposed on movement of foodgrains, even during the famine years of 1896–98 or 1907–09. In their evidence to the Famine Commission of 1898, the European traders were in support of the official attitude regarding trade, which naturally allowed higher profit margins during years of scarcities. 'I think the system of providing money for relief works, and leaving trade to furnish the grain was the most effective and the most economical which could have been adopted.'[72] Even the onset of famines did not lead the government to revise its opinion, as is evident in the following extract from the Famine Commission Report of 1880: 'We have no doubt that the true principle for the government to adopt as its general rule of conduct...is to leave the supply and distribution of food to private trade, taking care that every possible facility is given for its free action.'[73] We draw attention at this point to a rather historic communication between the Lieutenant-Governor of Bengal, Sir G. Campbell, and the Viceroy of India, Lord Northbrook, which took place during the famine of 1873 on questions connected with a ban on rice exports from India. Requests from the lieutenant-governor for a stoppage of rice export in view of a crop shortfall in Bengal was rejected by the viceroy who considered it '... improper to dearrange trade by stopping exports'. The latter sought to justify his action by pointing out that while exports of 'table rice' (the superior varieties), which comprised $\frac{1}{6}$ of the Bengal's rice exports '...was not suited for consumptions of ordinary people', they provided '...the growers the means which they require in order to provide themselves with cheaper varieties of food'; '...the remaining common rice exports were meant for the consumption of Bengal coolies in other colonies' (like Ceylon, Mauritius, and West Indies) and '...should not be interfered upon'.[74] The attitude of complacency towards the famine question in India continued to prevail amongst British administrators, as was revealed by the various witnesses to the Famine Commission of 1898.[75] Exports of rice continued from Bengal, Madras, and Burma, and the flow was unabated, according to statistics released by O'Connor in 1898,[76] during the famine years of 1896–98. The government was explicitly in favour of using the allocational norms of the market and viewed with disfavour any scheme of bypassing or disrupting this. '...The activity of private trade has been sufficient to distribute existing stocks so as to make good the deficiency in the out turn of the affected tracts, and food has always been purchasable and in some remote places at excessively high prices.... Private trade, we find, proved itself able to regulate the supply of food throughout India.' The above arguments advanced by the 1898 Famine Commission seem to be based on the 1881 Famine Commission's estimate regarding surplus foodgrains stock, at 5.1 million ton. The Famine Commission of 1899 revised upwards the estimate of Holderness—a government official. 'The surplus produce of India', according to the Commission, '... taken as a whole, still furnishes ample means of meeting the demands of any part of the country likely to suffer from famine at any one time', while conceding, that '...No doubt the high prices led to great and often painful economy of consumption'.[77] The above views held by British administrators in India on the efficacious market principle certainly reflected the contemporary ethos on the role of the market as the *deus ex machina*. In the context of a colonial economy the attitude was further conditioned by the fact that surplus grains (or other crops) exports provided, in addition to the home charges, profit in export trade, a business which was largely in control of the Europeans. No amount of starvation or death during famine years could, thus, weaken the supreme confidence of the government on the invisible hands of both the free market and of its agents which included the European and the indigenous traders. It was thus convenient for the British administrators to rely on the *laissez faire* doctrine, revived under the influence of utilitarians in England, especially in order to justify their complacency during the famine. Food prices, according to such views, always reached the level which was warranted by the forces of the market. The role of prices was to clear the market, and food 'available' (but unsold) at high prices in certain areas was thus 'justifiably' diverted to destinations, including foreign land, where those could be sold. Ample indications were found that foodgrains were available but unsold during the famine years. Several witnesses to the Famine Commissions, including the

European missionaries, pointed at a lack of purchasing power in the face of available supplies in the market.[78] Availability was no guarantee to an entitlement of food, which was influenced, amongst other things, by the buying power of the purchasers.[79] Thus market availability of foodgrains, which apparently rules out a scarcity situation, confirmed, in the above situation, a famine—an aspect conveniently overlooked by the British administrators in India.[80] In the more recent studies on the controversial role of foodgrain exports from colonial India, attention has been drawn to the possible stabilizing role of trade in the context of domestic consumption.[81]

Thus the ruling government in colonial India was, on principle, opposed to the idea of interfering with free market and the channels of trade even under the worst possible famine situation. Voices, however, were raised from different quarters within the economy which demanded positive steps on part of the government. Messers Gillander Arbuthnot and Company, traders in foodgrains from Calcutta, suggested (in their evidence to the Famine Commission of 1898) a ban on foodgrain export and a direct intervention on part of the government on import trade in foodgrains. Both were recommended as measures to curb prices at home.[82] According to Rev. Pelvot, a missionary, direct import of grains by the government could be of much help in alleviating price rise in the country during the famine of 1896–98.[83] Even a grain dealer from Calcutta, Brijraj, conceded that imports of Burma rice did help prices during the same famine and that '...government imports would have helped even more'.[84] Attention was directed, in certain quarters, to the possible negative effects of the newly expanding railroad and telegraphic network in the country. As argued sarcastically by an administrator from a native state '...In former famines only disjointed local areas were affected.... Now railways made it possible that we were starved to death as well as our neighbours.'[85] Even an indigenous grain dealer of Calcutta was ready to concede that '...Prices rose throughout India during this famine largely due to operation of railways. In the previous (1878) famine there was little movement of crops due to good harvests in some parts. In this famine bad harvest is also equally spread'. Spread of telegraphs, according to the grain dealer, '...helped merchants in keeping up prices throughout India.'[86]

Witnesses to the Famine Commission, drawn from an

unusually wide spectrum of society, included many Indians who were emphatic in pointing at the absolute and relative decline in the standard of living of the poorer sections of the country. 'A slow rise or no rise in prices of goods consumed by wealthier classes of people coupled with a sudden and continuous rise in prices of the grains consumed by the poor', was observed, along with 'large scale sales of jewellery and ornaments'.[87] The Famine Commission of 1898 came to a rather startling set of conclusions, especially when contrasted to the standard official view on the famine question. The following lines are worth quoting:

> The rise in prices...led to a considerable increase in the landholding and cultivating classes...and...in view of their standard of living and expenditure.... Beyond these (upper) classes there always has existed, and there still exists, a lower section of the community living a hand to mouth existence with a low standard of comfort, and abnormally sensitive to the effects of inferior harvests and calamities of season.... Wages of these people have not risen in the last twenty years in due proportion to the rise in prices of their necessaries of life... We may take this opportunity of remarking that in the evidence given before us many witnesses proved that in times of scarcity and famines in India the rise in prices of food is not accompanied by a rise in the wages of labour; on the contrary, owing to competition for the little employment available when agricultural employment falls off, the rate of wages offered and accepted is frequently below the ordinary or customary rate. Such wages in terms of famine prices are *not* subsistence wages for a labourer with dependents to support.[88]

Recommending an extension of relief works as a measure to increase temporary employment opportunities, the Famine Commission of 1899 came out with a rather progressive suggestion that remuneration on relief work should be set at a rate which was higher than the market rate, given that the market rate was below subsistence. Little attention, however, was given to the dietary implications of the relief rates which were often inferior to the jail diet.[89] Relief expenditure remained as the sole official response to the declines in levels of living thus ignoring the long-standing nature of the problem.

Worsened conditions for the poor were also indirectly evident in the nature of goods exported and imported by the country.

A large proportion of the value of the country's exports of commodities was utilized to import gold and silver primarily to meet the demand for coinage and also for hoarding within the country. Of the remainder, an average of 11 per cent was utilized to meet the demand for imports, the composition of which very closely reflected the demand coming from the richer sections of the community. Thus, cotton textiles and sugar alone comprised more than 50 per cent of total imports during the period which included, in addition, silk and woollens.[90] As for the composition of exports, the falling share of foodgrains in total crop output in the domestic economy was matched by a rise in the relative proportion of foodgrains in total exports, which, by 1890, was already 16 per cent of the total exports.[91] This explains the decline in the food availability figures relating to high export regions (e.g. Bengal) as a result of trade, as mentioned earlier. Bengal, however, remained a net importer of foodgrains *vis-a-vis* other regions within the country—a fact which *pari passu* implied a decline in availability for the rest of the country which also experienced a perceptible fall in the output growth. Such developments clearly were of least concern to the British officials in India, with their emphasis on fulfilling the immediate goal of administering the revenue targets set for the country. The rise in trade and its achieving the export surplus were, from the above angle, legitimately viewed with an optimism which spoke of their imperial alignments.

Notes

1. See S.J. Patel, 'Long-term Trends in Output and National Income', *Indian Economic Journal*, 1958. George Blyn, *Agricultural Trends in India, 1891–1947: Output, Availability and Productivity*, Philadelphia, 1966.
2. Adams and Craig, 'Prices in Nineteenth Century India', *Journal of Economic History*, 1979.
3. N.K. Thingalaya, 'A Century of Prices in India', *EPW*, 25 July 1969.
   Statistical Abstract of British India.
   See Michele B. McAlpin, 'Price Movements and Fluctuations in Economic Activity', in Dharma Kumar ed., *Cambridge Economic History of India, c. 1757–c. 1950*, Orient Longman, Delhi, p. 879.
4. George Blyn, *Agricultural Trends*, p. 253.

5. Ibid., p. 251.
6. The price indices were constructed with base at 1873 while the fixed weights related to 1953. The method followed by Thingalaya is not ideally suited for a comparison of price variations over time. In absence of detailed statistics relating to appropriate weights for 1873, we use, as a second-best series, Thingalaya's indices, following McAlpin in this regard.
7. K.L. Datta, *Report on the Enquiry into the Rise of Prices in India*, 5 Vols, Calcutta, 1914.
8. We have analysed, in the following pages, further evidence on tendency for increases in the relative price of inferior foodgrains during famines. *See*, in particular, evidence of James Edward O'Connor, director-general of statistics to the Famine Commission of 1899, East India (India) Reports of Commissioners, *Report of the Famine Commission and Evidences*, 1899, Vol. XXXIII c 9255, pp. 515–17. Data on sectoral price trends are also provided in Datta, *Prices in India*, Vol. II and Arun K. Ghosh, *An Analysis of Indian Price Structure from 1861*, Ph. D. thesis submitted to the London University in September 1949, pp. 52–63.
9. We draw attention at this point to the conclusions arrived at by the K.L. Datta Committee, mentioned above, that exports did help the cultivators in India, especially of crops including jute, cotton, oilseeds, and also wheat, probably by fetching higher prices in overseas markets. *See* K. L. Datta, *Prices in India*, Vol. I, pp. 128; 136–7, 139–40.
10. F.J. Atkinson, 'Rupee Prices in India, 1870–1908', *Journal of the Royal Statistical Society*, September 1909, pp. 496–576. *See also* F.J. Atkinson, 'Silver Prices in India', *Journal of the Royal Statistical Society*, March 1897 and March 1903.
11. F.J. Atkinson, 'Rupee Prices', 1909.
12. Ibid., pp. 565–6. See also Table. 3.8.
13. Adams and Craig, 'Prices in India', 1979.
14. The above observation relating to effects of railways on prices can be contrasted to the alternate view that railroads, by bringing in higher prices and commercialization, initiated productivity improvements in agricultural land cultivated. McAlpin, 'Impact of Trade on Agricultural Development: Bombay Presidency 1855–1920', *Explorations in Economic Hisotry*, Vol. 17, No. 1, 1980, pp. 32–3.
15. Adams and Craig, 'Prices in India', 1979.
16. Compound rates of growth (annual) relating to India's exports have been calculated as:

1834–35	to	1850–51	...	3.61	per cent
1851–52	to	1860–61	...	6.31	per cent
1861–62	to	1870–71	...	1.37	per cent
1871–72	to	1880–81	...	2.37	per cent
1881–82	to	1890–91	...	2.52	per cent

1891–92	to	1900–01	...	no	trade
1901–02	to	1910–11	...	4.80	per cent
1911–12	to	1920–21	...	3.00	per cent
1921–22	to	1930–31	...	–1.20	per cent

See K. N. Chaudhuri, 'Foreign Trade and Balance of Payments' in Dharma Kumar ed., *Cambridge Economic History*, p. 832.

17. McAlpin (1983) in Dharma Kumar ed., *Cambridge Economic History*
18. Ibid., p. 891.
19. K.N. Chaudhuri, 'Foreign Trade' in Dharma Kumar ed., *Cambridge Economic History*, pp. 812, 852–3.
20. N.K. Chandra, 'Long Term Stagnation in the Indian Economy', *EPW*, Annual Number, 1983, p. 519.
21. Foodgrains contributed to more than three-fourths of the value of agricultural output during 1900–1914, measured at 1928–29 set of prices. *See* Table 4.7.
22. A.K. Bagchi, *Private Investment in India 1900–1939*, New Delhi, 1975, p. 95.
23. George Blyn, *Agricultural Trends*, p. 288.
24. Mention may be made at this point of McAlpin's observations that in Bombay presidency there took place a rise in per capita sown area over 1891–1901—a phenomenon which, according to her, can be identified as a rise in 'intensity of cultivation', or in the index of agricultural prosperity. The author also observes an absolute and relative increase in cultivated area for cotton and for the 'high value' food crops, rice and wheat. All three commodities had a good market abroad—a fact which led the author to conclude that trade as well as extension of railways (the transport factor) contributed to output expansion in Bombay presidency area during the period. The rise in the 'intensity of cultivation' or in man/land ratio did fit in, according to the author, with a situation, where the well-off peasants were confronted with a 'utility maximizing function'. They were substituting leisure by work in response to favourable price movements.

    Observations relating to the rise in land/man ratio in Bombay presidency can be interpreted, in our judgement, by the perceptible declines in population as happened over 1891–1901 (see George Blyn, *Agicultural Trends*, p. 326). It is, however, difficult to accept as to why 'intensity of cultivation' should be defined in terms of labour available to cultivate units of land, especially when the latter was the scarce factor of production. Instead, it is far more instructive to proceed with conventional yield statistics, defined as output per unit of land. The latter, as indicated earlier, hardly responded to the pace of commercialization in agriculture. (Recall the fall in yield rate for cotton over 1896–1916 and the fact that most of it was grown in the Bombay–Sind area). We also have reservations in accepting the utility-maximizing postulate of McAlpin with its constraints which identify the status of the farmer with that of a rich peasant. It is also debatable to what extent the 'rich farmers' of the high export regions were responding to the brightened export prospects by introducing yield-raising innovations—a point we take up later. On the whole, increases in man/land ratio which came about in Bombay presidency because of de-population during the nineteenth century famines signified, instead, a pauperization process in the region. *See* McAlpin, 1980, p. 35.

25. *See* George Blyn, *Agricultural Trends*, pp. 327–8 for statistics.
26. Binoy Chaudhuri, 'Agrarian Economy and Agrarian Relations in Bengal', in N.K. Sinha ed., *History of Bengal, 1757–1905*, p. 247.
27. *See* Appendix, Table 5E in George Blyn, *Agricultural Trends*.
28. Excluding cotton textiles, the ratio was around 18 per cent. *Statistical Abstracts of British India* cited in Latham, *India and the International Economy*, p. 78.
29. It has been observed that price elasticity of substitution in cultivation between jute and rice were higher during 1905–06 to 1920–21 than during the earlier or later years. This indicates a considerable switchover in area cropped in the direction of jute, the acreage of which increased relatively over the period. *See* Saugata Mukherjee, 'Some Aspects of Commercialisation of Agriculture in Eastern India: 1891–1938' in Ashok Sen et al., *Perspectives in Social Sciences*, 2, Calcutta 1982, pp. 262–3. *See*, in addition, Table 4.5 for relative acreage figures for jute and rice. Also see Binoy Chaudhuri, *Growth of Commercial Agriculture in Bengal (1757– 1900)*, Vol. I, Calcutta, 1964.
30. M. McAlpin, in *Cambridge Economic History*, 1983, p. 885.
31. *See* Krishna Bharadwaj, *Production Conditions in Indian Agriculture*, Cambridge, 1974.
    Amit Bhaduri, 'A Study of Agricultural Backwardness under Semi-Feudalism', *Economic Journal*, March, 1973.
32. *See* for the facts and the arguments used in the paragraph and also for an excellent analysis of land legislation in late nineteenth century Bengal, Ashok Sen, *Perspectives*, pp. 11, 15, 16, 17, 21.
33. Ibid., pp. 17–28.
34. Ibid., p. 16.
35. Ibid., p. 18.
36. Ibid., p. 19.
37. Ibid., p. 27.
38. Neil Charlesworth, 'Rich Peasants and Poor Peasants in Late Nineteenth Century Maharashtra', in Cline Dewey and A.G. Hopkins ed., *The Imperial Impact: Studies in the Economic History of Africa and India*, London, 1978, p. 102.
39. Neil Charlesworth, 'Rich Peasants' in Hopkins ed., *Imperial Impact*, p. 107.

40. Satish C. Mishra, 'Commercialisation, Peasant Differentiation and Merchant Capital in Late Nineteenth Century Bombay and Punjab', *Journal of Peasant Studies*, 1982.
41. Binoy Chaudhuri, *Commercial Agriculture*, p. 31.
42. *Report on Agricultural Statistics for four districts in Jessore during 1873–74*, cited in Ashok Sen, *Perspectives*, p. 33.
43. Ibid., p. 39
44. Ibid., p. 41.
45. Rate of interest charged ranged between 9–12 per cent against immovable property, 12–18 per cent for small loans against pawns, 18–24 per cent for large loans on movable property, 18–36 per cent on petty loans to cultivators and 25 per cent on grain advances, see L.S.S. O'Maley, *Bengal District Gazetteers: Bankura*, Vol. XIV, Calcutta, 1908, pp. 108–9.
46. Evidence of Babu S.K. Das of Akalia, *Industrial Commission* 1916–18, Vol. XVIII, Calcutta, p. 483.
47. Dietmar Rothermundt, *Government, Landlord and Peasant in India: Agrarian Relations Under British Rule, 1865–1935*, Wiesbaden, 1978, p. 17.
48. Evidence of F.J. Cooke, deputy commissioner of Bilaspore. *See* East India (India) Reports of Commissioners: *Report of the Famine Enquiry Commission and Evidences* (FEC), 1899, Vol. XXXIII, c9255, pp. 95–6.
49. An agent from Ralli Brothers, which was a leading grain exporter was put the following question: 'When the high prices prevailed, did these cultivators who had grains to sell to the dealers, get prices as proportionately higher than usual, as those the grain dealers were selling at?' The agent replied '... cultivators were selling at little below market and dealers were benefitted by the rise in the market', *See FEC*, Minutes of Evidence, p. 104.
50. 'The largest export houses have many up country agents in the interior, who place contracts for purchases of grain for exports with native grain dealers'. Evidence from Ralli Brothers, cited in note (53), *FEC*, (1898) 1899, p. 104.
51. Evidence, 11 March 1898, *FEC*, 1898, p. 104.
52. Evidence by Rev. J. J. Lohr, *FEC, 1898*.
53. See evidence by Gurdayal, grain dealer of Calcutta, 25 January 1898, *FEC Report* 1899, p. 23.
'...Was there any ring and combination among grain dealers to keep prices high?' Babu Prabodh Chandra Chaudri (Messrs Dutt and Mitra, Produce Brokers of Calcutta).
'...Yes there was, in Calcutta market. The dealers said they could sell things daily at a fixed rate and simply follow each other... (with) information from the growing districts and chief producers', *FEC* 1899, 21–2.
54. *FEC*, 1899, pp. 515–17.

55 See Amit Bhaduri, 'The Evolution of Land Relations in Eastern India Under British Rule', *Indian Economic and Social History Review*, March, 1976.

56. Tapan Roychaudhury, 'Permanent Settlements in Operation: Backergunj, East Bengal', in R.E. Frykenberg ed., *Land Control and Social Structure in Indian History*, Madison, 1969.

57. McDonnel's Report on Foodgrains Supply and Famine Relief 1874, cited in Ashok Sen, *Perspectives*, pp. 60–1.

58. Glaziers Report on Rangpur-1876, cited in Ashok Sen, *Perspectives*, p. 23.

59. See, for details of the land systems, Ashok Sen, *Perspectives*, p. 33. '*Auggaira*' and '*adhihali*' respectively indicate rent paid in advance and rent paid at one half of cultivator's share.

60. In Bankura district produce rent fixed for the superior cultivator was at 3/4 of produce when cattle, plough and seed-crop were provided by the landlord, and 1/2 of produce when the inputs came from the tenant. In the Burdwan district the cultivator was to provide inputs against 1/2 of produce paid out as rent. Forms of under-tenure were subject to labour contracts in Birbhum where rent was fixed at (*a*) 1/2 of output plus straw from the field, as the ryot supplied inputs to the *kishan* or the under ryot. This system was known as *ardhabhag jot*; (*b*) 18/40 went as rent to ryot, and the remainder left for the *kishan* under what was known as *baisha jot*; (*c*) 3/5 of output and 4/5 of straw to the ryot as rent who has to provide, under the *pancha ardha bhag jot*, manure to the *kishan*; (*d*) fixed rent of *thika jot* which was fixed in advance and without reference to terms of contract. See *Bengal District Gazetteers*, L.S.S. O'Maley, *Bankura*, Calcutta, 1908, pp. 101–2, J.C.K. Peterson, *Burdwan*, Calcutta, 1910, pp. 108–9, and L.S.S. O'Maley, *Birbhum*, Calcutta 1910. p. 64.

61. Ibid.

62. Need to pay cash rent pressurized the cultivator to sell part of his produce at post-harvest price when it was the lowest. In case the proceeds were inadequate to meet the cash demand for rent and other needs of the cultivators, the latter got into debt at terms which further downgraded his economic status. See *Bengal District Gazetteers*.

63. P. Nolan, *Report on the Lower Classes of Population in Bengal*, Calcutta, 1888.

64. Letter of C.J.S. Faulder, collector, Birbhum District, to Burdwan division commissioner, 30 May 1888, cited in P. Nolan, *Report on Lower Classes*.

65. Memorandum on 'Material Conditions of Lower order in Bengal' by F.H.B. Skrine, 1892, cited in *Bengal District Gazetteers*: J.C.K. Peterson, Burdwan, p. 114.

66. *See* in particular, K. Mukherji, 'Levels of Living of Industrial Workers', and Jurgen Kuczynski, 'Condition of Workers (1880–1950), in V.B. Singh ed., *Economic History of India*, New Delhi, 1975, pp. 609, 660.
67. Average indebtedness of cultivators in Dholla district, according to Nolan, was at Rs. 150, which again was the same as two years of their net income. P. Nolan, *Report on Lower Classes*.
68. Arun Ghosh, 'Cyclical Trends in Indian Agriculture 1861–1913', *Indian Economic and Social History Review*, Vol. IV, 1967, pp. 177–201.
69. Binoy Chaudhuri, *Commercial Agriculture*, p. 266.
70. Ashok Sen, *Perspectives*, p. 19.
71. *See* Dietmar Rothermundt, *Government, Landlords, and Peasants in India*, pp. 58–85, and especially p. 79 for a historical account of the failure of state legislation to control indebtedness and land alienation among the agriculturists.
72. Evidence by Robert Steel, ex-president, Bengal Chamber of Commerce on 19 January 1898, *FEC*, 1899, pp. 11–12.
73. *FEC*, 1899, p. 355.
74. Letter of lieutenant-governor of Bengal, 17 November 1873; reply of the viceroy 12 November 1873, and minute by the viceroy on 30 January. *Report of the Indian Famine Commission*, 1885, c 3086, p. 124. Account and Papers, 1874, Vol. I, pp. 51, 54–5.
75. *See*, for an exception, the following: 'Of India as a whole it may be said with certainty that the food supply easily provides for the entire population under all known circumstances, and that in the late Bengal famine the export continued without any great diminution in spite of the local failure of crops'. Lecture delivered by Lieutenant-General R. Strachey on 18 May 1881, cited in *Report on the Famine commission*, 1881, c 3086, Appendix I.
76. During 1896–97 exports of rice amounted to 1.4 million cwt from British India excluding Burma and 25.8 million cwt from Burma. Of the latter, 6.5 million cwt were directed to British India, thus reducing the export figure (from Burma alone) to 19.3 million cwt. *Famine Enquiry Commission reports*, XXXII, 1899, pp. 3, 6.
77. *FEC*, 1899, pp. 356, 359.
78. '...By all means there was no lack of grain in their respective districts but their price was enormously high. The poor received no more alms and others had managed to live only a short period by the sale of their implement, jewels and very clothes. All had been compelled by sheer destitution and starvation to emigrate to other districts and to betake themselves to railway stations and chief centres in the hope of finding the necessaries of life'. Evidence given by Rev. Pelvot of Nagpur Roman Catholic Church to the Famine Enquiry Commission, *FEC*, 1899, pp. 15–16. Again, 'Grain could always be bought if a person has money to offer for

it'. Evidence of Rev. J.J. Lohr, North American Missionary in Raipur, *FEC*, 1899, p. 104.

79. *See* for a general understanding of the famine syndrome in terms of a distinction between direct entitlement right of food purchases, determined by initial endowment and other factors and trade-determined entitlement right, influenced by the price of food in terms of other commodities, Amartya Sen, *Poverty and Famines*, Delhi, 1981, pp. 45–51.
80. *See*, as a contrast, and for a general characterization of famine situations, 'Starvation is the characterisation of some people not having enough food to eat. It is not the characteristic of others being not given enough food to eat', Amartya Sen, *Poverty and Famines*, p.1.
81. Martin Ravallion, 'Trade and Stabilization: Another look at British India's Controversial Food Exports', *Explorations in Economic History*, 1986.
82. Evidence given by Gillander and Arbuthnot Company, grain dealers of Calcutta, *FEC*, 1899, p. 15.
83. Evidence given by Rev. Pelvot, *FEC*, 1899.
84. Evidence of Brijraj, Grain Dealer to *FEC*, 1899, p. 23.
85. Evidence given by Khan Bahadur Maulana Md. Hussein, diwan of Khairagarh, Central Province, *FEC*, 1899, pp. 105–8.
86. Evidence given by Kewal Chand, Calcutta agent, Seth Lachmandas, grain dealer, *FEC*, 1899, p. 22.
87. Evidence by Khan Bahadur Maulana Md. Hussein, *FEC*, 1899, pp. 105–6.
88. *FEC*, 1899.
89. See as a supportive evidence, Major J.L. Poyander, civil surgeon of Raipur, '...from a dietary point of view the diet for famine relief workers and minimum ration is inferior to the jail diet', *FEC*, 1899, pp. 115–18.
90. *Statistical Abstract of British India.*
91. Ibid.

CHAPTER 5

On Perspectives

The theoretical backdrop given in Chapter 1, on the specificities of the themes available in the literature on the empire–colony relations, and the analysis made in the subsequent three chapters of the pattern and the impact of colonial expropriations in India during 1890–1914, have prepared the stage for arriving at our concluding observations. We offer in the present chapter, the conclusions in the form of broad perspectives. For convenience, these broad perspectives, provided in Sections 5.1 to 5.3 can be divided into the following themes: (*a*) significance of the colonies in the British imperial system; (*b*) role of colonies as sources of surplus in the specific context of India between 1890 and 1914; (*c*) analogy between neo-colonies and the old forms of empire which seem to have in common similar tendencies for surplus appropriation, their utilization within the country, and transfers from the domestic economies which have largely remained stagnant. Our aim is to provide the reader, at end of this chapter, a broad idea of the issues raised in this volume, both as a study of colonial India in the historical context of the British empire, and as an approach towards an understanding of the international perspectives of the historical process of underdevelopment.

5.1 Colonies in the British empire

In the literature on British overseas trade and investment, divergent views prevail on the role of the empire in terms of the gains/losses it fetched to the ruling country.[1] While emphasis has been laid on external trade and investment as sources of profit, the analysis tends to overlook, in our judgement, the political context of British rule during the period especially in the overseas territories. Analysing the political context of dominance and power relations which originated from the formal rule of the crown in the British colonies, the advantages of an early start as an industrialized nation and the near monopoly over the channels of trade allowed Britain to enjoy greater economic benefits. Thus colonies (of which India was one of the foremost) held a key to the benefits presumably enjoyed by Britain from its international economic transactions during the period. We would try to focus attention on the above aspects in the pages that follow.

Assessing the gains Britain enjoyed from her overseas empire, we have tried to dispel the belief that the issue could be settled by the magnitude and profitability of investment alone in relation to the empire. Our position lends a broader perspective to the analysis of colonialism offered in the present volume—one which transcends the institutional realities of the formal empire by offering a theme which claims to interpret the international aspects of underdevelopment in general.

British involvement in overseas trade and investment during the days prior to First World War has raised certain questions in the literature.[2] These questions are:

(*a*) What were the direct benefits to Britain from trade, especially from within the empire? What were the implications of the tendencies observed which indicated a decline in the absolute supremacy of Britain as an industrial power?[3]
(*b*) Judging by the slower pace of home investment, was British overseas investment 'excessive' during the period? Thus, did the openness of the British economy (especially in terms of the high rate of overseas investment) account for its slow domestic growth?[4] Did access to the empire make for a difference in the outcome?

The issues are relevant for an understanding of the economic implications of the British empire during the period.

A negative merchandise balance which was maintained by Britain during the period fails to capture the range of the benefits the country achieved through external trade and payments. While the negative (merchandise) balance was incapable of generating income in the domestic economy, we can consider at least three more dimensions of British overseas trade, each one of which fetched gains to the country. These aspects included (*a*) the relatively low prices Britain paid for her imports of raw materials; (*b*) the composition of British overseas trade which changed to a pattern where British exports consisted mostly of manufactured articles while her imports comprised primary goods; and (*c*) profits were appropriated mostly by the British merchants who enjoyed exclusive rights on channels of overseas trade during the period. Political control of the empire made it possible for the British government and merchants to exercise direct control over the pattern of trade in relation to the colonies. De-industrialization in the colonies (as it happened in India during 1840–60),[5] followed as a direct consequence of the free trade policies of the colonial governments. This also changed the commodity pattern of British trade with her colonies, exports from which now consisted of raw materials and food.[6] Production of these was organized by the small peasants and agricultural labourers in the colonial economies, who had very little command over resources. It was possible for traders in the colonies to procure raw materials at low prices by exercising their bargaining strength *vis-a-vis* the peasants who were often forced to take up commercial cultivation. Traders, both local and overseas, enjoyed monopoly control over the trade channels which linked up the sources of raw material in the colonies to the centres of their final use in Britain and other industrial countries. The long experience in international shipping and other institutional support to maritime commerce (which included insurance and banking facilities) lent Britain a natural superiority in trade relations, with an ability to retain most of the profits from international trade. The magnitude of the benefit, though difficult to measure, was evident in the discrepancies between producer prices in the colonies and prices paid abroad for its final use. In the context of the empire, the ruling country often acted as the 'entrepot for the produce of the colonies' and in effect permitted '...a restricted world market for the primary products of the colonies.'[7] To Naoroji, the leading exponent of early nationalist arguments in India, profits on India's overseas trade, which were systematically appropriated by the British, provided additional sources of 'drain of wealth' from India.[8] Estimates have been provided, in a recent study, on Indo-British economic relations, for the possible margins of profits on India's merchandise trade during the forty years between 1858–59 and 1897–98. The estimate, net of expenses (roughly put at 25 per cent of profits realized), yielded a cumulative sum of £125.5 million for the period as a whole—a value which was more than a fifth of the cumulative sum of home charges paid by India over the same period. (In terms of this argument an estimate of the drain, when calculated by home charges alone, underestimates the actual drain by nearly 17 per cent.)[9]

Britain's overseas investment has been subjected to close analysis and scrutiny in the literature. The quantitative picture, indicated from the available statistical sources, has been fairly straight-forward in terms of the following three aspects: (*a*) that for Britain the proportion of overseas investment relative to home investment was high during 1870–1914 (ratio between overseas and home investment during 1865–1914 was at 2.1:1. Private flows alone maintained a ratio of 1.7:1 between overseas and home investment while for public funds the ratio was at 3.3:1);[10] (*b*) that average profits (or rates of return) on British overseas investment far exceeded the profitability of home investment, even after allowing for the respective risk premia. The yield on foreign securities (net of risk premium) was on an average 1.58 per cent higher than that on home securities during 1865–1914;[11] (*c*) that the magnitude of overseas investment, which was directed to the empire and other foreign nations, indicated that the empire was relatively less significant both in terms of its share in the aggregate flow of (overseas) investment and in terms of profitability. Within the empire the white-settled colonies (having rights of self-determination) offered better prospects, compared to the dependent crown-colonies, both in terms of the volume of investment and in terms of relative profitability.

The broad consensus on the quantitative dimensions of pre-World War I British overseas investment, which is given above, contrasts with the dissents and the divergent interpretations on the subject in the literature. The difference, incidentally, has a crucial bearing on the empire-colony issue which has concerned us in the present volume. Summing up the available positions, the following seem to emerge as three dominant (and sometimes divergent) views on British overseas investment during late nineteenth century.

(*a*) Flows of overseas investment from Britain has been consistent with the neo-classical paradigm of an optimal resource allocation and competitive equilibrium. Indeed, the rate of return, net of risk premium, which was higher on overseas investment served in terms of this argument a market-allocating function, a role which also explains the spurts in overseas investment relative to the pace of investment within the home economy.[12] (On a closer look a diminishing marginal productivity factor seems to provide the ultimate explanation of the pattern of capital flows from Britain in the rather static and competitive framework of analysis implicit in the neo-classical interpretations of economic history.)

(*b*) The spatial distribution in the rate of return on British investment abroad deserves a special emphasis. Thus the foreign countries (other than the empire) had been relatively important in terms of the share as well as the rate of returns on British overseas investment. Within the empire, the white-settled self-governing territories received the larger share and were capable of offering higher rates of return, compared to that obtained in the dependent crown-colonies.[13] Hence the dependent crown-colonies, as held by the above interpretation, were of little value to Britain in providing benefits through overseas investment. The argument has been used in a recent study to come to the extreme position that the empire did not bring any economic benefit to Britain during the period. The point takes us back to the debate which has recently been revived in the historiography on Britain and her colonies.[14]

(*c*) There remains an alternative opinion that British external investments in the past should be viewed as the outcome of the specific historical-institutional developments during the respective period. (The above viewpoint is clearly different from the competitive model of the perfect markets.) Extending the argument further, Britain's monopoly power over the international financial institutions of late nineteenth century is projected to explain the tendencies of 'high finance' in the London City in the midst of industrial retardation and technological obsolescence during the Victorian and Edwardian era. Citing the *Economist* of 1911, it has been observed by a researcher that London (of 1911) '...was more concerned with the course of events in Mexico than with what happened Midlands, and was

> more upset by a strike in Canadian Pacific than by one of the Cambrian collieries.'[15] The outcome not only related to the low share of home investment in total British investment but also to a rate of return which was comparatively low for home investment.

An eventuality, where Britain, the first industrial nation, had to emerge as a declining industrial power by the end of hardly a century has been characterized in a recent study as one of the inevitables, especially with steady increases in the investment income flows which resulted from past British investments (and other sources of invisible earnings from abroad). From a macro-economic angle, this amount remained as nondisposed savings in the domestic economy which were more easily lent abroad. (Recall the triennial averages during 1911–13, with £189.7 million investment income for Britain, the entire sum of which was exhausted in overseas investment amounting £207.7 million. Thus overseas investment income did not contribute to domestic expenditure in Britain during the period.) The nation also earned other invisibles which, at £181.6 million, roughly provided the finance for her trade deficit at £134.3 million.[16] It has thus been argued that 'in one way Britain's industrial stagnation was a direct consequence of her earlier manufacturing successes, which set going that fatal inexorable sequence of capital exports leading to inward payments later. Thus the high level of capital exports did damage not only, or not so much, because it simply withheld capital from Britain where it might have done some good, but because it created a growing mountain of inward obligations which not only disposed market signals to limit the growth of output at home, but did so in a most destructive way, by undermining enterprise.'[17]

Of the three interpretations, the last argument highlights the dual aspects of the British economy in terms of the opposite tendencies in finance and industry at the end of nineteenth century. The interpretation makes use of the institutional aspects of the domestic economy, especially in terms of the capital market. The framework, evidently far removed from the neo-classical paradigm of competitive equilibrium, has recently been questioned in some studies which continue to dwell on the allocative efficiency of Victorian England.[18] Absence of comparable informations on domestic securities in the London stock market and the consequent inability of the investor to judge the investment prospects at home and abroad reflected, in terms of one of the studies, the prevailing taste of British savers who treated the two prospects (of investment at home and abroad) as separate. It is thus inferred that the markets for home and foreign securities were effectively separate. Thus unlike what was suggested under the institutional approach, the market was fragmented. The lapses in the field of technological advances and industrial growth in the British Victorian economy, which was otherwise efficient, has been viewed in another study, as a clear case of 'market failure', and hence a deviation from what could otherwise be an Arrow-Debreu Pareto optimality situation for Victorian England.[19]

It is evident that British overseas investment during the last quarter of the nineteenth and the early twentieth century has been subject to at least two distinct interpretations. In terms of explanations incorporating the aspects included in (*a*) and (*b*) above, the phenomenon of heavy capital export from Britain is possible to reconcile with a competitive framework and an efficient market where the average investor displays rationality in his/her decisions. Lack of information or other rigidities, if any, in the market for domestic stocks are interpreted in a manner which retains the virtue and efficiency of the principles of market allocation.[20] The relatively higher rate of return on overseas investment is thus cited as an indirect evidence of the principles of efficiency operating in the market.

The vision of the British capital market seems to be rather different and much closer to reality in the historical–institutional approach provided in (*c*) above. We mention, below, the two major contributions of this approach. Both, incidentally, help towards a better understanding of the empire–colony relation. These are (*a*) emphasis on the institutional aspects of the activities in the London City in the age of high finance, which explains its ability to mediate international capital through specialized agencies; and (*b*) a reliance on the flow of investment income enjoyed by Britain which highlighted the continuing significance of overseas finance, both as a source of income and as a channel of fresh overseas investment. The growing significance of finance reduced, to secondary importance, the role of industry as a source of surplus to the British economy.[21]

The spatial aspects of British overseas investment and its rate of returns have led scholars like Huttenback and Davis[22] to arrive at the conclusion that the dependent colonies in the empire did not bring economic benefits to the investing country. In our judgement the argument can be contested by drawing attention to the flow of investment income to Britain, a substantial amount of which was from these colonies. We have indicated earlier that the entire finance for Britain's gross overseas investment around 1913 was, in fact, provided by investment income flows, which the country earned from abroad during the same period (see pp. 49–50). Since Britain's overseas investment in the old colonies within the empire started much earlier, it is reasonable to expect that the flow of investment income from these nations was providing for a substantial part of Britain's new investment in the white-settled colonies and other foreign countries during later years. In fact the investment income flows to Britain exceeded, during 1870–1914, her new overseas investment. The above lends support to the reverse-flow argument which projects England as a rentier nation by late nineteenth century. (The reader may recall the statistics offered in pp. 49–50 dwelling on the theme of the reverse flow to Britain during 1870–1914.) We have hinted, earlier in this chapter, at the fact that Britain's new investment at £201.7 million over 1911–13 fell short of the invisible income at £371.3 million (of which interests and dividends were at £187.9 million). In terms of one of the comprehensive estimates, the foreign government loans publicly issued and subscribed in London during 1860–79 amounted to £320.7 million. The sum was nearly double the £161.9 million loan offered to colonies, including India, over the period. In addition, loans amounting to another £232.0 million were extended to railways and other companies located between the foreign countries and the empire.[23] The share of India seems to have been rather large in British railway and other overseas industrial investment during the period, as evident in the £150 million of such investment in India over 1857–71.[24] In terms of a different estimate, the cumulative receipts of India on guaranteed railway loans alone amounted to £69.5 million over 1860–79. Thus, of the £232.0 million British investment in railways and other companies (during 1860–79), at least half seem to have been invested within the empire (including India). It may be recalled that the period of formal annexation of the British empire started, with the acquisition of India, and with the granting of self-governing status to Canada in 1867.

While the formal annexations continued till 1927, most of the empire was consolidated by 1913. The share of the empire in overseas investment on railways and other companies can be put in terms of the calculations mentioned above at 60 per cent of aggregate British overseas investment under the same head over 1860–79. The rate of return on investment in the empire, which averaged a steady 6 per cent by 1870s, was roughly of the same order at 5.81 per cent average, for British overseas investment as a whole over the next fifty years. The new British investment in the empire dropped to 36 per cent of the aggregate British external investment, as measured by the capital called up during 1870–1914.[25] However, such declines, in our judgement, fail to establish that the empire was of little significance in providing the source of British overseas investment income, the flows of which were crucial in providing the financial resources for new overseas investments from the country.

We can, at this point, sum up our position on colonies as sources of profit for British overseas investment. The relative decline in new investments in the direction of the old colonies, which were under the direct rule of the British crown, did not, as observed earlier for the period 1870–1914, reduce their significance to Britain as sources of investment income. The above was evident in the large British investments in railways and other ventures and the loans offered to the colonial governments during the 1860s. Colonies in the dependent territories continued to provide financial resources to the ruling country during the later years, supporting the flow of new investment to other areas. Investment income from abroad (of which the contribution from the dependent colonies was not inconsequential) also seem to have supported consumption expenditure in the British economy. (An indirect evidence of above has been provided earlier (p. 150). (Thus investible surpluses from domestic savings plus investment income from abroad exceeded in Britain, her investment between home and overseas during the period as indicated by historical statistics available for 1870–1941.)

Research on profitability of the empire for Britain, during pre-First World War years—a theme on which there has been a revival of interest in recent research—should not, however, convey an impression that the issue can be settled by the records on the rate of return on British portfolio investment alone. Indeed, income (profits) on past investment represented only one out of the four possible sources of colonial surplus for the ruling nation. The remaining ones mentioned at the beginning of the present study in Section 1.1 include profits on trade and tributes paid on political grounds, covering the civil and military claims on the subordinate government. Moreover, the discretionary control, by the ruling nation, of the official reserves of colonial governments also provided sources of income to the ruling nation. We have, in this section, so far looked at the significance of Britain's colonies from the point of view of the benefits appropriated by Britain through overseas trade and investment. To complete the picture, we need to recognize the supplementary sources through the stream of unilateral transfers from the colonies, and through unconditional surrender of the official reserves held by the colonies to meet the liquidity demand in London—the financial centre of the ruling nation. These were utilized by the latter for overseas investment.[26]

In the literature, data on issue of new securities in London for 1865–1914 have been compared to Britain's overall balance in current account (OBCA) over the same period.[27] A rough correspondence between the two series on an average indicate that most of Britain's current account surpluses were invested abroad on a long-term basis over the same period. The above, however, was combined with a certain discrepancy during 1896–1905,[28] when the new issues exceeded the OBCA returns. Combining the results of research on the pattern and composition of Britain's short-term assets and liabilities, it is possible to explain the excess of the new issues of long-term securities in London over Britain's OBCA during the period, by net accumulations of short-term liquidities on part of Britain. The spurt in the short-term liquidities during the period was, however, not accidental if one recalls the newly opened branches of foreign and colonial banks in London and the compulsions, especially on part of the colonial governments, to maintain their official reserves in gold and sterling located in London. In a recent work[29] data has been provided on the short-term liabilities of Britain which arose due to the foreign official and private reserves held in the City. The figures help us explain the observed excesses of British long-term investment over current account balance which inevitably were financed by making use of these short-term liabilities. The picture fits in well with our argument that in the context of empire, the ruling nation could have an additional economic advantage because of its ability to make use of the financial reserves of other countries (and especially those of the colonies) which were usually maintained in London—the financial centre of the world. Reserves kept with the London City thus provided the benefits of financial intermediation to Britain which could earn a margin of profit by lending them on a long-term basis.

Our analysis so far has been around the theme of investment income flows and their significance for British balance of payments. We will now briefly dwell on the important theme mentioned above on the institutional approaches to British overseas investment in the nineteenth century. The theme relates to the significance of the evolving power structure in determining the pattern of the empire–colony relations—one which includes aspects of dominance as well as conflicts both in the empire and in the ruling nation. Literature on related themes refer to the singularity of the London City as a clearing house for most international transactions concerning trade and finance. It can be observed that the economic agents who conducted business in the City created a milieu which was far remote from the order of a perfectly competitive market. As it has been observed rather correctly in a classic work on the subject, '...interest percentages apart, the movement of capital and of foreign policy came from springs of action, and were largely in the hands of men (in London) who were of a common social group. Institutional relations were irrelevant when there was such an camaraderie of personalities between politics and banking. Banking houses had partners sitting in the House of Commons with greater regularity than in the direction of the Bank of England. There needs to be no scandal in these relations.'[30] Thus the financial oligarchy which characterized the London City was consistent with the rise of finance capital and its close links to industry in that age of high finance and imperialism.[31] The uneven power relations between the British and the colonial administration or other financial/commercial bodies often led to the settling of disputes (on matters concerned with distribution of official expenses etc.) in favour of the stronger party, which inevitably comprised the British. Differences of opinion were also common on matters concerning commerce and the monetary (currency) management. The conflicts and the typical manner in which those were resolved reflected, in case of colonial India, the underlying pattern of dominance and power relations in the empire–

colony relations. This included the British government, and sometimes the Bank of England, which wielded supreme authority over the hierarchical structure. The remaining characters included, in a descending order of significance, the Government of India, the European (or Anglo-Indian) commercial community in India, and the local Indian business community.

5.2 Colonial sources of surplus and the related spoliations: India 1890–1914

In the preceding section, we had focused on the functional role of the British colonies as sources of surplus for the ruling nation. Issues relating to colonial India, offered earlier in this book and in the rest of the present chapter, can now be linked up to the historiography on Britain and her empire.

To repeat a theme we have advanced earlier, colonies within the formal empire were used by ruling nations to procure surpluses which came through four possible channels. The first included the political tribute, which comprised the civil and military expenditure of the empire levied on the colonies. The second comprised the 'profits on trade' realized by the ruling nation, often by virtue of its political control of the colonies. The third source consisted of the investment outlet provided by the colonies. Income flows from these enjoyed by the ruling nation could provide a significant contribution to its new investments in other areas (this happened in Britain during 1870–1914). Finally, the official reserves of the colonial governments, which were maintained in London—the money centre of the imperial nations since late nineteenth century—provided short-term liquidity which could even be used by Britain to finance the long-term capital issues subscribed in the City.

These channels of colonial expropriations open to the ruling nation were all significant in the context of colonial India. We have indentified, in Chapter 2, the flow of tributes from colonial India, consisting of the annual home charges and other remittances to Britain. Ordinarily treated as invisibles, the home charges, (on a closer look at the underlying accounting jugglery) seemed to originate in the political rule of the British in India (see p. 73–87). While the entire sum of the home charges was provided for (under the head of 'Expenditure Abroad') in the budget through taxes and other revenue raised within India, an appropriation, by the India Office in London, of equivalent (or more after 1905) sterling through CBs sold against India's export surpluses implied that the net revenue earmarked against home charges in India could be used to reimburse the CBs sold. The procedure, as has been indicated earlier, froze the proceeds of India's net exports from abroad. Thus the nation not only transferred the sterling proceeds of her net export earnings to England (to settle the home charges), but was also forced to go through a simultaneous contraction in official expenditure in the domestic economy which was of an equivalent amount in Indian rupees (*see* pp. 49–73).

Unlike the financial tributes and their remittances abroad, profits on trade as a source of surplus for the ruling country has always been relatively difficult to quantify. We have mentioned earlier the direct evidence relating to the high margin of profits enjoyed by the British in trade in India and of the available estimates.

Profits (or income) on investments provided a ready source of earnings to the British in colonial India. The period of heavy investments, especially in railways during the 1860s, led, along with other investments, to a steady flow of interests paid out by India. Indeed, in the annual home charges, which was around £18 million during 1912–13, interest charges amounted to £11 million.[32] While the accounting transfers gave the false impression that the entire amount of interest payments was against borrowings for productive public works expenditure, it was certainly correct to say that the sum reflected interest payments alone. Thus investment income flows accounted for nearly 70 per cent of the contractual home charges borne and paid out by India by 1913 (*see* Table 2.1 for estimates relating to home charges etc).

Colonial India also proved to be a ready source of short-term liquidity to Britain. As we have indicated earlier (*see* pp. 128–55), London City was in a position not only to transfer and retain most of the nation's gold and sterling reserves, but actually did make use of them nearly free of interest charges to finance transactions in the City. Indeed, India Office's reserves with the Bank of England often proved difficult to be withdrawn by the SOS, even under pressure from the India government which wanted to make use of the official reserves for its regular purchases of silver needed for coinage. While interest was hardly paid on the SOS's deposits with the Bank of England (possibly since these were kept as demand deposits), the Bank lent the money to commercial banks and other borrowers in the City at the prevailing market rate. In addition, India Office also subscribed directly to the sterling loans or bonds sold in London. It was rather evident, from the account given above on the transfer of India government's official reserves to London and on their deployment with the Bank of England and/or the London stock market that India Office provided sources of additional liquidity to the London money market, and thus helped it to profit from its role as a financial intermediary (*see* pp. 186–220). The India Office's balances in the money centre were also important as a source of the frequent conflicts between the Bank of England, the India Office, and the rest of the government and/or the commercial interests in India. (Use of India Office's reserves, its size and location were already a major issue of these conflicts in 1913 when a memorandum was submitted to the Royal Commission on Indian Currency.) Conflicts were inevitably resolved in favour of the dominant party, as was the case with the continued rejection of India Office's demands (backed by the official and private commercial interests in India) for release of sterling at Bank of England for purchase of silver. The Bank of England clearly had the authority to reject the demand and even maintain the monopoly over silver purchase contracts for the India government. Arguments provided by the Bank of England justifying its attitude indicated that the India Office's purchase of silver could upset the London money market by reversing the price trends of silver (and hence of gold) in the City. Clearly it became important for the British government and its financial agent (the Bank of England) to closely monitor and control the portfolio balance decisions of the India Office (pp. 186–220). Contraction in money supply and availability of credit in India often resulted as a consequence of the typical resistance of the monetary authorities in India and Britain, to allow the India government to lend directly to the public. The scarcity of silver, which often resulted as a consequence of the disapproval by these authorities of India government's requests for silver purchases in London, created additional reasons for a tapering off of supply of money in India (it may be recalled that despite the use of paper money, rupee coins remained the major component of money supply in India during the pre-War period, and hence, minting of rupee coins was all the more important). The reader can here recall the shortage of silver and the consequent scarcity of rupee coins in India during 1898–1900 and 1912–13 which, with the stringency of credit in India, prompted the commercial community, including the Bank of Bengal Governor, Martin Lindsay, to demand easy credit from the presidency banks. Both demands were rejected—the first (for silver purchase) by the Bank of England, and the second (for easy credit) by the India Office in conjunction with the British government. The outcome reflected the balance in power relations between the various agents in India and in London which shared an interest in Indian monetary policy (*see* pp. 186–220 for details on the aspects relating to monetary policy in colonial India).

On the whole, monetary stringencies experienced by the Indian economy during the period was one of the consequences of the colonial government's policy of transfers abroad of export surpluses on a regular basis and of the official reserves as and when it was possible. Thus colonial monetary management during the period denied the country the possibility of an expansion in the monetary base as might have otherwise resulted from the reserves accumulated by the country under the prevailing gold exchange standard. In reality, the rules of the game under automatic adjustment of the price–specie flow were never implemented in India where supply of money and credit were controlled by the respective authorities who dominated policy. Nor could the country's net export revenue generate income within the national economy which was forced to remit nearly an equivalent sum of annual tributes. Colonial administration in India thus made use of its political power to expropriate surpluses for Britain along all the four possible channels which we have mentioned at the beginning of this section.

We now dwell briefly on the analysis offered in Chapter 4 on the weak links between surplus generation under colonial administration and the growth performance within the domestic economy. With the export surplus from the country indicating rough magnitude of the real transfers in colonial India, the rising exports and the pace of commercialization left little dynamism in terms of real activities in the economy. We have drawn attention, as an explanation, to the pattern of distribution and the disposal of the agricultural surpluses which remained within the economy. These surpluses included the rent, the interest, and profits on internal trade (export trade was entirely controlled by foreign agency houses while the local trade was in the hands of local *banias* and *beparis*). While the level of the agricultural surplus distributed, relative to what was left to the cultivators, was rather high, there remained very little incentive, under the prevailing organization of production in agriculture, for the money-lenders or the mercantile agents in grain trade to come forward and invest in land. Land legislation in colonial India was inadequate from the angle of generating a climate for steady investments in land. Thus little incentives, if at all, were forthcoming from the rent-seeking landlords or their intermediaries to introduce yield-augmenting investments in cultivation. It was also clearly impossible for the peasants, who were left with a slender margin of subsistence, to invest in land they cultivated. As we have observed earlier, the standard of living of the cultivators seems to have fallen sharply over the period (*see* pp. 167–71 for the arguments and Table 4.10 for figures relating to the cost of living index for the cultivating families between 1891–92 and 1913–14).

Export expansion from India during late nineteenth and early twentieth centuries thus failed to generate agricultural growth in India. For the two regions of relatively higher export expansions, viz. the Bombay and Bengal presidencies, growth in export crop production was explained by the shifts in acreage from other crops to exportables. The above, however, had very little to do with the near stationary or declining yield rate in crops used for home consumption or for export. Export expansions, primarily of agricultural output in India, thus failed to initiate yield-raising innovations in cultivation and much of the expansion in export crop output was achieved through switches in production. The switches were particularly important for the inferior grains for which the acreages as well as output fell as a consequence. However, crop selections and the production switches were not functions of relative prices. This could be observed from the fact that prices of inferior grains rose faster than those of exportables. The organization of cultivation was thus subject to factors other than price which had a bearing on selection. These factors included the system of cash advances (*dadan*) against commercial crops and use of usury and land mortgages as tools of coercion. Unlike what is claimed in the literature, the peasant had very little opportunity to act as a 'rational agent' for allocation of resources in these circumstances. Simultaneously, interests of merchants who gained from handling the trade (internal and external) in export crops matched that of the ruling state which was keen on securing the sterling proceeds of India's net exports. It is, however, important to realize that there existed landlords and usurers, or even traders, in India, who did not directly participate in export trade. However, they had their own share of surplus, in the form of rent, interest, or profits which was either spent on unproductive consumption, or reinvested to plough back surpluses along the same channel of activities. Details of the internal–external division of the surplus appropriation in colonial India and the inability of the system to stir domestic growth have been offered in more detail given earlier in Chapter 4.

India's links with Britain and the rest of the world reflect a roughly similar pattern during the later years of colonial rule in the country, especially with the very limited direct gains enjoyed by the national economy from the growing levels of external transactions.[33] The pattern was evident with the controls exercised by the British rulers on the composition and the proceeds of India's exports during the First World War. Supply of strategic war materials was secured by the British through payments arranged on priority basis against exports of these goods from India. The arrangement also worked as an incentive in India to switch to strategic exports since a large part of export under non-strategic heads remained unpaid with selective sales of CBs against strategic exports alone. Unpaid export earnings of India comprised its War Loans to the British government which were to be paid back at end of the War. In the meantime the rising international price of silver during the War years created pressure on the rupee rate and the rupee floated upwards in 1917. Uncertainties in the world silver market introduced a new constraint for colonial monetary policy in India and the rupee rate which was fixed back at 2s at end of the War had soon to be revised as silver prices tumbled down in the post-War period. Measures were taken to prevent further depreciation of the rupee by stopping sales of CBs during 1921–23. The need to protect the rupee rate during the period of falling silver prices also led the monetary authorities to take recourse to direct remittances of sovereigns and silver during 1921–23. The arrangement helped Britain to sort out problems in regard to operating bimetallism in the colonies in the face of changing silver prices. However, the annual liabilities of the India Office, which by the twenties, were much larger than the annual home charges of the SOS in London, led to a situation where Reverse Council Bills (RCBs) were sold in India in order to release the India Office's sterling reserves for the purpose of meeting its own expenditure. It is interesting to note that RCBs were sold during 1921–23 despite the surpluses in India's trade balance. Unlike the pre-War sale of the RCBs during 1907–09, when the rupee rate tended to fall due to the adverse turn in India's balance of trade, the situation during 1921–23 was one where the drop in rupee rate happened due to the decline in world silver prices (in terms of gold). The consequent pressure on the rupee rate was sought to be arrested by the monetary authorities through disbanding of CB sales and a revival of RCBs in order to release the SOS's sterling reserves for revenue purpose. Evidently, the continuation of silver coinage in India which was also in support of the bimetallic standard faced additional constraints with the fluctuation in silver prices. The officials adopted policies which suited the colonial administration by avoiding gold as the base of currency system in India and by retaining the silver rupee at an exchange rate which did not hurt the export interests in the ruling country. The underlying design was rather evident to the Indian public, the vocal sections of which protested against the harmful effects of the overvalued rupee, especially from the angle of the country's industries. A need to procure sterling in London pushed the India Office to accept the RCBs when sale of the CBs was not advisable in view of the downtrend in silver prices and the consequent pressures on the rupee rate. The growing liabilities of the India Office led it to borrow afresh during 1921–23, which, interestingly, coincided with its repayment of War Loans and a release of sterling through sale of RCBs during the same period. At home, industrial interests in Britain also supported the fixing of the rupee rate, especially when the market trends could depreciate it further. On the whole the exigencies of economic policy in colonial India thus continued to be guided during the 1920s by the dominant economic interests in Britain—both private and official.

During the thirties the magnitude of India's merchandise surpluses went down and the shortfall in net export revenue was made good by net export of gold, often procured as distress sale in India. The country's exports, which comprised primary goods, experienced steep price shortfalls. Thus export performance had very little or none of any dynamic effects in the domestic economy as during the earlier years. Thus the stationary pattern of the domestic economy and the expropriative character of the colonial government, both of which were prominent in the pre-First World War years, continued to prevail during the subsequent years of colonial rule.

5.3 The predicament of neo-colonies: Can history provide a lesson?

It would perhaps not be too far-fetched to seek an analogy between colonial experiences in general and the developments in the politically independent Third World. The processes of backwardness and underdevelopment often weave a familiar story, with the economically dependent nations showing no signs of dynamism despite the growing levels of foreign trade and capital inflows. The colonial tributes and the drain of wealth have been substituted, in the politically independent neo-colonies of the post-Second World War, by flows of royalties, dividends, interest payments, and technical fees on foreign capital which often are accepted at non-negotiable terms. Attitude of the local bourgeoisie, or that of the ruling state has been oriented by the prospects of gaining access to some of the benefits through collaborations. Given the uneven bargaining strength of these national governments, the political tribute of the earlier years continues in the form of debt peonage and the various demands of foreign capital on the host economies. Profits on trade are similarly continued, with the high share of the foreigners, achieved by means of their control over trade channels which are manipulated by the industrial countries. With norms set by the international credit market and the IMF defining credit-worthiness, the developing countries are often forced to be cautious about the level of their official reserves since these usually provide them access to the world money markets. The reserves, which are normally maintained as deposits with the international banks, have, in recent years, been a channel of reverse capital flows from the Third World. The above process has been matched by a compulsion to generate and maintain export surpluses, especially in the big debtor countries of Latin America. Even lesser debtors in Africa have recently been forced to cut back imports and trade deficits, largely as a consequence of the diminished flow of international credit which now has been diverted away from the developing areas. Resource transfers from the Third World thus parallel the colonial mode of expropriations and resource transfers through trade surpluses of the colonies.

The analogies are not perfect, nor should one draw complete parallels between the empire–colony and the neo-colonial situations. The method and the underlying process of surplus appropriation, its transfer abroad and the utilization of the rest in the domestic economy have, however, continued to be similar, providing a justification of our enquiry into the experience of colonial India in the context of the empire.

Notes

1. See for a defensive account of the empire, Lance E. Davis and Robert A. Huttenback, *Mammon and the Pursuit of Empire: The Political Economy of British Imperialism 1860–1912*, Cambridge, 1986, pp. 1–117.
   See *also* for counter-arguments, M. Edelstein, *Overseas Investment in the Age of High Imperialism*, New York, 1982, and M. Edelstein, 'Foreign Investment and Empire 1860–1914', in F. Floud and D. McCloskey eds., *The Economic History of Britain since 1770*, London, 1981, Vol. II, p. 90.
   The recent controversy, in *Economic History Review* on the empire reflects a revived interest in the topic. See, in particular, Sidney Pollard, 'Capital Exports, 1870–1914: Harmful or Beneficial?', *Economic History Review*, Vol. 38, 1985, pp. 489–514.
   Peter Temin, 'Capital Exports, 1870–1914 : An alternative Model' and Sidney Pollard, 'Comment on Peter Temin's Comment', *Economic History Review*, Vol. XL, No. 3, August, 1987, pp. 453, 459–60.
2. See, in addition to references cited in (1), William P. Kennedy, *Industrial Structure, Capital Markets and the Origins of the British Economic Decline*, Cambridge, 1987, pp. 10–14, 109–20.
   D.H. Aldcroft, 'The Entrepreneur and the British Economy 1870–1914', *Economic History Review*, 1964, pp. 17, 113–14. S.B. Saul, 'Britain and the World Trade', *Economic History Review*, Vol. VII, 1954, pp. 49–66.
3. See, in particular, Sidney Pollard, 'Capital Exports', 1985, Lance E. Davis and Robert A. Huttenback, *Mammon*, pp. 73–177. M. Edelstein, *Overseas Investment*, 1982, pp. 9–44, 163–70.
4. Davis and Huttenback, *Mammon*, p. 39.

5. A.K. Bagchi, 'Deindustrialisation in India in the Nineteenth Century', *Journal of Development Studies*, January, 1976.
6. Latham, *India and the International Economy*, Croom Helm, 1969.
7. A.K. Bagchi, *Political Economy of Underdevelopment*, Cambridge, 1982, p. 32.
8. *See* Chapter 2.
9. A.K. Banerji, *Indo-British Relations*, pp. 133, 168.
10. The ratios relate to the minimum estimates of investment, provided by Huttenback and Davis. *See* Davis and Huttenback, *Mammon*, p. 4.
11. M. Edelstein, *Overseas Investment*, p. 139, Davis and Huttenback. *Mammon*, p. 81.
12. British overseas investment in the empire as a proportion of similar investment by Britain in other foreign nations worked out to be an average of 0.63 over 1865–1914. Within the empire the ratio of British investment in the self-governing white-settled colonies to that in other dependent British colonies (excluding India) was at 7.9 over the same period. The ratio however, comes to 40.0 when other dependent colonies include India. British investment in foreign countries was also relatively lucrative in terms of the rate of return when comparison is made to that in the empire. As it is explicitly stated, '...overall there is little evidence to indicate that financial investment in the Empire was particularly profitable, whether the yardstick is domestic or foreign rates of return'. *See* Davis and Huttenback, *Mammon*, pp. 40–1, and p. 80.
13. Ibid.
14. Ibid., p. 11.
15. F.N. Paish, 'The London New Issue Market', *Economica*, N.S. 18 (1915), p. 2, and *Economist*, 20 May, 1911, p. 1059. Both are cited in Pollard, 'Capital Exports', 1985, p. 508.
16. Sidney Pollard 'Capital Exports', p. 511.
17. Ibid., pp. 510, 512.
18. *See*, in particular, Peter Temin, 'Capital Exports', 1987, and William Kennedy, *British Economic Decline*.
19. *See*, for a rather mechanistic attempt at an application of Pareto optimality properties to interpret British investment in nineteenth century, William Kennedy, *British Economic Decline*, 1987, pp. 10–14, 146–7.
20. Sidney Pollard, 'Capital Exports', 1985, p. 46.
21. *See* for the theoretical argument in the context of the international economy during the eighties, Sunanda Sen, 'Swings and Paradoxes in the international capital market: A Theoretical Note', *Cambridge Journal of Economics*, June, 1991.
22. Huttenback and Davis, *Mammon*, p. 11, also L.H. Jenks. *The*

Migration of British Capital, p. 425.
23. Ibid., p. 283.
24. Huttenback and Davis, *Mammon*, p. 27.
25. Ibid., p. 335, and M. Edelstein, *Overseas Investment*, p. 496.
26. S. Lindert, *Key Currencies and Gold*, Princeton, 1975, pp. 16–35.
27. *See* Edelstein. Overseas Investment, pp. 15–20 for the argument. *See also* Lindert, *Key Currencies*, and Mathew Simon, 'The Pattern of New British Portfolio Foreign Investment. 1865–1914' in A.R. Hall ed., *The Export of Capital from Britain*, London, 1968, pp. 15–44.
28. Ibid.
29. Lindert, *Key Currencies*, p. 19.
30. Jenks, *Migration of Capital*, p. 285.
31. *See* V.I. Lenin, *Imperialism*.
32. *See* Chapter 2.
33. Analysis attempted in the next few pages of the post-1914 developments in colonial India is rather tentative and less than complete. We have found the following, among others, as useful readings for Indian economy during 1914–39. Reports of Royal Commissions of Currency and Finance (RCC) by Babington Smith Committee (1926) and Hilton-Young Committee (1931). Government of India, *Summary Report of Royal Commissions on Currency and Finance*, Simla, 1931.
S.E. Harriss, *Monetary Problems of British India*, New York, 1931.
A.K. Banerji, *India's Balance of Payments*, Bombay, 1963.
D.N. Gurto, *India's Balance of Payments 1920–1960*, Delhi, 1961.
Raymond Goldsmith, *Financial Development*.
B.R. Tomlinson, *Political Economy*.
See, in addition, Sunanda Sen, 'Imperial Rule in India and India's External Economic Transactions: 1833–1947' in A.K. Bagchi and S. Bhattacharya ed., *Economic and Social History of India* (forthcoming).

Bibliography

Books and journals

Adams, Brooks. *Law of Civilization and Decay: An Essay in History, 1986*, New York, 1943.

Alavi, Hamza et al. *Capitalism and Colonial Production*, London, 1982.

Aldcroft, D.H. 'The Entrepreneur and the British Economy 1870–1914', *Economic History Review*, 1964.

Ambedkar, B.R. *History of Indian Currency and Banking*, Vol. 1, Thaker and Co., Bombay, 1947.

Ambirajan, S. *Political Economy and British Policy in India*, Cambridge, 1978.

———. *Political Economy and Monetary Management: India 1766–1914*, Affiliated East–West Press, Madras, 1984.

Anstey, Vera. *Economic Development in India*, London, 1911, pp. 509–10.

Atkinson, F.J. 'A Statistical review of income and wealth in British India', *Journal of the Royal Statistical Society*, Vol. 65, 1902.

———. 'Rupee prices in India, 1870 to 1908: with an examination of causes leading to present high level of prices', *Journal of the Royal Statistical Society*, Vol. 72, September, 1909.

———. 'Silver prices in India', *Journal of the Royal Statistical Society*, Vol. 60, 1897.

Bagchi, A.K. 'Towards a correct reading of Lenin's theory of imperialism', in P. Patnaik ed. *Lenin and Imperialism*, Orient Longman, Delhi, 1986.

———. *Private Investment in India 1900–1939*, Cambridge University Press, 1972.

———. *The Evolution of State Bank of India, The Roots, 1806–1867*, Parts 1 and 2, Oxford University Press, Bombay, 1987.

———. *The Political Economy of Poverty*, Cambridge University Press, 1982.

Baker, C.J. *An Indian Rural Economy 1880–1955, The Tamilnad Countryside*, Clarendon Press, Oxford, 1984.

Banerji, A.K. *Aspects of Indo-British Economic Relations*, Bombay, 1982, pp. 176–206.

______ *India's Balance of Payments: Estimates of Current and Capital Accounts from 1921–22 to 1938–39*, Bombay, 1963.

Barbour, D. *The Theory of Bimetallism and the Effects of the Partial Demonetization of Silver on England and India*, Cassell, London, 1885.

Barratt-Brown, M. *Economics of Imperialism*, Spokesman Books, 1984.

______. *Essays on Imperialism*, Spokesman Books, 1972.

______. *Models in Political Economy*, Penguin, 1984.

Bayly, C.A. *Rulers, Townsmen, and Bazaars*, Cambridge, 1938.

Beaud, M. *A History of Capitalism 1500–1980*, London, 1984.

Bhaduri, A. 'The Evolution of Land Relations in Eastern India under British Rule', *Indian Economic and Social History Review*, March, 1976.

______. 'A Study of Agricultural Backwardness under Semi-feudalism', *Economic Journal*, March, 1973.

Bharadwaj, K. 'A note on commercialization in Indian Agriculture' in K.N. Raj et al. ed. *Commercialization in Indian Agriculture*, Delhi, 1985.

______. *Production Conditions in Indian Agriculture*, Cambridge, 1974.

Bhatia, B.M. *Famines in India*. London, 1963.

Bhattacharya, S. *Financial Foundations of the British Raj, 1858–1872*, Simla, 1971.

Blyn, G. *Agricultural Trends in India 1891–1947: Output, Availability and Productivity*, University of Pennsylvania Press, Philadelphia, 1966.

Bose, A. 'Foreign Capital' in V.B. Singh ed. *Economic History of India 1857–1956*, Allied Publishers, New York, 1965.

______. 'Foreign Capital' in V.B. Singh ed. *Economic History of India 1857–1956*, Allied Publishers, Delhi, 1975.

Brunyate, J.B. *An Account of the Presidency Banks*, Superintendent of Government Printing, Calcutta, 1900.

Buchanan, D.H. *The Development of Capitalistic Enterprise in India*, First edition, Macmillan, New York, 1934. Reprinted, Frank Cass, London, 1966.

Catanach, I.J. *Rural Credit in Western India 1875–1930: Rural Credit and Co-operative Movement in the Bombay Presidency*, University of California Press, Berkeley, 1970.

Chablani, H. *Studies on Indian Currency and Exchange*, Oxford University Press, Bombay, 1931.

Chandra, Bipan. 'Lenin and the nationalist liberation movements' in *Nationalism and Colonialism in Modern India*, Orient Longman, Delhi, 1979, pp. 297–322.

______. *Growth of Economic Nationalism in India*, Peoples Publishing House, New Delhi, 1966.

______. 'Reinterpretations of India's economic history' in Bipan Chandra ed. *Nationalism and Colonialism in Modern India*, Delhi, 1979.

Chandra, N.K. 'Long-term Stagnation in the Indian Economy', *EPW*, Annual Number, 1983.

Charlesworth, N. *British Rule and the Indian Economy*, London, 1982.

Chaudhuri, B.B. *The Growth of Commercial Agriculture in Bengal, 1759–1900*, Calcutta, 1964.

Chaudhuri, K.N. 'India's International Economy in the nineteenth century: A historical survey', *Modern Asian Studies*, 2.1, 1968.

______. 'Foreign Trade and Balance of Payments', in Kumar and Desai ed. *Cambridge Economic History of India, Vol. 2*.

Chaudhuri, K.N. and Dewey, C. ed. *Economy and Society: Essays in Indian Economic and Social History*, New Delhi, 1979.

Child, Josiah, ed. *Discourse of Trade*, 1775.

Coyayee, J.E. *The Indian Currency System*, University of Madras, 1930.

Dadachanji, B.E. *Economic History of India*, Allied Publishers, Delhi, 1965.

Darling, N. *The Punjab Peasant in Prosperity and Debt*, 1925.

Datta, K.L. *Report on the Enquiry into the Rise of Prices in India*, Superintendent of Government Printing, Calcutta, 1914.

de Cecco, M. *Money and Empire: The International Gold Standard, 1890–1914*, Blackwell, Oxford, 1974.

Dewey, C. and Hopkins, A.J. *The Imperial Impact: studies in the Economic History of Africa and India*, London, 1978.

Digby, W. *Prosperous British India: A Revelation from Official Records*, T.F. Unwin, London, 1901.

Dobb, M. Sweezy, P. et al. 'The Transition from Feudalism to Capitalism', *Science and Society*, 1950–53.

Doraiswami, S.V. *Indian Finance, Currency and Banking*, Madras, 1915.

Doss, Tincowry, *A Practical Treatise on the Currency Question*, S.B. Doss, Calcutta, 1887.

Dubey, V. 'Railways' in V.B. Singh ed. *Economic History of India*.

Dutt, R.C. *The Economic History of India in the Victorian Age*, Vol. 2, London, 1906. Reprinted, Publications Division, Government of India, Delhi, 1980.

Dutt, R.P. *India Today*, Manisha, Calcutta, 1970.

Edelstein, M. *Overseas Investment in the Age of High Imperialism*,

New York, 1982.

______. 'Foreign Investment and Empire' in Floud and McCloskey ed. *The Economic History of Britain since 1770*, Vol. 2, London, 1981.

Feinstein, H. *National Income, Output and Employment in the UK*, Cambridge, 1972.

Findlay, Shirras G. *Indian Finance and Banking*, Macmillan, London, 1920.

Fischer, W. et al. ed. *The Emergence of a World Economy*, Vol. 2.

Floud, F. and McCloskey, D. *The Economic History of Britain since 1770*, Vol. 2, London, 1981.

Frykenberg, R.E. ed. *Land Control and Social Structure in Indian History*, University of Wisconsin Press, Madison, 1968.

Gadgil, D.R. *The Industrial Revolution of India in Recent Times, 1860 to 1939*, OUP, Bombay, 1969.

Gallaghar, J. and Robinson, R. 'The Imperialism of Free Trade', *Economic History Review*, 1953.

Ganguly, B.N. *Dadabhai Naoroji and the Drain Theory*, Bombay, 1965.

Gaylor, J.L. Richards, Irene, and Morris, J.A. *A Sketch-map Economic History of Britain*, London, 1975, p. 175.

Ghosh, A.K. *An Analysis of the Indian Price Structure since 1861*, Ph. D dissertation, London School of Economics, 1949.

Ghosh, D.N. *Banking Policy in India*, Bombay, 1979.

Goldsmith, R.W. *Financial Structure and Development*, Yale University Press, New Haven, 1969.

______. *The Financial Development of India, 1860–1977*, New Haven, 1983.

Gopal, S. *British Policy in India 1858–1905*, Orient Longman, Bombay, 1975.

Government of India, *Reports of Currency Committees*, Calcutta, 1931.

Gunder Frank, A. *Capitalism and Underdevelopment in Latin America*, 1971.

______. 'On some questionable questions about Marxist theory and international capital flows', *Radical Political Economy Review*, 1976.

Gurto, D.N. *India's Balance of Payments, 1920–1960*, S. Chand, Delhi, 1961.

Habib, I. 'Banking in Mughal India' in T. Roychaudhury ed. *Contributions to Indian Economic History*, K.L. Mukhopadhyay, Calcutta, 1960.

Harris, S.E. *Monetary Problems of British India*, New York, 1931.

Headrick, Daniel. *The Tools of Empire: Technology and European Empire in the Nineteenth Century*, New York, 1983.

Heston, A. 'National Income' in Kumar and Desai ed. *Cambridge Economic History*.

Hobson, C.K. *The Export of Capital*, London, 1904.

Howard, H.F. *India and the Gold Standard*, Thacker Spink and Co., Calcutta and London, 1911.

Hurd II, J. 'Railways and the expansion of markets in India 1861–1921', *Explorations in Economic History*, July, 1975.

Huttenback, R.A. and Davis, L. *Mammon and the Pursuit of Empire: the Political Economy of British Imperialism 1860–1912*, Cambridge, 1986.

Jenks, L. *The Migration of British Capital*, Knopf, New York, 1927.

———. 'British experience with foreign investment', *Journal of Economic History*, December, 1944.

Jevons, H.S. *Money, Banking and Exchange in India*, Government Central Press, Simla, 1922.

Kennedy, W.P. *Industrial Structure, Capital Markets and the Origin of the British Economic Decline*, Cambridge, 1967.

Keynes, J.M. *The Collected Writings of John Maynard Keynes*, ed. D. Moggridge, Vol. 15, *Activities 1906–1914*, Macmillan, London, 1971.

———. 'Rise in prices 1907–1909', Editorial Comments in *Madras Mail*, 10 April 1909.

———. 'Notes on sea-borne trade of India' Supplement to *Indian Trade Journal*, 22 September 1910.

———. 'Review of Theodore Morison: Economic Transition in India', *Economic Journal*, 1911.

———. 'Rise in Prices 1907–1909', *Economic Journal*, 1909.

———. *The Collected Writings of John Maynard Keynes*, ed. D. Moggridge, Vol. 1. *Indian Currency and Finance*, Macmillan, London, 1971.

———. *The Collected Writings of John Maynard Keynes*, Vol. 11, *Economic Articles and Correspondence, Academic*, ed. D. Moggridge, Macmillan, London, 1983.

———. *Collected Writings*, Vol. 1, *Indian Currency and Finance*, London, 1913.

Krishnamurthy, S. 'Real wages of agricultural labourers in the Bombay Deccan, 1874–1922', *Indian Economic and Social History Review*, 24 (2), January–March, 1987.

Kuczynski, J. 'Conditions of Workers 1880–1950' in V.B. Singh ed. *Economic History of India*.

Kulke, H. and Rothermundt, D. *A History of India*, Beckenham, 1986, New Delhi 1987.

Kumar, D. *Western India in the Nineteenth Century*, University of Toronto Press, Toronto, 1968.

Kumar, D. and Desai, M. ed. *The Cambridge Economic History of India, Vol.2, 1757–1970*, Orient Longman, Delhi, 1982.

Kumar, Dharma. 'The fiscal system' in *Cambridge Economic History of India*, Vol. 2.
Latham, A. *India and the International Economy*, Croom Helm, 1968.
Lenin, V.I. *Collected Works*, Vol. 22, Moscow, 1964.
———. *Imperialism, the Highest Stage of Capitalism*, Peking, 1960.
———. *The National Liberation Movement in the East*, Moscow, 1969.
———. 'Notebooks on imperialism (1915–16)' in *Collected Works*, Vol. 39, Moscow, 1969.
Lindert, S. *Key Currencies and Gold*, Princeton, 1975.
Luxemburg, Rosa. *Accumulation of Capital*, translated by Tom N. Bottmore, London, 1963.
Macpherson, W.J. 'Investment in Indian railways, 1845–1875', *Economic History Review*, 8, No. 2, 1955–56.
———. 'Economic development in India under the British Crown 1858–1947' in A.J. Youngson ed. *Economic Development in the Long Run*, Allen & Unwin, London, 1971.
Maddison, A. 'Alternative estimates of the real product of India, 1900–46', *Indian Economic and Social History Review*, 22 (2), April–June, 1985.
———. *Class Structure and Economic Growth: India and Pakistan since the Moghuls*, Allen & Unwin, London, 1971.
Manser, W.A.P. *Britain in Balance*, Penguin, 1971.
Martin, Montgomary. *The Political, Commercial and Financial Aspects of the Anglo–East Empire in 1832*.
Marx, Karl. 'The Future Results of the British Rule in India' in *Marx-Engels Reader*.
McAlpin, M. 'Impact of Trade on Agricultural Development: Bombay Presidency 1855–1920', *Explorations in Economic History*, Vol. 1, No. 1, 1980.
———. 'Price Movements and Fluctuations in Economic Activity' in Kumar and Desai ed. *Cambridge Economic History*, Vol. 2.
McLane, John. 'The Drain of Wealth and Indian Nationalism at the Turn of the Century' in T. Roychaudhury ed. *Contributions to Indian Economic History*, Vol. 2, Calcutta, 1963.
Melotti, Umbretto. *Marx and the Third World*, London, 1977.
Mill, J.S. *History of British India*, Vol. 3.
Mishra, S. 'Commercialization, Peasant Differentiation and Merchant Capital in Late Nineteenth Century: Bombay and Punjab', *Journal of Peasant Studies*, 1982.
Mitchell, B.R. *Abstracts of British Historical Statistics*, Cambridge, 1962.
Morison, Theodore. *Economic Transition in India*, London, 1911.
Morris, M.D. et al., *Indian Economy in the Nineteenth Century: A Symposium*, Delhi, 1969.

Mukherjee, M. *National Income of India, Trends and Structure*, Statistical Publishing Society, Calcutta, 1969.

Mukherji, K. 'Levels of Living of Industrial Workers' in V.B. Singh ed. *Economic History of India 1857–1965*.

Mun, Thomas. *England's Treasure by Forraign Trade*, 1664.

Murray, Robin. 'The Internationalism of Capital and the Nation-State' in Hugo Radice ed. *International Firms and Modern Imperialism*, Penguin, 1975.

Naoroji, D. *Essays, Speeches and Writings*, ed. C.L. Parekh, Bombay. 1887.

______. *Poverty and Un-British Rule in India*, 1873.

______. *Poverty and Un-British Rule in India*, London, 1901.

Nolan, P. *Report on the Lower Classes of Population in Bengal*, Calcutta, 1888.

Nurkse, R. *Patterns of Trade and Development*, Stockholm, 1979.

O'Connor, J.E. *Review of the Trade of India for 1884–1885*, Government Central Press, Simla, 1885.

______. 'Note on the influence of low rate of exchange on the trade of India', *Review of the Trade of India for 1885–1886*, Simla, 1886.

Paish, F.N. 'The London New Issues Market', *Economica*, 1915 and *Economist*, 20 May 1911.

Paish, G. 'Great Britain's Capital Investments in Individual Colonial and Foreign Countries', *Journal of the Royal Statistical Society*, 1910–11.

Palat, Ravi et al. *Review*, I, Summer, 1976.

Pandit, Y.S. *India's Balance of Indebtedness, 1898–1913*, George Allen and Unwin, 1937.

Patel, S.J. 'Long-term Trends in Output and National Income', *Indian Economic Journal*, 1958.

Platt, D.C.M. 'Canada and Argentina: The first preference British investor', *Journal of Imperial and Commonwealth History*, XIII (3), May, 1985.

Pollard, S. 'Capital Exports, 1870–1914: Harmful or Beneficial?', *Economic History Review*, 2nd series, XXXVIII (4), November, 1985.

______. 'Comments on Peter Temin's Comment', *Economic History Review*, XL, 1987.

Prakash, V. 'An Estimate of Stock of Precious Metals in India' in V.K.R.V. Rao et al. ed. *Papers on National Income and Allied Topics*, Vol. 1, Asia Publishing House, New York, 1960.

Ranade, M.G. *Essays on Indian Economics*, Bombay, 1898.

Radice, H. *International Firms and Modern Imperialism*, Penguin, 1975.

Ravallion, M. 'Trade and Stabilization: Another Look at British India's

Conventional Food Exports', *Explorations in Economic History*, 1986.

Rothermundt, D. *Government, Landlord and Peasant in India. Agrarian Relations under British Rule, 1860–1935*, Wiesbaden, 1978.

———. *The Indian Economy under British Rule*, New Delhi, 1983.

Roychaudhury, T. 'Permanent Settlement in Operation, Backergunj, East Bengal', in R.E. Frykenberg ed. *Land Control and Social Structure in Indian History*, Madison, 1969.

Saul. S.B. *The Myth of the Great Depression 1873–1896*, Macmillan, London, 1969.

Sen, A.K. *Poverty and Famines*, Delhi, 1981.

Sen, Sunanda 'Swings and Paradoxes in International Capital Markets', *Cambridge Journal of Economics*, June, 1990.

———. 'Free Trade Imperialism in South-East Asia', *Studies in History*, January–June, 1980.

———. 'Trade as a Handmaiden of Colonialism: India during Late Nineteenth Century to First World War', *Studies in History*, Vol. IV, Number 1, January–June, 1982.

Singh, V.B. ed. *Economic History of India*, New York.

Stein, Berton and Washbrook, David. 'Eighteenth Century India: Historiography, Perspectives, and Proposition', London, 1987 (mimeo).

Strachey, John Richard. *The Finances and Public Works of India*, London, 1882, p. 259.

Szymanski, Al. 'Marxist Theory and International Capital Flows', *Radical Political Economy Review*, 6 (3), 1974.

Temin, P. 'Capital Exports, 1870–1914: An Alternative Model', *Economic History Review*, Vol. XL, No. 3, August 1987.

Thavaraj, K. 'Capital Formation in the Public Sector in India: A Historical Study, 1898–1938' in V.K.R.V. Rao et al. ed. *Papers on National Income and Allied Topics*, Vol. 1, Asia Publishing House, New York, 1960.

Thingalaya, N.K. 'A Century of Prices in India', *EPW*, 25 July 1969.

Thomspon. E.P. *The Making of the English Working class*, London, 1963.

Thorner, D. and Thorner, A. 'The Working Force of India, 1857–1946', Bombay, 1960 (mimeo).

Thorner, Daniel. *Investment in Empire*, Philadelphia, 1950.

Tomlinson, B.R. *The Political Economy of the Raj, 1914–1947*, Cambridge, 1979.

Vakil, C.N. *Financial Developments in Modern India, 1860–1924*, D.B. Taraporevala Sons, Bombay, 1925.

Viner, Jacob. *Canada's Balance of International Indebtedness, 1900–*

1913, Harvard University Press, Cambridge, 1924.

Wallerstein, Immanuel. *The Capitalist World Economy*, Cambridge, 1979.

______. *The Modern World System: Capitalist Agriculture and the Origins of the European World Economy in the Sixteenth Century*, New York, 1976.

Warren, Bill. 'How International is Capital?' in Hugo Radice ed. *International Firms and Modern Imperialism*, Penguin, 1975.

Whitcombe, E. *Agrarian Condition in Nothern India*, Vol. I. *The United Provinces under British Rule 1860–1900*, University of California Press, Berkeley and London, 1972.

Wingate, George. *A Few Words about the Financial Relations with India*, London, 1859.

Official reports

Bengal District Gazetteers, O'Mally L.S.S., *Bankura*, Volume XIV, Calcutta, 1908. Peterson, J.C.K., *Burdwan*, Calcutta, 1910.

British Parliamentary Papers, Statistical Abstract of British India, 1914–16.

East India, Report of Commissioners, *Report of the Famine Commission and Evidence, 1885* and *1899*, (FEC).

Glazier's Report on Rangpur, 1876.

Government of India, *Indian Currency and Banking Enquiry Committee Report*, 1930.

Government of India, *Reports of Currency Committee*, Calcutta, 1931.

Report of the Industrial Commission, 1916–18.

Royal Commission on Indian Currency (Babington Smith Committee), 1926.

Royal Commission on Indian Currency (Fowler Committee), *RCC 1898*, London, 1898,

Royal Commission on Indian Currency (Herschell Commission), *RCC 1893*, London, 1893.

Royal Commission on Indian Currency (Hilton–Young Committee), 1931.

Royal Commission on Indian Currency and Finance (Chamberlain Committee) *RCC 1914*, London, 1914.

Royal Commission, *Final Report on Expenditure of India* (Welby Commission), London, 1900.

Statistical Abstract of British India, Indian Department of Commercial Intelligence and Statistics, New Delhi, annually.

Journals and newspapers

Cambridge Journal of Economics.

Economic History Review.

Economic Journal.

Economic and Political Weekly.
Exploration in Economic History.
Indian Economic Journal.
Indian Trade Journal.
Journal of Economic History.
Journal of Peasant Studies.
Madras Mail.
Modern Asian Studies.
Review.
Radical Political Economy Review.
Science and Society.
Studies in History.
Times of India, November 1913.
Times, November 1914.

India Office Library records

IOR/L/F/5/4.
IOR/L/F/5/29.
IOR/L/F/7/214 (Financial Collections file 1-7).
IOR/L/F/7/220.
IOR/L/F/7/224.
IOR/L/F/7/421.
IOR/L/F/7/442.

Private Papers

Benthal papers, South Asian Studies, Cambridge University.
Keynes *Papers*, Marshall Library, Cambridge (File IB/2 and IB/3, 53 A7).
Meston Papers, India Office, London (IOR/Eur MSS/F 136/14).

Author Index

Subject Index